Clues to Lower Mississippi Valley Histories

# Clues to Lower Mississippi Valley Histories

*Language, Archaeology, and Ethnography*

DAVID V. KAUFMAN

UNIVERSITY OF NEBRASKA PRESS, LINCOLN

Portions of chapters 5, 6, and 7 have previously appeared
in "Two Siouan Languages Walk into a Sprachbund," in
*Advances in the Study of Siouan Languages and Linguistics,*
edited by Catherine Rudin and Bryan J. Gordon, 39–62
(Berlin: Language Science Press, 2016) and "The Lower
Mississippi Valley as a Linguistic Area," in *Oxford
Handbook of Language Contact* (Oxford: Oxford University
Press, 2019).

**RECOVERING**
**LANGUAGES&LITERACIES**
**OF THE AMERICAS**

This book is published as part of the Recovering
Languages and Literacies of the Americas initiative.
Recovering Languages and Literacies is generously
supported by the Andrew W. Mellon Foundation.

*Library of Congress Cataloging-in-Publication Data*
Names: Kaufman, David V.
Title: Clues to Lower Mississippi Valley histories:
language, archaeology, and ethnography / David V.
Kaufman.
Description: Lincoln: University of Nebraska Press, 2019
Includes bibliographical references and index
Identifiers: LCCN 2019002943| ISBN 9781496209979
(cloth: alk. paper) | ISBN 9781496222237 (paperback) |
ISBN 9781496214935 (pdf)
Subjects: LCSH: Indians of North America—Mississippi
River Valley—Languages. | Mississippi River Valley—
Languages. | Anthropological linguistics—Mississippi
River Valley. | Languages in contact—Mississippi River
Valley. | Language and culture—Mississippi River Valley. |
Mississippi River Valley—History—To 1803.
Classification: LCC PM451 .K38 2019 | DDC 497/.5—dc23
LC record available at https://lccn.loc.gov/2019002943

Set in Merope Basic by Tseng Information Systems, Inc.

To my parents
And to all the scholars who came
before, upon whose shoulders
I stood in writing this book

# CONTENTS

## PART ONE. GEOGRAPHY, ARCHAEOLOGY, PEOPLES, AND LANGUAGES

## PART TWO. LANGUAGE CONTACT

## ILLUSTRATIONS

## TABLES

## ACKNOWLEDGMENTS

A book is never the work of just one person but several. I would like to thank my dissertation adviser, Dr. Carlos Nash, who so expertly and kindly guided me through the production of my dissertation. I also want to thank the late Dr. Robert Rankin for being my mentor and encouraging me to study Siouan linguistics, which later led me on to researching and studying other, including non-Siouan, Native American languages, making a comparative work like this possible. I also want to thank my friend and colleague Dr. Alice Beck Kehoe, who has helped me in so many ways through this book-writing process. I want to thank the anonymous reviewers of earlier drafts of the book for their comments and suggestions. I want to thank numerous other colleagues, including Drs. Pam Munro, Jack Martin, Aaron Broadwell, David Costa, and Daniel Hieber, as well as many other friends who have been enormously supportive through the arduous process of research and writing. Last, but certainly not least, I thank the editor Matthew Bokovoy and other University of Nebraska Press staff for their encouragement, comments, suggestions, and guidance through preparation and production.

*Yakoki!*

Fig. 1. The Lower Mississippi Valley. Created by author based on National Park Service 2010.

The Mississippi Valley (see fig. 1) is the heartland of early North American civilizations. The region is rich, diversified, and at the center of transportation to every part of eastern North America and to Mesoamerica (Mexico). The Lower Mississippi Valley (LMV) was home to the earliest mound-building societies and some of the most impressive kingdoms seen by Spanish and French explorers. The languages of the region are key to the realities experienced by these indigenous peoples, their histories, and their relationships. Much of this book focuses on relationships that constitute what linguists call a *sprachbund* (a German term meaning 'language union'), or language area, ca. 500–1700 CE. As I set out these relationships, archaeological and ethnohistorical data fall into place. This is a history of North America that dates back many centuries before the European invasions and the establishment of the United States.

The main premise of this book is that, in addition to archaeology and ethnography, languages can inform us about events of the past. Linguistic evidence can help us discern cultural and social patterns of the past and can help us trace movements and contact among peoples (Silver and Miller 1997, 314). While the main focus of this book is on language and, more specifically, language contact, I also incorporate and synthesize archaeological and ethnographic evidence with the language evidence where appropriate. That is, if we extend the archaeological concept of *artifact* to include words and grammatical concepts—things also made by humans—then we can include language evidence in interpreting archaeological records.

Linguists and archaeologists often do not consult with each other, and syntheses between these disciplines have been lacking. In this book I attempt such a synthesis and preliminary analysis of certain aspects of linguistics and archaeology as they pertain to the LMV and the elucidation of its history. Perhaps not every non-linguist will be convinced of the significance of the data I adduce, but the language relations, and the sprachbund they form, are telling to a linguist. For example many archaeologists will insist that there is little or no evidence of contact between the North

American Southeast and Mesoamerica. Yet there is probable *linguistic* evidence for such contact that goes unacknowledged. Borrowing, or copying, of vocabulary between languages implies human interaction among those speaking the languages; even in the absence of *material* evidence, such linguistic evidence should be seriously considered and evaluated.

The North American Southeast has long been hypothesized as a sprachbund (see, for example, Sherzer 1976 and Martin 1994), but there has been little systematic in-depth analysis of the region in comparison with better-known language areas such as Mesoamerica (Campbell, Kaufman, and Smith-Stark 1986; Thomason and Kaufman 1988), the Balkans (Friedman 2009; Tomić 2006), and South Asia (Emeneau 1956; Masica 1976). In this book I incorporate such a systematic in-depth analysis, examining the degree of linguistic contact among the peoples of the LMV and how the languages have been shaped by such contact. In addition this book will demonstrate broader linguistic contacts with regions outside of the LMV, including with other possible language areas to the east and west. It will also become clear that discursive and pragmatic features such as focus- and topic-marking, which have been generally little studied in analyses of language areas, play a major role in the LMV. Further, word borrowings, which include exchanges of "basic" vocabulary and several calques (semantic translations), suggest intense contact and intercommunication within the area.

It is my hope that linguists, anthropologists, historians, and anyone with a general interest in Native America will profit from reading this book, gaining more insight into the history, peoples, and languages of the LMV and its importance to the history of North America. It is a history rooted in the rich multiethnic and multilingual diversity of this region for many centuries, if not millennia.

## METHODOLOGY

The methodology employed for part 1 is to report on what archaeologists have noted in the literature on the LMV. I will elaborate more on the methodology for part 2 in chapter 4, but for now suffice it to say that methodology for that part of the book consists primarily in the perusal of written sources, both published and unpublished, since most of the LMV languages are no longer spoken. Part 2 is divided into three sections: Phonetics and Phonology, Morphology, and Words and Calques. For the first two sections of part 2, preexisting lists of phonetic and grammatical traits, or features, taken from Sherzer (1976) and Campbell (1997) were used, to which I added certain features gathered in my own research. The number of features occurring in each LMV language is counted. These features are also weighted according to such factors as overall crosslinguistic occurrence or uniqueness in the LMV sprachbund and peripheral languages. This will yield the "most LMV" features—those closest to the LMV sprachbund norm. Data for the Words and Calques section was primarily gathered from dictionaries and lexicons in order to establish the extent of likely word and calque borrowing between LMV and peripheral languages. The occurrence of *basic* vocabulary loans across LMV languages was also analyzed for the purpose of discovering the *degree* of language contact in the LMV.

## ARRANGEMENT

This book is divided into two parts and a conclusion. Part 1 (chapters 1–3) contains an overview of the geography, geology, and environment of the LMV; a brief history of the LMV through the categorical prism of archaeological periods, including a discussion of mound-building, agriculture, and trade; a sketch of the peoples of the LMV and their movements and migrations; and an overview of LMV languages. Part 2 (chapters 4–7) offers a discussion of language contact and of the region's status as a sprachbund. The conclusion offers a synthesis of the first two parts, combining archaeological, ethnohistoric, and language contact data to see what conclusions we can ultimately derive from this cross-disciplinary analysis.

# ABBREVIATIONS

Grammatical Terms

| | | | | |
|---|---|---|---|---|
| 1 | first person | | CONN | connective |
| 1p | first person plural (we) | | CONT | continuative |
| | | | CONTR | contrastive |
| 1s | first person singular (I) | | COP | copulative |
| | | | DAT | dative |
| 2 | second person | | DECL | declarative |
| 2p | second person plural (you all) | | DECS | decessive |
| | | | DEF | definite (article) |
| 2s | second person singular (you) | | DEM | demonstrative |
| | | | DET | determiner |
| 3 | third person | | DIM | diminutive |
| 3p | third person plural (they) | | DIR | directional |
| | | | DS | different subject |
| 3s | third person singular (he, she, it) | | DU | dual |
| | | | EMPH | emphatic |
| ABL | ablative | | ERG | ergative |
| ABS | absolutive | | EVID | evidential |
| ACC | accusative | | EXCLAM | exclamation |
| AGR | agricultural | | F | feminine |
| ALL | allative | | FOC | focus |
| ANIM | animate | | FUT | future |
| AOR | aorist | | GEN | genitive |
| ART | article | | HAB | habitual |
| ASRT | assertive | | IMPF | imperfective |
| AUX | auxiliary | | INACT | inactive |
| CAUS | causative | | INAN | inanimate |
| CMP | completive | | INC | incompletive |
| COM | comitative | | INCHO | inchoative |
| COND | conditional | | INDF | indefinite |

| | | | |
|---|---|---|---|
| INDIR | indirect | PROX | proximate |
| INF | infinitive | PRT | particle |
| INFER | inferential | PRTP | participle |
| INST | instrumental | PST | past |
| INTENS | intensive | PT | patient |
| INTER | interrogative | PURP | purposive |
| IRR | irrealis | PVB | preverb |
| LOC | locative | QT | quotative |
| M | masculine | REC | reciprocal |
| MOD | modal | REDUP | reduplication |
| NEG | negative | REM | remote |
| NEW.TOP | new topic | RFL | reflexive |
| NM | new mention | RL | realis |
| NOM | nominative | SEM | semelfactive |
| NZR | nominalizer | SG | singular |
| OBJ | object | SOV | subject-object-verb |
| OPT | optative | | (constituent order) |
| OSV | object-subject-verb | SR | switch reference |
| | (word order) | SS | same subject |
| PAUS | pause | STAT | stative |
| PERF | perfective | STG | something |
| PERS.PRO | personal pronoun | SUB | subordinate |
| PHR.TRM | phrase terminal | SUBJ | subject |
| PL | plural | SUF | suffix |
| PLURACT | pluractional | TEMP | temporary |
| POSS | possessive | TNS | tense |
| PREV | previous mention | TOP | topic |
| PRO | pronoun | | |

## Non-grammatical Terms

| | | | |
|---|---|---|---|
| ANAT | anatomical | BOT | botanical |
| APS | American Philosophical Society | GA | Gulf-Atlantic |
| | | IE | Indo-European |
| BAE | Bureau of American Ethnology | LMV | Lower Mississippi Valley |

| | | | |
|---|---|---|---|
| MTL | Mobilian Trade Language (Mobilian Jargon) | PM | Proto-Muskogean |
| | | PSL | Plains Sign Language |
| | | RGV | Rio Grande Valley |
| OVS | Ohio Valley Siouan | ZOOL | zoological |
| PCA | Proto-Central-Algonquian | | |

Clues to Lower Mississippi Valley Histories

**1**

# Geography, Archaeology, Peoples, and Languages

# ONE

# Geography and Environment

The geography and environment of the LMV was conducive to the development and maintenance of a sprachbund. The myriad waterways of the region, including one of the world's longest rivers, provided excellent communication and trade routes. At the same time the area offered enough isolation to provide a degree of autonomy and the maintenance of separate cultures and languages (Matras 2009).

For this book I define the LMV as an area extending from about 260 miles (418 km) west of the Mississippi River eastward to Mobile Bay on the Gulf of Mexico—a total of about 380 miles (612 km)—and about 425 miles (684 km) northward from the Gulf of Mexico toward the vicinity of the Tombigbee and Arkansas Rivers, an area encompassing 144,600 square miles (496,600 sq km). This area encompasses present-day southern Arkansas, Mississippi, and Alabama, southeastern Oklahoma and eastern Texas over toward central Alabama, and all of the modern states of Louisiana and Mississippi. This definition includes a broader territory than other definitions of the LMV (e.g., Rees and Livingood 2007, 1) in order to include languages that were undoubtedly an intimate part of this proposed sprachbund (e.g., Atakapa and Choctaw-Chickasaw), though geographically somewhat removed from the Mississippi Valley itself.

## THE GULF OF MEXICO

The LMV borders the northern Gulf of Mexico. The Gulf covers about 598,458 square miles (1,550,000 sq km). Its greatest east-to-west breadth is about 1,118 miles (1,800 km); its south-to-north extent is approximately 808 miles (1,300 km). There are thirty-three major rivers emptying into the Gulf, draining "a continental area nearly double its size." The Gulf of Mexico "is a large, isolated sea" with a surrounding catchment zone including much of the Mesoamerican and Southeastern culture areas (Wilkerson 2005, 58). Several of the rivers (detailed below) entering the Gulf are located in the LMV.

## MOBILE BAY

Mobile Bay, located near modern Mobile, Alabama, is between 8 and 18 miles (13–29 km) in width. The bay enters the Gulf of Mexico between Dauphin Island and Mobile Point. The earliest known eyewitness account we have of Mobile Bay is by the Spaniard Alonso Álvarez de Pineda, who in 1519 entered this bay, which he named Bahía Espíritu Santo (Bay of the Holy Ghost) (Swanton 1946, 150; Walthall 1980, 247). He and his small fleet sailed a short distance up the Río del Espíritu Santo (now known as the Mobile River), where he reported sighting "some forty Indian villages along the shoreline" (Walthall 1980, 247). Unfortunately this is the limit of his account; however, the report is enough to infer the large population in this region at the time, supporting the idea of Mobile Bay's importance as a large port and trading center. The origin of the name, which has also been spelled *Mabila, Mauilla,* and *Mavila,* is unknown, but it may be from Choctaw *moeli* 'paddle' (Walthall 1980, 218), probably in reference to the primary means of entering and exiting this port.

Mobile Bay appears to be the "trait core" area of the LMV sprachbund and was likely the primary port on the north shore of the Gulf (Tanner 1989). The bay was likely a major crossroads, not only for east-west travel along the Gulf but also for north-south travel on the six rivers draining into it from the northern interior: the Mobile, Alabama, Tombigbee, Black Warrior, Coosa, and Tallapoosa Rivers.

The abundance of rivers and other waterways in the region is likely what primarily contributed to the development of the LMV as a sprachbund. This multitude of aquatic routes formed an ancient highway network that would have served as the quickest means for linking peoples and goods in the region.

## RIVERS

### Mississippi

The Mississippi River, the lower valley of which is the focus of this book, is the longest river in North America, draining with its major tributaries—the Missouri and Ohio Rivers—an area of approximately 1.2 million square miles (3.1 million sq km), or about one-eighth of the entire continent. The name *Mississippi* was first applied by French missionaries in the seventeenth century, deriving the name from Ojibwe (Algonquian) *mishi* 'big' + *ziibi* 'river.' The French had originally named the river Fleuve Colbert and Fleuve Saint Louis. Rising in Lake Itasca in Minnesota, the Mississippi River flows almost due south across the continental interior, collecting the waters of its major tributaries approximately halfway along its journey to the Gulf of Mexico through a vast delta southeast of modern New Orleans, a total distance of 2,350 miles (3,780 km) from its source, emptying into the Gulf near the modern town of Venice, Louisiana, near Barataria Bay. The lower Mississippi River is a meandering alluvial river, meaning that the channel loops and curls along its floodplain, leaving behind meander scars, cutoffs, oxbow lakes, and swampy backwaters. The valley is bordered by a line of bluffs up to 200 feet (61 m) high. The eastern bluff line is interrupted by a few small streams while several large river valleys that cross the Great Plains, such as the Arkansas and the Red, cut through the bluffs on the western side (Bense 2009, 14). The Mississippi forms a north-south environmental corridor extending from the Upper Midwest to the Gulf of Mexico, providing a broad range of plant and animal species that contributed to indigenous economies (Bense 2009, 168) and a flyway from Canada and the northern United States down to the southern end of the Mississippi Valley, which is a refuge for wintering fowl (Smith 2009).

Several smaller rivers drain into the Mississippi, including, in approximate geographical order from the Gulf of Mexico northward, the Red, the Yazoo, and the Arkansas. The Atchafalaya is a distributary to the west of the Mississippi while the Pearl, Tombigbee, and Mobile are to the east of it—the latter two in modern Alabama while the Pearl is in the modern state of Mississippi.

### Red

The Red River has its confluence with the Mississippi about 216 miles (348 km) upstream from the latter's mouth. The Red River rises in the high plains of modern eastern New Mexico, flowing southeast through modern Texas and Louisiana to a point northwest of present-day Baton Rouge, where it enters the Atchafalaya River, which flows south to Atchafalaya Bay and the Gulf of Mexico. The Red River is 1,290 miles (2,080 km) long and drains an area of some 93,000 square miles (241,000 sq km). (This river is often called the Red River of the South to distinguish it from the Red River of the North, which is in the northern United States and Canada, flowing northward through Minnesota and Manitoba and emptying into Lake Winnipeg.)

### Yazoo

The Yazoo River has its confluence with the Mississippi about 285 miles (459 km) upstream from the latter's mouth. The Yazoo is formed by the confluence of the Tallahatchie and Yalobusha Rivers north of modern Greenwood, Mississippi. It meanders about 190 miles (306 km) generally south and southwest, much of the way in parallel to the Mississippi River, which it joins at the modern town of Vicksburg.

### Arkansas

The Arkansas River is a large tributary of the Mississippi River whose confluence with the Mississippi is about 396 miles (637 km) upstream from the latter's mouth. The Arkansas River rises in the Rocky Mountains of what is now central Colorado and flows generally eastward for 1,460 miles (2,350 km) through the modern states of Kansas, Oklahoma, and Arkansas before entering the Mississippi 40 miles (64 km) northeast of present-day Arkansas City, Arkansas. The river's drainage basin covers 161,000 square miles (417,000 sq km).

### Atchafalaya

The Atchafalaya River is a distributary of the Red and Mississippi Rivers in modern Louisiana. It branches southwest from the Red River near a point in what is now east-central Louisiana. The name *Atchafalaya* derives from Choctaw or Mobilian Trade Language (MTL) *acha* 'river' + *falaya* 'long.' The Atchafalaya flows generally south for about 140 miles (225 km) to Atchafalaya Bay, an inlet of the Gulf of Mexico. Its length, including the Red River, is 1,420 miles (2,290 km), and its drainage area is 95,100 square miles (246,300 sq km).

### Pearl

The Pearl River rises in modern east-central Mississippi and flows southwestward into modern Louisiana, emptying into the Gulf of Mexico. The river divides into two streams, the East Pearl and the West Pearl, which parallels the East Pearl several miles to the west. The Pearl is approximately 411 miles (661 km) long, draining about 7,600 square miles (19,700 sq km).

### Tombigbee

The Tombigbee River is formed in modern northeastern Mississippi and flows south and southeast for nearly 525 miles (845 km) to merge with the Alabama River; the two form the Mobile River about 45 miles (70 km) north of the modern city of Mobile, Alabama. The Tombigbee drains about 21,100 square miles (54,600 sq km). The name *Tombigbee* derives from Choctaw *itombi* 'trunk, box, coffin' + *ikbi* 'maker,' the river being so called because a trunk- or box-maker inhabited one of the river's branches (Byington and Swanton 1915, 216).

### Mobile

The Mobile River is located in what is now southwestern Alabama. It is formed by the confluence of the Tombigbee and Alabama Rivers. The river enters Mobile Bay after a southerly course of 45 miles (72 km) through the Mobile-Tensaw delta region. With its tributaries it drains some 44,000 square miles (114,000 sq km), making it the sixth-largest river basin in the United States. The Mobile River drains into Mobile Bay, on which the city of Mobile now stands. This bay extends 35 miles (56 km) south from the mouth of the Mobile River to its Gulf outlet.

## GEOLOGY

Most of the LMV falls within the Coastal Plain of the northern Gulf of Mexico and ranges from sea level at the coast to about 300 feet (about 91 m) in the upland regions (Walthall 1980, 13). It is an area featuring flat expanses to low, rolling hills and shallow valleys, a region of meandering rivers and innumerable swamps, some vast, "thickly covered with cypress and cane" (Hudson 1976, 15).

## FLORA AND FAUNA

The flora of the rich coastal plain includes edible wild vegetables and fruits like blackberries, palmetto, gooseberries, grapes, varieties of acorns, prickly pears, sea grapes, and several plants (Hudson 1976, 15). The trees that grow on the plain are broadleaf deciduous species, such as white hickory, swamp chestnut oak, laurel oak, and white oak, and evergreen species and several species of pine, including southern white pine, shortleaf pine, longleaf pine, and loblolly pine (Walthall 1980, 15). There are broad floodplains along the coast with forests of cypress and several species of oak (Walthall 1980, 15). The LMV was home to deer, specifically white-tailed deer (*Odocoileus virginianus*), the primary prey for human hunters in the Mississippi Valley and Southeast well back into millennia BCE (Smith 2009; Hudson 1976). Bear provided food, oil (for cooking), and skins. Other animals hunted or caught included panther (cougar), beaver, otter, raccoon, muskrat, opossum, squirrel, rabbit, snakes, turtles, terrapins, alligators, crawfish, crabs, clams, mussels, and oysters (Hudson 1976, 17–18).

The LMV, with its multitude of rivers, streams, lakes, and swamps as well as the Gulf, provided a good year-round abundance of fish (Brain and Porter 1990; Hudson 1976; Kniffen, Gregory, and Stokes 1987; Smith 2009; Yerkes 2005). Catfish and sturgeon were among the most important fish caught and eaten, together with several species of smaller fish like shad, suckers, bass, perch, sunfish, and mullet (Hudson 1976, 282).

Birds, especially migratory waterfowl, also provided a major source of sustenance, with about two dozen species of ducks, geese, and swans following this flyway corridor annually as they flew toward their southern wintering grounds and the coastal marshes of Louisiana, making for an almost inexhaustible food supply through the fall, winter, and spring (Smith 2009, 173). Turkeys and passenger pigeons[1] were also widely available and hunted (Hudson 1976, 280).

Now that we have a better idea of the geography, geology, and flora and fauna of the LMV, we can explore the region's archaeology and history.

# TWO

# Archaeology and History

In this chapter I summarize the claims, within a framework of established archaeological periods, put forth by archaeologists who focus on the LMV. The building of monumental earthworks (especially mounds) and the establishment of trade and agriculture contributed to the history of the LMV and will be discussed here.

## ARCHAEOLOGICAL PERIODS

We can view LMV history through the prism of established North American archaeological periods. We see these periods in tables 1 and 2.

By means of comparison, the Archaic period in North America[1] correlates more or less with the Stone and Bronze ages in the Near East and the Paleolithic-Bronze Age in Western Europe. The beginning of the North American Woodland period correlates with the Mesoamerican Formative, or Preclassic, period until ca. 250 CE. After 250 CE the Classic period extends up until ca. 900 CE, about the time of the Classical Maya "collapse." The North American Mississippian period roughly correlates with the Mesoamerican Postclassic period until ca. 1515 CE. Further, the Mississippian period correlates with the Plaquemine period in the LMV.

Each of the periods in tables 1 and 2 correlates with certain archaeological characteristics and developments. Paleoamerican (formerly called Paleoindian) is the first recognized cultural stage in the Southeast as well as in all of North America. The exact date for the beginning of the Paleoamerican stage is still unknown. The beginning of this period is open to further refinement based on the most recent findings and dating methods; thus the Paleoamerican period may have begun much earlier than Bense's hypothesized date of 13000 BCE. Characteristic of the Paleoamerican period is the hunting of Pleistocene big game, including the now extinct mammoth

Table 1. North American archaeological periods

| PERIOD | YEAR RANGE |
| --- | --- |
| Paleoamerican | ?–8000 BCE |
| Archaic | 8000–1000 BCE |
| Woodland | 1000 BCE–1000 CE |
| Mississippian | 1000–1700 CE |

Table 2. Archaeological periods further refined in the LMV

| PERIOD | YEAR RANGE |
| --- | --- |
| Poverty Point | 1600–500 BCE |
| Tchula (Tchefuncte) | 500 BCE–1 CE |
| Marksville (Hopewell) | 1–500 CE |
| Troyville (Baytown) | 500–700 CE |
| Coles Creek | 700–1200 CE |
| Plaquemine (Mississippian) | 1200–1720 CE |

After Roe (2007, 23, 28)

and mastodon, using high-quality, lanceolate-shaped stone spear points (Bense 2009, 4).

## Archaic

The Archaic was the longest archaeological period in the Southeast. Characteristic of this period are such pivotal cultural developments as notched and stemmed triangular stone spear points, ground and polished stone artifacts, and containers of stone and pottery (Bense 2009, 5). The oldest known ceramics in North America, called Stallings Island pottery, appeared on the Atlantic coast in what is today northeastern Florida and southeastern Georgia during the Archaic, ca. 2500 BCE.

The first long-distance trade to develop in the region was during the Archaic period. It was also during the Archaic that we encounter the first and oldest known mound complex in the Americas in what is now northeastern Louisiana: Watson Brake, dated to ca. 3500 BCE. These mounds antedate those of Mesoamerica by about two thousand years. Watson Brake has an oval earthen embankment enclosing 22 acres, ranging from 2 to 5 feet tall, measuring 900 feet from end to end and 600 feet across. Along the top of the embankment are eleven conical earthen mounds (Little 2009, 110).

During the late Archaic and early Woodland periods, the Poverty Point (1600–500 BCE) culture arose in the LMV. The Poverty Point culture involved the construction of mounds and earthworks, a long-distance trade network, and an advanced stone lapidary industry (Bense 2009, 99). Poverty Point peoples achieved a high level of skill in stonework. Stones come from as far away as the Appalachian Mountains, the Piedmont region, the Rocky Mountains, the Ouachita Mountains, and the Great Lakes (101). Poverty Point peoples hunted, gathered, fished, and grew bottle gourds and squash. In addition to steatite, sandstone, and fiber-tempered pottery, they used bottle gourds and squash as containers (100–101). Poverty Point culture settlements contained semicircular and horseshoe-shaped earthworks with one or more mounds (101), such as those at its flagship site of Poverty Point (see fig. 2). The Poverty Point site, near current Epps, Louisiana, dating to ca. 1600 BCE, is one of the largest earthen mound complexes in North America. The site includes a set of earthworks nearly a mile long in the form of a semi-octagon. These earthworks contain elevated terraces "upon which small houses had been erected" (Little 2009, 107).

The first pottery appeared in the LMV during the Archaic: a ceramic tradition called St. John's (Saunders and Hays 2004, 3) at Poverty Point. The many small groups of hunter-gatherers living along the Gulf Coast and in the LMV presumably used this pottery.

## Woodland

A diffusion of pottery throughout the LMV along with a growth of elaborate mortuary rituals and an increase in long-distance trade characterize the Woodland period. This period saw the cultivation and storage of many types of plants, and an increase in the construction of burial mounds (Bense 2009, 5).

The Woodland Tchula (500 BCE–1 CE), or Tchefuncte, peoples were the first to fully adopt ceramics for cooking and storage. The dart and atlatl (spear thrower) were their primary weapons (Kidder 2004, 546). Limited subsistence data during this time period suggest an "exclusive reliance on wild plants and animals" (547). Tchula populations were descendants of the

Fig. 2. Photograph of stairway leading up Mound A, Poverty Point.
© 2017 John W. Hoopes.

Poverty Point people, yet, unlike their predecessors, there is no evidence of Tchula people trading over long distances (548).

It was during the middle Woodland period, ca. 500 BCE–100 CE, that the Adena ceremonial complex developed in the central Ohio Valley, a complex that incorporated different local and regional cultures (Bense 2009, 121). While geographically distant from the LMV, the Adena culture is peripherally important since it seemingly precipitated the later Hopewell ceremonial complex (discussed below), which had a broad effect on the Midwest and Southeast, including on the LMV. Adena started with simple mounds atop shallow, bark-lined grave pits, each containing one body buried with utilitarian grave goods. By ca. 200 BCE mortuary buildings were constructed that contained individuals with both utilitarian and ornamental grave goods placed in shallow pits prior to burning the building. A mound was built over the burned mortuary building. New mortuaries were often built on top of the mound; this cycle was repeated several times (Bense 2009, 121).

Later Adena log tomb burials were more elaborate and included distinctive prestige items such as copper bracelets, finger rings, adzes, celts, marine shells, crescents and sheets of mica, many types of ground and polished stone gorgets (chest ornaments), zoomorphic pipes, and stone tablets with inscribed geometric designs and bird images (Bense 2009, 122).

Mortuary ceremonialism increased in complexity. By ca. 1 CE, the Adena complex at first overlapped with, then gave way to, the Hopewell ceremonial complex, which lasted until ca. 500 CE. Hopewell was named after the family who owned a farm in Ohio that included "large geometric earthworks" containing a village and burial mounds. Hopewell ceremonialism included mound centers on a grand scale often enclosed by geometric earthworks in the shape of octagons, parallel lines, and circles up to 50 acres in size (Bense 2009, 122). Hopewellian culture included "flamboyant burial customs" (Fagan 1995, 411) such as elaborate tombs with great numbers of grave offerings and exotic artifacts, including copper, marine shells, mica, obsidian, shark and alligator teeth, and meteorites (Bense 2009, 122). While Hopewell ceremonialism was most elaborate in the Ohio Valley, Hopewell eventually spread its artistic symbolism and iconography throughout much of the Midwest and South, including into the LMV at

Marksville, anticipating the Mississippian Culture (see below) whose geographic sphere of influence some five hundred years later closely mirrored that of Hopewell.

The Marksville (1–500 CE) period demonstrates classic middle Woodland traits such as mound-building, mound burials, and long-distance trade in exotic goods. The Marksville culture represented the Hopewell ceremonial sphere in the LMV and participation in the Hopewellian iconographic pattern. Marksville mounds and earthworks were scattered throughout the LMV (Kidder 2004, 550). The Marksville culture's flagship mound complex was the Marksville Mounds, now a Louisiana state historic site. The site contains three conical and two rectangular platform mounds (Bense 2009, 143) surrounded by a 3,300 foot-long semicircular earthwork ranging between 3 and 7 feet tall (Little 2009, 103). Early and late Marksville period sites in the Mississippi River delta and along the coast are poorly documented (Kidder 2004, 548). Marksville people maintained frequent contacts with populations to the north and east of the Mississippi Valley (551).

Baytown (Troyville) (500–700 CE) period settlements and social organization were highly variable. Baytown populations displayed a complex pattern of settlement organization with burial mounds usually low and conical or rounded in shape (Kidder 2004, 553). Baytown and Coles Creek period pottery contained small pieces of crushed pottery called grog, sometimes along with sand, grit, bone, and shell. Vessels included beakers, bowls, and globular jars (Bense 2009, 176). The Troyville Mounds formed the Baytown culture's flagship site, located near modern Jonesville, Louisiana (see fig. 3). The mounds were built at different times between 1 and 700 CE. Troyville was one of the largest mound sites in Louisiana, but little remains today of the site, which was almost totally destroyed, especially after the United States Civil War (Little 2009, 109). Thirteen mounds once stood at the site. The largest mound consisted of two terraces surmounted by a cone (Kidder 2004, 554), which was 75 feet tall with a base of 160 by 250 feet (Little 2009, 109). Troyville contained the second-largest pyramidal mound in Native North America (after Monks Mound, of the later Cahokia).

Although mound-building began in the Archaic period, the construction of mounds with large, leveled public squares, or plazas, was a main component of late Woodland and later Mississippian cultural history. Silty

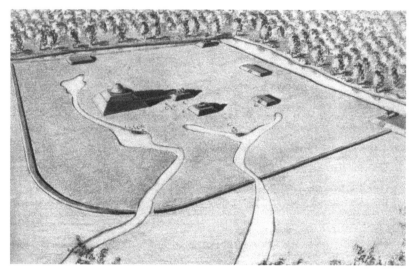

Fig. 3. Reconstruction of Troyville Mounds, by Dee Turman, from *The Illustrated Encyclopedia of Native American Indian Mounds and Earthworks* (2009; 2016).

clays ranging in hue from black to red and white were used to cover the mounds, contrasting them with "the green leafy landscapes in which they sat" (Pauketat 2007, 99).

The LMV was home to the first known earthworks and earthen mound complexes to appear in the Americas. It is believed that mounds began primarily as either effigy mounds in the shape of animals such as birds and snakes or as burial mounds in which were buried certain deceased members of a particular society. Mounds also represented a legitimization of power and rulership. Mounds were physical symbols of elevated position and ways to legitimize power by symbolically connecting nobles with their ancestors, who often were buried in the mounds. Since emerging political and social elites were competing for power and prestige, mound-building is thought to have been a means of allowing individuals and groups to express status and power (Kidder 1998; Kidder 2004; Steponaitis 1986).

The construction of mounds and plazas led, in the nineteenth century, to the "mound builder" controversy (Brain 1988, 48) over who exactly built the thousands of earthen mounds and earthworks dotting the middle and southern regions of North America, including in the LMV. Since few

Europeans and Euro-Americans believed that the ancestors of the modern Native North Americans they encountered could have been "civilized" enough to organize and engineer the building of these massive earthen monuments and complexes, alternative theories of the mounds' creators were developed with "energy and zeal" (Mann 2003, 71–73). Hypotheses as to the identity of the builders included a lost tribe of Israel, the Toltecs of Mexico (MacLean 1879), Hindus from India (Fagan 1995, 30), Vikings, and refugees from Atlantis (Mann 2003, 71–73)—anybody but the indigenous peoples who were already here and remained.

During the late Woodland period in the LMV mound centers expanded into sociopolitical centers, with platform mounds (flat-topped mounds often topped by structures) becoming the primary mound type. The Coles Creek period (700–1200 CE) witnessed increasing cultural change from egalitarianism to ranked lineages with centralization of power in a small group of elites and ranking of communities (Bense 2009, 178). Coles Creek sites were generally larger than those in earlier times (Kidder 2004, 554); settlements consisted of a plaza, rectangular in shape with platform mounds along the sides (177). Coles Creek mounds changed from simply covered burials to platform mounds atop which foundations for perishable structures, such as houses or temples, were built with burials later deposited in them. Long-distance trade appears infrequent and there is little evidence of contacts with groups outside of the LMV (Kidder 2004, 554). Both Troyville (Baytown) and Coles Creek settlements "were very abundant in the Mississippi Valley," with more sites than from any earlier period, representing "both population growth and mobility" (Bense 2009, 176). Not only was there population growth during the Late Woodland period in the LMV but increasing social integration as evidenced by the construction of ceremonial centers, apparently "to attract and organize dispersed populations" to public ceremonies (Girard, Perttula, and Trubitt 2014, 37). Although the development and rituals of later Woodland period LMV mound centers demanded leadership, "evidence does not indicate that power and prestige were based on, or symbolized by, military conquest or wealth accumulation ... Burials at ceremonial centers were communal, not reserved for elites. Little or no individual or group status differentiation is evident by mortuary programs at Troyville or other Late Woodland period centers" (37–38). This situation would soon change, however, during the Mississippian Culture period.

### Mississippian-Plaquemine

The Mississippian Culture arrived in the LMV ca. 1200 CE. (Plaquemine is the LMV version of the broader Mississippian cultural complex and is thus referred to here as Mississippian-Plaquemine.[2]) Mississippian-Plaquemine towns had mound-and-plaza combinations that were often built over "substantial Late Woodland villages" (Brown 2003, 210). Large Mississippian mound complexes included Lake George (Holly Bluffs), Anna (see fig. 4), Medora, Winterville, and the Grand Village of the Natchez (Fatherland; see fig. 5) sites, which tended to combine elements of Coles Creek architecture with that of Mississippian-Plaquemine.

Mississippian cultural ideology consisted of a geographically broad politicoreligious tradition based on "artifacts, symbols, motifs, and architectural groupings" displaying physical evidence of ritual activities practiced by numerous ethnic groups (Reilly and Garber 2007, 1). This ideological and artistic tradition began ca. 700 CE and spread throughout much of the northern Plains down to the Gulf of Mexico and beyond, ranging from what is now Wisconsin to northern Florida, and from the southern Appalachians to just west of the Mississippi River where Chitimachas and Caddoans lived; Atakapas appear to have had limited participation in Mississippian-Plaquemine culture). Although the Mississippian "collapse" occurred before the European invasions, the Mississippian period is considered to have officially ended in 1731 with the French destruction of the Grand Village of the Natchez, who were the last remnants of true Mississippian Culture, in modern-day Natchez, Mississippi.

Certain ceramic sets of the lower Yazoo Basin, where Siouans are known to have settled with the Tunicas at Haynes Bluff (see fig. 6) and other settlements, "may identify the Ofo" (Brain 1988, 393). A "thrust from the north," while not necessarily an "invasion," produced a new phase in the Lake George region to which the term *Mississippian* can be applied in a full cultural sense (Phillips 1970, 13). While being relatively new arrivals to the LMV during the late sixteenth and seventeenth centuries, Biloxis and Ofos were likely already Mississippian in culture before their southward migrations,

Fig. 4. Reconstruction of Anna Mounds site, by Dee Turman, from *The Illustrated Encyclopedia of Native American Indian Mounds and Earthworks* (2009; 2016).

Fig. 5. Reconstruction of the site later occupied by Natchez, Grand Village of the Natchez (Fatherland), by Dee Turman, from *The Illustrated Encyclopedia of Native American Indian Mounds and Earthworks* (2009; 2016).

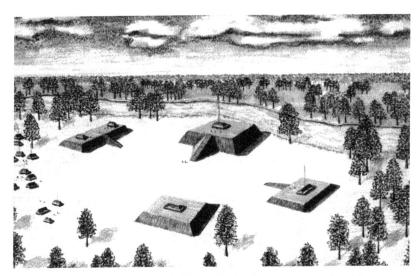

Fig. 6. Reconstruction of Haynes Bluff Mounds site, by Dee Turman, from *The Illustrated Encyclopedia of Native American Indian Mounds and Earthworks* (2009; 2016).

the latter bringing Mississippian-style ceramics such as Old Town Red pottery, a red-filmed pottery of "northern connection" (Brain 1988, 393) that shows up in the Yazoo River basin.

Mississippian iconography includes the swastika, the eye-in-hand motif, the skull and bones motif, the bilobed arrow motif, a feathered (and sometimes horned) serpent, and a representation of the Birdman or Falcon Impersonator, often including a forked-eye motif likely associated with warfare and the military (Reilly and Garber 2007, 5). The Mississippians, despite their advances and achievements in sociopolitical organization and agriculture, were not necessarily peaceful agrarians. Warfare is a major theme in Mississippian art, and "there is evidence of warfare and organized violence throughout Mississippian history" (Birmingham and Goldstein 2005, xiii). Many Mississippian settlements were walled in and heavily fortified (xiii), indicating that attacks and the threat of violence were an ongoing concern for these farmers. As will be seen, most Mississippian cities were abandoned by ca. 1450, "when their inhabitants walked away" (La Vere 2007, 135), possibly succumbing to climatic changes at the beginning of the Little Ice Age, which lasted ca. 1300–1850. (The same fate befell Chaco in the Southwest around the same time.[3])

The sheer grandiosity of many Mississippian settlements warrants further discussion; I will highlight a few of these settlements here. The first, Cahokia, was physically located far north of the LMV, near modern St. Louis. Yet, despite its peripheral location, this ancient city was the largest in North America north of Mexico and has been called the capital of Mississippian Culture, thus warranting further discussion here. A discussion of two other major Mississippian settlements in the LMV, Moundville and Bottle Creek, will follow.

## MAJOR MISSISSIPPIAN PERIOD SETTLEMENTS

### Cahokia

One of the most important North American Plains settlements was known as Cahokia, a "true archaeological behemoth" (Pauketat 2007, 48), the core of which is now preserved as an Illinois state park. Archaeologists named this city Cahokia after a Native group that had later lived in the area (Birmingham and Goldstein 2005, x). What inhabitants of the city called it is unknown (xi). Cahokia (Old Cahokia) was originally established ca. 700–800 CE (Pauketat 2009) near the Mississippi River and modern St. Louis in a Mississippi floodplain called the American Bottom.

Cahokia (New Cahokia) was rebuilt ca. 1050 to become the largest city north of Mexico. It thrived during the Medieval Warm Period, as did Chaco in the Southwest. Cahokia's population exceeded ten thousand; there were at least twenty thousand to thirty thousand more people in the surrounding farming settlements that ranged for fifty miles in each direction (Birmingham and Goldstein 2005, 2). Cahokia contained more than 120 mounds (Alt 2012, 497). Monks Mound, the largest, covered four-fifths the area of the Pyramid of the Sun at Teotihuacan (Mexico) and was even larger in area than the Pyramid of Khufu in Egypt (Birmingham and Goldstein 2005, 2). Cahokia grew to the size of an average ancient Mesopotamian city-state, was about as large as early Andean capitals such as Moche and Tiwanaku (Peru), and was larger than London at the time (Pauketat 2009, 26).

Cahokia covered over five square miles (almost 13 sq km). In its center was a large plaza surrounded by large earthen platforms and other mounds, or "packed-earth pyramids" (Pauketat 2007, 99), along with a two-mile-long palisade that walled off this urban core from the rest of the city (Birmingham and Goldstein 2005, 21). According to Birmingham and Goldstein, "dense residential districts ringed the Cahokia center along with other ceremonial places" (2005, 21).

Cahokia's influence spread far and wide, radiating in all directions, to the southeast and southwest as well as north, including to the top of a narrow bluff as far north as Trempealeau in modern western Wisconsin on which a pyramid-and-causeway complex stood (Boszhardt, Benden, and Pauketat 2015, 68). Its influence also spread into the northern LMV around the Yazoo Basin.

We do not currently know who inhabited Cahokia and what language(s) they spoke, although there is some ethnohistorical evidence of Dhegiha Siouan occupation of the area (see Kehoe 2007). But it is likely that many, or even most, Midwestern, southern, and Plains peoples were somehow "entangled in a history that began at Cahokia" (Pauketat 2009, 38). Cahokia may indeed have been a multicultural and multilingual city, home to speakers of Siouan, Caddoan, Algonquian, and perhaps other languages.[4]

Cahokia is often considered to be the headquarters of Mississippian symbolism and ideology. Ironically, however, there is no evidence of Cahokia being "Mississippian" until about the time of its collapse, ca. 1200 CE (Alice Kehoe, pers. comm., 2016). Cahokia was by far the largest settlement in Mississippian times in North America, and its influence spread to other parts of the Southeast and LMV. I will now discuss two other major Mississippian cities that were influenced by, and outlasted, Cahokia.

### Moundville

Moundville (see fig. 7), near modern Tuscaloosa, Alabama, dated to ca. 1250 CE, was the largest Mississippian-period settlement in the North American Southeast. Located on a bluff above the Black Warrior River, the Moundville complex covered 200 acres and included twenty mounds (Bense 2009, 221).

At Moundville, social stratification is apparent, with two internal ranks evident within the elite stratum. These social ranks had specific burial loca-

Fig. 7. Photograph of a section of Moundville mounds on the Black Warrior River, Alabama. © 2017 John W. Hoopes.

tions and grave goods. Elite individuals were buried in or near platform mounds and were accompanied by stone palettes, copper axes, infants, and single skulls. Commoners, who made up 95 percent of the population at Moundville, were buried either with no grave goods or with items appropriate to their particular age and gender (Bense 2009, 221–23). Moundville reached its climax ca. 1400 CE, at which point it was home to about three thousand people (221). This large settlement then went into decline, like Cahokia, its population dispersing.

### Bottle Creek

Bottle Creek was built and became a major mound city, located in modern Alabama, ca. 1250 CE, around the time of the decline of Cahokia (Walthall 1980, 269). Bottle Creek was situated in the Mobile-Tensaw delta just north of Mobile Bay and had eighteen mounds and various "non-mound habitation areas" (Brown 2003, 1). Bottle Creek is known to have had "early connections" with Moundville to the north (224).

The principal mound at Bottle Creek is a flat-topped pyramidal mound about 46 feet (14 m) tall (Brown 2003, 1). Bottle Creek's location in a swampy, flood-prone delta likely made year-round habitation difficult, if not impossible. It has been speculated that this location was chosen for this huge mound complex because the site itself was "sacred" (220). However, I believe this location may have been chosen for more practical reasons: it was situated near a probable high-activity trading port (Mobile Bay), near several salines, or salt springs, situated along the Tombigbee River, as portrayed on a map dated ca. 1816 by Thomas Freeman, surveyor general for lands south of Tennessee (as appears in Waselkov and Gums 2000, 40, fig. 23). Thus, Bottle Creek may have served as another center of the trade in salt (Galloway 1995, 62), as well as in other items. Bottle Creek itself may have served as a principal port in the region, showing evidence of a man-made 656 foot (200 m) canal at the site (Rodning 2003, 198).

Like Cahokia and Moundville before it, Bottle Creek went into decline, with its population dispersing and mound construction ceasing by ca. 1550. Bottle Creek continued to be occupied to some degree up until the mid-eighteenth century, but by this time the great mound city was no more than a necropolis, or "a repository for the dead," like Moundville had become before it (Brown 2003, 222).

Other important Mississippian-period sites that were on the periphery of the LMV and are believed to have had contact with Cahokia are Spiro (see La Vere 2007) in modern eastern Oklahoma and Aztalan (see Birmingham and Goldstein 2005) in modern southern Wisconsin.

### TRADE

The Southeast had been a major center of long-distance trade at least as far back as the fourth millennium BCE, even preceding the development of mound-and-plaza architecture (Brown, Kerber, and Winters 1990, 273; Jefferies 1996, 225; Johnson 1994, 100).[5] Long-distance trade fluctuated in intensity at various times in LMV history (Kidder 2004; Johnson 1994). Items traded included chert, copper, ceramics, galena, soapstone, meteoritic iron, and marine shell (Johnson 1994). The three most highly valued materials were copper, marine shells, and freshwater pearls (Brown, Kerber, and Winters 1990, 260).

Salt was another highly valued commodity that is often overlooked and little mentioned in the literature. In the early eighteenth century, salt was an important trade commodity among Caddos. Reports of salt production and trade in the Caddo region date back to de Soto's expedition (Girard, Perttula, and Trubitt 2014, 117). The Chitimachas and Atakapas may have also been salt producers and traders. Their western and eastern territorial boundaries, respectively, bordered on Petite Anse—what came to be called Avery Island—about two miles from Vermilion Bay, now known for its production of McIlhenny Tabasco sauce (Avery salt, white wine vinegar, and Avery-grown red peppers being primary ingredients of the sauce) (Kurlansky 2002). Avery Island is a salt dome. Archaeologists have discovered this region to be the location of an ancient saltworks "in the manner of the early Romans," in which brine (water saturated with salt) was evaporated in pottery that was then broken. Ceramic sherds used for salt evaporation, dating back to at least a thousand years ago, covered about a five-acre area of Avery Island (Kurlansky 2003, 272).

The Tunicas were also salt producers and traders, as were likely the Biloxis. Unfortunately, little is currently known about how various Native American groups participated in salt production (Girard, Perttula, and Trubitt 2014, 117). I concur with White that salt as a product of socioeconomic interaction in the Gulf region (and in Native America in general) needs more investigation (White 2005, 310).

Unfortunately no unified theory of trade has arisen in regard to the Southeast (Johnson 1994, 116). However, it is likely that "interregional alliances" played a large role in ritual exchange (Johnson 1994, 115; Brown, Kerber, and Winters 1990, 253). The establishment in various places of merchant colonies, especially among stronger groups, likely also played a large role in trade, just as it did in the ancient Near East, Europe, and other places.

Some archaeologists believe that Poverty Point served as a major trade center, with marine shells and fiber-tempered ceramic sherds from western Florida (Kehoe 1998, 154) and copper artifacts from the Great Lakes dating back to 4000 BCE (Brown, Kerber, and Winters 1990, 273). The LMV's prime location along the Mississippi River ensured a navigable north-south route of transport; its location along the Gulf Coast ensured an east-west and circum-Gulf route.

Cahokia may have influenced the LMV ca. 1050–1200 CE in the realm of ceramics (Wells and Weinstein 2007). There is "unmistakable evidence of direct contact" between Cahokia and the LMV, primarily in the Yazoo Basin region (52). This contact is evident at the Winterville, Shell Bluff, and Lake George (Holly Bluff) sites (55). The last shows evidence of occupation by Tunicas and Ofos (a Siouan group) (Brain 1988). Caddoans, on the northwest periphery of the LMV, were known for their production of pottery and salt, which they certainly traded with Atakapas, Chitimachas, and others in the LMV. Caddoans also cultivated and traded maize, a commodity they likely received from the Southwest, that they also traded to other LMV groups, including Biloxis and Ofos.

Unfortunately, "archaeologists and historians are still enormously biased in favor of explaining cultural interaction in the past as a result of travel over land … when for most of the human past it was much more difficult and far less relevant than water travel" (White 2005, 14). Although trade and contact also occurred on foot, the plethora in the LMV of bayous and other waterways, including the Gulf itself, would have made water transportation the most efficient means of trade and movement. As Wilkerson observes, "trade and movement by water is likely to have been not only commonplace, but also a virtual necessity, from very early in the history of sedentary life on the Gulf Coast" (2005, 60). The fact that the majority of chert found at Poverty Point was from modern Illinois, Indiana, and Missouri rather than from the Appalachian Mountains suggests that this chert from the Middle Tennessee Valley arrived in Poverty Point via the Tennessee, Ohio, and Mississippi Rivers rather than overland (Johnson 1994, 110).

The placement of the Bottle Creek site in Alabama, in the middle of a swampy river delta north of Mobile Bay, in itself attests to the importance of water travel as a force in shaping Mississippian Culture and settlement (Rodning 2003, 195). Indigenous canals have been identified at localities along the Gulf Coast; a canal in Bottle Creek, possibly engineered and constructed by its inhabitants, has also been found (198).

The primary craft of travel and trade was the dugout canoe. To make the canoes, fire was used to hollow out a single log of bald cypress, poplar, or pine, although some larger ones were made of cottonwood (Hudson 1976). Canoes could reach enormous proportions and were used for warfare as well as for trade and transportation. That at least the largest canoes were likely seaworthy appears evident from the discovery of certain species of barnacles at Bottle Creek that may have arrived in boats coming "across Mobile Bay or the Gulf itself" (Rodning 2003, 203).

## AGRICULTURE

The LMV groups discussed here, with the exception of the Atakapas, were likely heavily involved with agriculture. Principally due to the drop-off of rainfall in the western reaches of the LMV, Atakapan groups were not major agriculturalists and largely remained fishermen and hunter-gatherers, sometimes hunting bison in the interior (Swanton 1946, 802).

Ancient North America, as with ancient Mesopotamia, Egypt, and China, was home to some of the world's first farmers. The first evidence for a shift from hunting and gathering to farming in North America appears midcontinent through the Central Mississippi Valley as early as ca. 4000 BCE (Smith 2011). Evidence for the early use of domesticated Native American crops is strongest on the northern periphery of the LMV (Kidder 2004, 552). As part of a floodplain, the LMV served as a limited center of agricultural production of primarily native North American cultigens from at least ca. 2000 BCE on. However, the LMV was not a major agrarian center until ca. 1200 CE, with the arrival of intensive maize agriculture from the north (Kidder and Fritz 1993). This was the beginning of the Mississippian-Plaquemine culture in the LMV, although the Yazoo River basin in the northern LMV had stronger ties with Mississippian Culture to the north even before this. The linguistic evidence, particularly the lack of loans related to plants and agriculture, suggests that LMV groups likely already did at least some small-scale farming before their migrations into the LMV.

These early North Americans, like ancient Mesopotamians and Egyptians, took advantage of the yearly river floods that provided optimal growing conditions and fertility. Three of the four plant species domesticated in eastern North America (marsh elder, chenopod, and *Cucurbita pepo* gourds) are floodplain weeds brought forth on an annual basis by spring flooding (Smith 2011, S477).

Native seed crops were not cultivated "as major foods south of northern Alabama" (Fritz and Kidder 1993, 7). At the Reno Brake site in north-central Louisiana, there is evidence of the consumption and use of acorns (*Quercus* spp.), pecans, and fruits such as grape (*Vitis* spp.), persimmon (*Diospyros virginiana*), and palmetto (*Sabal minor*) (7). There is indirect evidence (chipped stone bifaces and flakes exhibiting a high degree of polish) of hoe cultivation in Poverty Point, but the *C. pepo* squash is the only potential cultigen well documented in archaeobotanical assemblages in Poverty Point (ca. 1500 BCE) (Fritz and Kidder 1993).

Farming increased in intensity after the advent of Mississippian-Plaquemine culture ca. 1200 CE. Although maize first entered the Mobile Bay region ca. 1500 BCE, this crop does not hold high prominence in the LMV until the time of Mississippian-Plaquemine influence. Maize arrived in North America from Mesoamerica, first in the Southwest ca. 3000 BCE, then later in the Southeast ca. 1500 BCE, at Lake Shelby (Clark and Knoll 2005; Fearn and Liu 1995, 109), in modern-day coastal Alabama near Mobile Bay and ca. 400 BCE at the north end of the Tombigbee River in what is now northeastern Mississippi (Fearn and Liu 1995, 110).[6] Rather than first occurring, as one might expect, in regions closer to Mesoamerica, the first securely dated evidence of maize (based on pollens) in eastern North America occurs about 144 miles (232 km) east of the Mississippi River near Mobile Bay, which, as earlier suggested, was a Native American "principal port" (Tanner 1989).

Now that we have an idea of the geography, geology, and archaeological history of the region, we can now focus on the peoples, their migrations, and languages.

# THREE

# Peoples, Migrations, and Languages

In this chapter I provide an overview of the peoples and languages of the LMV (see fig. 8) as well as explore known and probable movements of peoples both within and into the LMV, as much as this can be known or inferred. After some general remarks on peoples, migrations, and languages of the LMV, I will explore these three topics individually under each specific group. MTL, a pidgin or trade language not associated with a particular people, will be discussed separately toward the end of the chapter.

## PEOPLES

The LMV, along with the rest of the North American Southeast, was one of the most densely populated regions of North America (only the Northwest coast, present-day California, and the Southwest Pueblo area had higher population densities) (Sherzer 1976; Kroeber 1939). Peoples in the LMV region include Atakapas, Biloxis, Chitimachas, Choctaw-Chickasaws, Natchez, Ofos, and Tunicas. Each of these peoples had carved out a niche in the LMV, as described by Kroeber:

> The Natchez and their neighbors lived in a habitat of River-bottom and Transition Forest, the Chickasaw largely in Deciduous; the Choctaw . . . chiefly in the Pine . . . the Chitimacha, and the supposedly Muskogian [*sic*] tribes downstream from New Orleans, in a region of prevailing marsh grassland. (1939, 63)

Atakapas, Chitimachas, and Natchez may have inhabited the LMV for a long period of time. Biloxis, Choctaw-Chickasaws, Ofos, and Tunicas, on the other hand, appear to have undertaken long-distance migrations at various times and, in the case of all but the Choctaw-Chickasaws, evince multiple movements within the LMV that were primarily due to the on-

Fig. 8. Map of primary peoples and languages mentioned in this book. Those in larger font indicate LMV peoples and languages while those in smaller font are considered peripheral. Map by author.

slaught of European invaders and the harsh consequences thereof, including increasing hostilities, violence, and slave raids.

## MIGRATIONS

Unfortunately, with the exception of Tunicas, Biloxis, and Ofos, little is known about early movements and migrations of people in the region. We must rely on scanty archaeological, linguistic, and oral narrative evidence to determine the origins and locations of most LMV groups prior to Spanish and French documentation of the sixteenth century. Oral histories used in tandem with linguistic and archaeological data, when available, can help us to pinpoint origins and migrations; such oral narratives will be discussed here along with some linguistic and archaeological data.

## LANGUAGES

The LMV languages represent different linguistic genetic families; Ataka-pan, Chitimachan, Muskogean, Natchesan, Siouan, and Tunican. Choctaw and Chickasaw are Muskogean languages, while Biloxi and Ofo are Siouan. The other languages are isolates, like Basque in Europe, with no known current linguistic relatives.[1]

The languages discussed here are Atakapa, Biloxi, Chitimacha, Choctaw-Chickasaw, MTL, Natchez, Ofo, and Tunica. MTL, or Mobilian Jargon, is a pidgin, one of a few that occurred in North America (others include Chinook Jargon in the Northwest and Delaware, or Unami, Jargon on the East Coast). It was used as a lingua franca in intensive trade and contact in the Mobile Bay region and throughout much of the LMV and southeastern United States. In pre-European times the Southeast was linguistically complex. However, this area was among the first to suffer European encroachment. Thus, some languages and also entire language families went extinct long before linguistic scholars were able to document them. European documents refer to many groups and languages that are now unknown to us and lost to history.

The LMV languages are typologically and grammatically quite different from Indo-European (IE) languages like English, Spanish, French, and German. The LMV languages, with the exception of MTL, are polysynthetic in nature, meaning that they are "languages which share a high number of morphemes per word" (Mithun 1999, 38). LMV languages thus structurally resemble the agglutinative Finno-Ugric, Kartvelian (Southern Caucasian), and Turkic languages of Central Asia more closely than IE languages. Like many other indigenous American languages, LMV languages (with the exception of MTL) rely heavily on affixation, by which prefixes and suffixes are added primarily to verb roots in order to convey a large number of distinct ideas within a single word (Boas 1911, 74). In English, these ideas would take several separate words to convey. These indigenous languages are "head-marking" languages, the "head" word usually being a verb. A single verb in these languages can serve as an entire sentence unto itself.

LMV languages range from mildly synthetic to heavily polysynthetic. Here is an example of the latter from Natchez, arguably the most polysynthetic LMV language. The first line demonstrates the actual utterance.[2] The second line shows the breakdown of the morphemes involved in the utterance, while the third line gives the meaning of each morpheme. The fourth line gives a free translation of the utterance, in this case of the one word:

(1)   *ʔokšene·škuya*
      *ʔok-še-ne-···škʷ-ya*
      stick.on-QT-IMPF-EMPH-AUX-ART
      'and he was really sticking them on'
      (Kimball 2005, 391)

Here we can clearly see the polysynthetic nature of Natchez in that several morphemes in the form of suffixes are added to the "head word" verb ('stick on' in this case), making the single Natchez word equivalent to an entire sentence in English. Most LMV languages, while structured similarly, are less extreme in this regard than in this Natchez example. The Natchez example also demonstrates that, as in all of the LMV languages (again with the exception of MTL), verbs are the most highly inflected category. Nouns, on the other hand, are relatively uninflected, although Tunica has the unique feature that all nouns, regardless of animacy, are marked with masculine or feminine gender, as in, for example, Spanish and French. All LMV languages are verb-final, following a subject-object-verb (SOV) sentence pattern, with the exception of MTL, which is object-subject-verb, or OSV, when an object exists.

Both three- and five-vowel systems are attested in the LMV. Western and Eastern Muskogean languages have three-vowel (*i, a, o*) systems, as does peripheral Caddoan. MTL also has a three-vowel (*e, a, o*) system, though with considerable variance in phonetic realization (Drechsel 1996, 261). Other LMV languages have five-vowel (*i, e, a, o, u*) systems.

Biloxi and Choctaw-Chickasaw show heavily developed systems of subject reference tracking (switch reference), while Natchez shows topic tracking. Biloxi and Choctaw-Chickasaw have systems of evidentiality, while all of the LMV languages show various degrees of discourse or pragmatic marking, such as focus-marking. Switch reference, evidentiality, and discourse marking are perhaps the most unfamiliar concepts to speakers of

English and other Indo-European languages, though being more familiar to speakers of, say, Turkic and other Central Asian languages.[3]

Two languages in the LMV, Tunica and Natchez, have been noted to have retroflex sibilants (Rankin 1988). This retroflexion may have spread from the greater Gulf-Atlantic sprachbund (see below), since such retroflexion also occurs in the Eastern Muskogean languages Muskogee (Creek), Hitchiti, and Alabama, as well as in peripheral Siouan Quapaw (Rankin 1988). Nasalized vowels occur in Atakapa, Biloxi, Choctaw-Chickasaw, and Ofo. MTL has "nondistinctive nasalized variation" (Drechsel 1996, 257). Nasal vowels also occur in Natchez, but only in phrase-final position, as a form of declarative marker. The bilabial fricative /ɸ/, written <f>, is not common in North America, but it occurs in the LMV and Gulf-Atlantic region among all Muskogean languages as a reflex of Proto-Muskogean $*x^w$. It also occurs in one Siouan language, Ofo (as its name implies), possibly through diffusion from Muskogean. Atakapa also has the /ɸ/ phoneme, but it is rare. The voiceless lateral fricative /ɬ/ occurs in the Muskogean languages, including in MTL, and in Atakapa. The phoneme /x/ is found in the Siouan languages Biloxi and Ofo as well as in Atakapa. The phoneme /kʷ/ is found only in Natchez. The phoneme /tl/ occurs only in Atakapa and is likely a reflex of /ɬ/.

Vowel harmony, also a feature of many Mesoamerican languages, is found in Natchez. Natchez has pitch accent with four pitch contours: high, mid, rising, and falling (Kimball 2005, 396). All LMV languages share a quinary (base 5) number system, as opposed to, for example, the vigesimal (base 20) system typical of Mesoamerican and the Coahuiltecan (Rio Grande Valley region) languages.

Haas proposed a tenuous genetic relationship among Natchez, Tunica, Atakapa, Chitimacha, Muskogean (what she collectively called the "Gulf" languages), and Siouan, saying that Siouan languages were "at least distantly related to the Gulf languages" but that she was "not yet ready to publish the evidence for this statement" (1958, 233–34). She conceded that there was a lack of material on Proto-Siouan, and did not pursue this idea any further. The modern consensus of most linguists, including me, is that such a relationship is not adequately supported and cannot be verified.

Chafe (1976) proposed a genetic link among the Siouan, Caddoan, and Iroquoian language families, but again little has been done on this proposed relationship and it remains unverified.

Haas (1958) presented a somewhat stronger case for a possible genetic affiliation between the Gulf languages and Algonquian, based primarily on phonetic and phonological evidence. Much of this evidence is less than convincing, however. For example, she proposed a relationship between the Proto-Central-Algonquian (PCA) *kwan- 'swallow' and Proto-Muskogean (PM) *kʷalak-, Natchez -akun-, Tunica kɔra, Chitimacha kaač-t-, and Atakapa kul, which seems a bit of a stretch. She does demonstrate a few more convincing links, such as PCA *pak- 'beat,' Natchez paak-, Tunica pɛka, and Atakapa pak. However, the similarities are more likely due to diffusion, or possibly even to onomatopoeia, than to a genetic relationship. The Biloxi term *pakpakhayi*, referring to a type of woodpecker, supports the onomatopoeic interpretation in this case, though this does not rule out the possible sharing of an onomatopoeic term among languages, which does happen. LMV languages also borrowed from Algonquian languages, as attested by the PCA word for 'eye' *ški:nšekw (Haas 1958, 245), borrowed as Choctaw *niškin* (Byington and Swanton 1915, 445) and MTL *nešken* (Drechsel 1996, 280), possibly arriving via contact with Algonquian languages to the north.

### The Periphery

Around the periphery of the LMV were Algonquian Shawnee and Siouan Quapaw to the north and the isolate Euchee (Yuchi) to the northeast. To the east were the Eastern Muskogean languages (including Muskogee [Creek], Alabama, Hitchiti, and Koasati [Coushatta]), Cherokee, Catawba, and Timucua. I incorporate these languages into a separate but adjoining language area: the Gulf-Atlantic (GA) sprachbund. Toward the west and southwest were the isolates Karankawa[4] and Tonkawa along with the languages of the Rio Grande Valley region (including Coahuiltec, Cotoname, and Comecrudo). I incorporate these languages into another separate but adjoining language area: the Rio Grande Valley (RGV) sprachbund. To the south of this region, in north-central Mexico, there is Huastec, a Mayan language long separated from its linguistic sisters farther south. Just beyond Huastec are Nahuatl (Aztec) and Totonac. The GA and RGV language areas overlap somewhat with the LMV sprachbund, demonstrating a continuum of language contact, and thus trade, from the Atlantic coast all the way along the Gulf into north-central Mexico.

I will now discuss individual groups of the LMV, in alphabetical order, along with their languages and what is known of their migration history. MTL will be discussed last as an independent entity that was used as a second (or even third or fourth) language for trade and contact by many groups in the LMV region.

### ATAKAPAS

The Atakapas are located along the Gulf Coast in what is now southwestern Louisiana and southeastern Texas, where they have been located at least since European contact in the sixteenth century. Atakapans, who are thought to have included Akokisas, Opelousas, Bidais, and Patiris, inhabited marshy regions of the coast as well as inland prairies and pine forests. Groups of Atakapans lived on Vermilion Bayou, on Mermentou River, and on lakes near the mouth of the Calcasieu[5] River (Swanton 1946, 93).

The Atakapas called themselves *Yokiti* and *Takapo* (Gatschet and Swanton 1932) as well as *Išak*, meaning simply 'people.' The name *Atakapa* is an exonym bestowed upon them by speakers of a Western Muskogean language, meaning 'man-eater,' apparently due to the supposed Atakapan custom of ritual cannibalism. According to Atakapa narrative, the wife of the Western Atakapa chief Lo came to found a new nation of Atakapas "yonder toward the rising sun" (Gatschet and Swanton 1932, 11), or Sunrise People, those who came to speak the Eastern Dialect (see text in appendix). Western Atakapas, or Sunset People, who spoke the Western Dialect, lived around Lake Charles. Swanton estimated a population ca. 1805 of between 1,000 and 3,500 (Swanton 1946, 94).

Atakapas were part of what archaeologists call the Mossy Grove culture, which extended from about the Sabine River west to the Colorado River in southeastern Texas (Ricklis 2004, 191). They were principally fishermen, although they also hunted white-tailed deer and bison. Although Atakapas may have practiced farming on a small scale, they were not known to be intensive agriculturalists. They alternated between living in coastal regions and farther inland in different seasons.

Atakapas received pottery from the Karankawas and Caddoans. They traded heavily with Chitimachas. Atakapas traded dried and smoked fish and such items as shark teeth with other LMV groups (Swanton 1946). Atakapas, along with Chitimachas, were likely salt producers and traders, both living in close proximity to the Avery Island salt dome.

Although Atakapas are not known to have heavily participated in Mississippian-Plaquemine culture, there is evidence of heavy population growth and at least incipient societal stratification about the time of the arrival of Mississippian-Plaquemine culture ca. 1200 CE, indicating the emergence of an elite class that may have come about through cultural influence from the east.

## Migrations

An Atakapa story states that, after a great flood, Atakapan ancestors ended up in "the mountains of northwest Texas beyond San Antonio" (Swanton 1911, 348, 363), probably in the Texas hill country. This tells us nothing, however, about earlier migrations. The Atakapas may have been in place along the Gulf Coast for a very long time, perhaps millennia.

## Language

Atakapa is a now extinct isolate language spoken until the early twentieth century by several small groups along the Gulf Coast between Vermilion Bay, Louisiana, and Galveston Bay, Texas, and up the Trinity River (Mithun 1999, 344). Atakapa is a moderately polysynthetic, head-marking language, as in the following example:

(2)  *tepuk*    *neš*    *hihulat*
     tepuk    neš    hi-hul-at
     peach    tree    INDF-plant-CMP
     'They planted peach trees.'
     (modified from Gatschet and Swanton 1932, 9)

Vowels are /i/, /e/, /a/, /o/, and /u/, both oral and nasal; there was apparently also vowel length but this was not consistently marked by Gatschet and

Swanton. Consonants are stops /p/, /t/, /k/, and /ʔ/; fricatives /f/ (rare), /š/, /h/, and /x/; voiced sonorants /m/, /n/, /ŋ/, /l/, /w/, and /y/; and laterals /tl/ and /ɬ/. The Atakapa phonemes /tl/ and /ŋ/ are unique in the LMV; there is the possibility that the latter is a dialectal variant of vowel + /n/, thus *wan* or *waṇ* 'walk' (Gatschet and Swanton 1932, 141). The operation of stress in Atakapa is not clearly understood, although stress appears to have been phonemic, as the pair *ka'khaw* 'sun' (Gatschet and Swanton 1932, 178) and *kakaw'* 'water' (Gatschet and Swanton 1932, 180) attest, apparently showing first-syllable stress in the former and final-syllable stress in the latter, in addition to an apparent difference in the phonetic quality of the middle *k* (aspiration in the former and no aspiration in the latter) (Kaufman 2014b, 77).

Verbal prefixes include objective pronominal prefixes in three persons and two numbers, reflexive, and reciprocal. Verbal suffixes include subjective pronominal suffixes in three persons and two numbers, usitative, future, continuative, volitional (sometimes used for future), perfect, a negative, and tense (Mithun 1999, 345). Atakapa has at least two forms of past tense, reflecting the aspectual distinction between complete and incomplete action. Atakapa, like Natchez, does not appear to have a distinction between alienable and inalienable possession. Like Chitimacha, Atakapa verbs have two conjugation paradigms with agent-patient semantic alignment. Atakapa and Chitimacha both have a focus and assertive suffix -*š*. The Atakapa -*š* can also serve as a definite article.

There may have been various Atakapan languages in the LMV, including Bidai, which went extinct early on, and Opelousa. Jean Béranger had elicited a supposed forty-five-word Atakapan vocabulary in 1721 that Swanton designated as Akokisa, an undocumented group that lived on Galveston Bay. Although Gatschet and Swanton (1932) incorporated Béranger's Akokisa vocabulary into his Atakapa dictionary, it is uncertain whether this vocabulary actually reflects the Akokisa language (Goddard 2005, 38).

Swanton (1932) divided Atakapa-speaking groups into two major subgroups, Western Dialect (WD) and Eastern Dialect (ED). The three varieties noted herein, including Akokisa, based on the Gatschet-Swanton data, show relatively minor phonological and lexical differences among them. The number systems, however, seem to diverge drastically between WD and ED.

Extant data for the Atakapa language is very limited. The earliest vocabulary of Atakapa was collected in 1721 by the French sea-captain explorer Jean Béranger, who carried off nine of the "Indians of that region," all of whom escaped shortly thereafter. Béranger collected forty-five words of the language (Gatschet and Swanton 1932, 2). An ED vocabulary of 287 entries was collected in 1802 by the Spanish commander Martin Duralde. In 1885 Gatschet collected WD material in consultation with Louison Huntington and Delilah (or Delia, as she was also known) Moss in Lake Charles, Louisiana. Gatschet's material consists primarily of words and phrases, but he transcribed about four and a half pages of text from Louison Huntington (Gatschet and Swanton 1932, 5).

Swanton (1932) compiled and edited a 181-page, bidirectional Atakapa-English dictionary, containing about eight hundred headwords with some sample sentences and verb conjugations, incorporating the earlier material from Gatschet. This dictionary includes nine texts. The only Atakapa grammar available is the twenty-eight-page Swanton (1929) article, which provides a good overview of phonetics and phonology, morphology, and syntax, including detailed remarks on the use of affixes, and one annotated text with gloss and free translation.

We are currently preparing an Atakapa Ishak grammar and dictionary (Southworth and Kaufman, forthcoming) for learners, to assist with language revitalization efforts. This book will incorporate all of the above data with an updated orthography in a user-friendly format for ease of reference.

### BILOXIS

Biloxis, who call themselves *Tanêks* (Dorsey and Swanton 1912, 5), settled the farthest south of any currently known Siouan group. Biloxis and Ofos are Ohio Valley, or Southeastern, Siouans who may have been a single group prior to ca. 800 CE. Biloxis and Ofos acquire separate terms for an object for the first time with the arrival of the bow, ca. 400–600 CE (Biloxi *ąksaapixti* and Ofo *šleka* [Dorsey and Swanton 1912, 329], the latter possibly a borrowing from Lakota *awosleca* 'to split by shooting upon' [Buechel and

Manhart 2002, 33]). Similarly, beans arrived in the Southeast ca. 1100 CE and gained separate terms in Biloxi and Ofo (Robert Rankin, pers. comm., 2007). This linguistic evidence suggests a Biloxi-Ofo split around 600–1100 CE.

Biloxis are traditionally thought to have first made contact with Europeans in 1699, when they met the French explorer Iberville while living on the Pascagoula River near Mobile Bay (Swanton 1946, 96; Goddard 2005, 9). (The modern resort city of Biloxi, Mississippi, and Biloxi Bay are named for them.) However, Biloxis may also have been "the Istanane [Estanani] mentioned in narratives of the Spanish expeditions of 1693 to survey Pensacola Bay, said to be a very numerous tribe living 'along a western bayou in Mobile Bay'" (Swanton 1946, 96; Waselkov and Gums 2000, 25; Goddard 2005, 9). *Annocchy* may have been another name for Biloxis (Waselkov and Gums 2000, 26). But Biloxis may have had even earlier contacts with Spaniards in the late sixteenth century, during the Juan Pardo *entradas.*[6] Given the prior Spanish estimate of the Biloxis (Estananis) as being "very numerous," smallpox epidemics may have reduced their numbers considerably. The population of Biloxis was estimated between thirty and seventy, from 1805 to 1829 (Swanton 1946, 98).

## Migrations

A discussion of Biloxi (and Ofo) migrations must begin with the apparent *Urheimat*, or homeland, of Siouan-speaking peoples and the long-distance migrations of Proto-Siouans. There has been a long-standing debate on the exact homeland of Siouan-speaking peoples. Much of the debate has focused on the opposing views of Swanton (1943), a linguist, and Griffin (1942), an archaeologist. Swanton posited that the Siouan homeland was likely located in the Ohio Valley prior to ca. 1000 CE, while Griffin posited that it was in the Allegheny Piedmont region of modern-day Virginia and the Carolinas. I suspect that Swanton's position is closer to the mark. Part of Griffin's argument against an Ohio Valley Siouan Urheimat is his contention that the "historic evidence available on the Tutelo indicate that they were in the Piedmont area at the time of the first contacts and does not indicate that they had ever been in the Ohio Valley" (1942, 279). However,

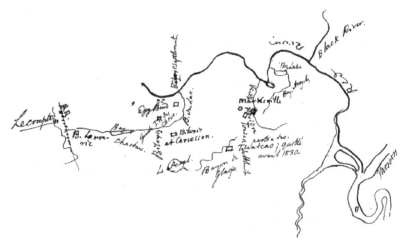

Fig. 9. Hand-drawn map by Albert Gatschet (1886) showing location of Biloxi and Choctaw settlements near Marksville, Louisiana, on the Red River just west of the Mississippi (after 1776).

the linguistic data (see below) indicates that the Tutelos may indeed have inhabited the Ohio Valley.

Much of Swanton's evidence for an Ohio Valley origin of Siouan peoples comes, rightfully, from the oral narratives of Siouan speakers themselves. Swanton specifically states, "according to the traditions of western Siouan tribes, they, or at least some of them, formerly lived toward the east, the Ohio river being in some cases specifically mentioned" (1943, 49). He further states that "all of the [Siouan] traditions speak of a movement from the east to the west covering a long period of time … [Their homeland] seems to have been situated … among the Appalachian mountains" (49). The Omahas, in particular, "remember a tradition that their ancestors once dwelt at the place where Saint Louis now stands" (50). This would place the Omahas, as well as possibly other Siouan groups, in the vicinity of the large city of Cahokia, occupying the American Bottom region in the vicinity of modern East St. Louis. Siouan Osage and Omaha oral narratives of the priestly class have been linked to several features at Cahokia (Kehoe 2007). This supposed Siouan westward migration from east to west is also supported by what the "Berthold Indians" (likely Hidatsas[7]) of Fort Berthold, North

Dakota, reported to Dr. Washington Matthews of the U.S. Army: "Long ago the Sioux were all to the east, and none to the West and South, as they now are" (Riggs [1893] 2004, 181).

> In those times the western plains must have been very sparsely peopled … in comparison with the present, for the old men now living, and children of men of the past generation, say that they traveled to the southwest … to a country where the prairie ceased, and were gone from their village twenty-one moons. Others went to the north to a country where the summer was but three moons long. (181–82)

Ancestral Biloxis likely originated in the western Appalachian, or Cumberland Plateau, region near modern Knoxville, Tennessee. They were likely part of what archaeologists call the Dallas Phase, which is the latest Mississippian culture found in modern eastern Tennessee (Kimball 1994, 72). The Dallas Phase included mound-and-plaza towns surrounded by a palisade, or wall. Kimball endorses a connection between the Dallas Phase and the Eastern Muskogean Koasati (Coushatta) people, one of his primary arguments being Dallas Phase house-building techniques. The Koasati word for 'wall' is *čakpá*, which refers to the four sides of a house rather than an individual wall, suggesting that walls are considered a unit (Kimball 1994, 72). Biloxi also has no single word for 'wall' but instead has the word *thipsohe*, literally 'house corner,' similarly suggesting that the walls of a house are a unit. This suggests that both Koasatis and Ohio Valley Siouans were part of the Dallas Phase, living close to each other in the same region and both likely part of the Mississippian kingdom of Coosa.

A couple of toponyms in the region seemingly containing the Biloxi word for 'salt,' *waasi*—*Ouasi-oto*, the old name for Cumberland Gap, and *Guasi-le*—suggest that Ohio Valley Siouans, including Biloxis and their ancestors, occupied this region (Kaufman 2016, 40n4) and may have been salt producers and merchants. Further support for this origin comes from the Juan Pardo documents of the late sixteenth century. He is mentioned meeting with several chiefs in the southern Appalachians, including with one named Atuqui (Hudson 1990, 96, 219, 231), or Atuki, which means 'raccoon' in Biloxi.

Later, Biloxis "appear at various places and at various times in the documentary record. They seem to have either gone through a series of movements throughout the late seventeenth century or were divided into several towns stretching from present-day central Alabama to the Gulf coast" (Ethridge 2010, 174). After their meeting with Europeans in 1699, Biloxis moved ca. 1702 to "a small bayou between New Orleans and Lake Pontchartrain," then ca. 1722 they settled on the Pearl River on a site once occupied by the Acolapissas (Colapissas). Between then and 1730 "they seem to have drifted back to the neighborhood of the Pascagoula River." A French map of 1733 "shows a Biloxi site on Alabama River at the mouth of Bear Creek" in modern Alabama. It is unknown whether this may represent a site established during a Biloxi migration southward toward the Gulf from the Cumberland Plateau, but it remains a possibility, although it could also be a group that splintered off from the main body of Biloxis on the Pascagoula. In 1763 Biloxis moved west of the Mississippi, settling near the mouth of the Red River. After this time, many Biloxis fused with the Tunicas and Choctaws, though a "large body" of Biloxis "went to Texas and established themselves on a stream in Angelina County, still called Biloxi Bayou" (Swanton 1946, 97). Biloxis eventually united with Tunicas, an unrelated group. The Tunica-Biloxi Tribe was federally recognized in 1981, situated on an old Spanish land grant in modern Marksville, Louisiana.

### Language

Figure 10 shows the Siouan language family. Proto-Siouan is thought to have split into three distinct branches possibly as early as 1000 BCE: Missouri Valley, Mississippi Valley, and Ohio Valley (Southeastern) — the last being most relevant to the present study. The italicized forms indicate the major subgroups (Dakotan, Chiwere, and Dhegiha) of the (upper) Mississippi Valley branch. Note that the Mississippi Valley branch of Siouan does not include Biloxi and Ofo, because these latter languages are likely to be, like Tutelo, from the Ohio Valley region in origin and are intrusive to the Mississippi Valley. (An asterisk follows extinct varieties.)

Biloxi is a now extinct Ohio Valley (also called Southeastern) Siouan language, closely related to Ofo. The autonym may be related to the Biloxi term *tani* 'to be in advance of another' and *tąniki* 'first' (Dorsey and Swanton 1912, 5), thus perhaps 'the first ones.' Biloxi was spoken in southern

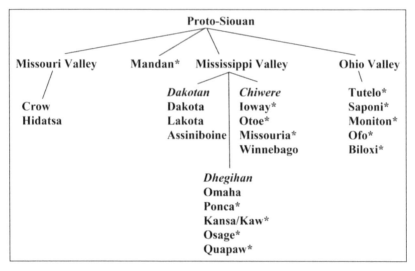

Fig. 10. Siouan Language Family (after Rankin 2006). Created by author.

Mississippi when French Canadians first encountered them in 1699. Later, as they were forced westward, the language was spoken in Louisiana and eastern Texas. The last known native semi-speaker of Biloxi, Emma Jackson, died in 1934. The few remaining members of the Biloxi nation currently share a small reservation with the Tunicas (see below), a linguistically unrelated group, in Marksville, Louisiana.

Biloxi is a mildly polysynthetic, head-marking language:

(3)  *tahôôxk*   *nǫpa*   *ko*   *x-khu.khu*       *ǫ*      *daha*      *dąde.*
     horse     two    ?    1-give.REDUP    do    PL.OBJ    FUT
     'I will give two (of the) horses to each (man).'
     (Dorsey and Swanton 1912, 210)

Verbs are subject to noun incorporation. Biloxi lost the active-stative split common to other Siouan languages. Deictics follow nouns in Biloxi. Negation is optionally periphrastic with a prefix *ka-*, but the suffix *-ni* alone is sufficient. The plural suffix *-tu* can be added to any noun or stative verb, but is optionally employed; often the singular/plural distinction goes unmarked. A dual verbal form exists only for verbs of motion and for positional auxiliaries. A type of nominal case system exists, although, as in Choctaw, suffixed forms for accusative (object) and locative seem to be largely speaker-centered and not obligatory. Biloxi stress is poorly understood.

In 1886 Albert Gatschet, a linguist with the Bureau of American Ethnology (BAE), traveled from Washington DC to Louisiana to collect cultural and linguistic information. While there, Gatschet met with Jim Sam (full-blood Biloxi), Bankston Johnson (half-Biloxi, half-Alabama), Juliane Dilsey, Maria Dilsey, Matt Caddy (full-blood Biloxi), Ben Austin, John Dorsey, Betsey Joe Johnson, and William Johnson (half-Biloxi, half-Tunica) (Gatschet 1886).

Gatschet produced a word-list of Biloxi vocabulary, which proved that Biloxi was a Siouan language and not Muskogean, as previously thought due to its geographic location near Muskogean languages. For example Gatschet found the following correlations between Biloxi and Dakota (northern Plains Siouan): Biloxi *sûpi* or *s'pi* 'black' and Dakota *sapa* 'black'; Biloxi *akpe* 'six' and Dakota *sha'kpe*. This word-list was never published but is available through the Smithsonian (MS 1347, Smithsonian Institution National Anthropological Archives). Later, James Dorsey,[8] a missionary-linguist who had worked extensively on Siouan languages, visited the same area on the Red River where Gatschet had been. Dorsey met with language consultants Maria Johnson, Betsey Joe Johnson, and Bankston Johnson (Dorsey and Swanton 1912), these last two having been visited by Gatschet six years prior.

Seventeen years later, in 1912, Swanton posthumously gathered Dorsey's material in order to edit and publish it. Swanton produced a dictionary of the Biloxi and Ofo languages (1912), which contains about 2,400 lexical items (2,000 Biloxi and 400 Ofo items), with some sample sentences and many elicited phrases and verbal paradigms. This work includes thirty-one Biloxi narrative texts, which are presented in the Dorsey-Swanton orthography with interlinear glosses. These are sometimes followed by notes on vocabulary items and grammar in the text, followed by an English translation. The texts, ranging from cultural narratives to two letters translated into Biloxi from Omaha, are the primary texts from which the bulk of the vocabulary in the dictionary is drawn. The Ofo portion of the dictionary does not include texts.

The dictionary is usable, but the orthography employed is complex. Some lexemes are arranged under supposed "roots" that do not exist or are due to mistaken analysis or false etymologies. Such factors can make using the dictionary laborious and misleading. Dorsey used diacritics such as <û> and <ŭ> to indicate the difference between /u/ and /ə/. Unfortunately, Swanton switched some (but not all) of Dorsey's diacritics, replacing, for instance, Dorsey's /û/ with /ŭ/, thereby leaving uncertain the phonetic values of some of Dorsey's vowel diacritics. Following the convention of the time Swanton also organized lexical items by what he perceived to be stems, which were often missegmented morphemes that are not useful in word construction. The indexing of the dictionary is also problematic, and numerous items have been misplaced (Haas 1969a, 287).

In an effort to make the material on Biloxi easier to use, I developed and produced a revision to the Biloxi language portion of the original Dorsey-Swanton dictionary (Kaufman 2011). I developed a standardized orthography that captures the phonetic differences in vowel quality, such as the difference between orthographic <o>, which corresponds to [o], and orthographic <ô>, which is [ɔ], after Haas and Swadesh (1968). I also reorganized the dictionary's headwords, using complete non-segmented Biloxi lexemes as headwords, which improves word search.[9]

Paula Einaudi (1976) wrote a grammar of Biloxi as her doctoral dissertation. Her 184-page grammar is overall a good overview of Biloxi. However, she does not adequately cover discourse features such as evidentiality marking. She does not analyze many Biloxi particles, instead concluding that "nominal particles remain the thorniest problem of Biloxi syntax" (149). Einaudi's orthography also unfortunately conflates certain phonemic distinctions, for example, /ə/ and /u/ to simply /u/, thereby obliterating the phonemic distinction between them, which can lead to phonetic and semantic inaccuracies.[10]

Sources on related Siouan languages that I consulted include a Lakota dictionary (Buechel and Manhart 2002), an Osage dictionary (Quintero 2009), a Dakota grammar (Riggs [1893] 2004), and an Osage grammar (Quintero 2006).

### CHITIMACHAS

The French first encountered the Chitimachas at the end of the seventeenth century, situated in what is now southwestern Louisiana around

Grand Lake (Mithun 1999, 387; Swanton 1919, 8) and between the Bayous Lafourche and Teche and the Gulf of Mexico. It is in this region, which the Chitimachas called Šeyti (Swadesh 1939, 67),[11] where several archaeological mound sites (16SM5[12] Hipinimtc Namu; 16SMY2 Okunkiskin; 16SMY10 Qiteet Kutingi Namu [see fig. 1.2]), known to have been inhabited by them, are found (Rees and Livingood 2007, 78–87). Chitimachas called themselves *panš* 'people,' or *Sitimaša*.

Chitimachas are first discussed in 1699 with French colonization of the area (Swanton 1946, 119). "Washa and Chawasha, two small tribes immediately to the east" were also Chitimachan, speaking the same or a similar language (Goddard 2005, 13). After a Chitimacha warrior killed the missionary Jean-François Buisson de Saint-Cosme in 1707, French colonists took many Chitimachas, among others,[13] as slaves to work in their own fields or to Saint-Domingue in the Caribbean to work on plantations there. A census of 1930 confirmed a population of fifty-one (Swanton 1946, 121). A revitalization program of the language has been instituted (Daniel Hieber, pers. comm., 2010).

## Migrations

Chitimacha tradition holds that they were originally situated in the region where the Natchez came to be located, near modern Natchez, Mississippi (Swanton 1946, 23). Chitimachas then moved southward to their present location in southern Louisiana. As with the Atakapas, there are no other known migration stories.

## Language

Chitimacha is an isolate, formerly spoken in what is now southwestern Louisiana, along the Gulf Coast near Vermilion Bay, Louisiana, and along the Atchafalaya River basin, the region which the Chitimachas called Šeyti (Swadesh 1939, 67). European explorers reported that two small groups, Washa and Chawasha, also spoke languages similar to Chitimacha but these languages are undocumented (Goddard 2005, 13; Rowland and Sanders 1927, 32; Swanton 1919, 8). Much of the extant data for Chitimacha is as yet unpublished, and I have had to rely heavily on these unpublished sources, predominantly copies of handwritten field notes produced by Swadesh. Chitimacha currently has a vigorous language revitalization program in place, with partial help from the Rosetta Stone Foundation.

Chitimacha is a moderately polysynthetic, head-marking language, as shown in this example:

(4)  *cu·k'š*        *cu·k'š*        *še·nink*      *hup*        *hi*       *nicwiʔi*

    cu-k'-š        cu-k'-š        še·ni·nk      hup        hi        ni·cw·iʔi

    go-PRT-FOC     go-PRT-FOC     pond-LOC      to there    water     move.upright-3s

    'He went and went till he came to the edge of a pond.'

    (Daniel Hieber, pers. comm., 2013)

Stress falls on the first syllable (Mithun 1999, 387). Vowels are long and short /i/, /e/, /a/, /o/, and /u/. Consonants are stops /p/, /t/, /c/, /č/, and /k/; ejectives /p/, /t/, /c/, /c/, and /k/; the glottal stop; fricatives /s/, /š/, and /h/; and sonorants /m/, /n/, /w/, and /y/. Nasals may be syllabic.

As in other LMV languages, a Chitimacha verb alone may form a complete clause. Only some nouns, primarily those referring to humans, have plural forms. Chitimacha has a subject suffix only for the first person; second and third persons are unmarked. Postpositions may mark location, directions, instruments, beneficiaries, and companions. As in most other LMV languages, auxiliary verbs distinguish position—horizontal, vertical, and neutral—though one Chitimacha innovation is that the horizontal positional may be derogatory when applied to humans. Tense/aspect/mode distinctions include future, aorist (past or present), continuative, usitative, necessitative, desiderative, imperative, polite imperative, hortatory, permissive, conditional, gerund, and gerundive (Mithun 1999, 388).

Swanton published a short, fifty-six-page monograph (1919), in which he proposed that Atakapa, Chitimacha, and Tunica were all related in a stock he named "Tunican." Swanton gives historical background on the three languages; a discussion on the comparison of phonetics, grammatical categories, syntax, and pronominal systems; a tabular comparison of structural elements; and a comparative vocabulary for Chitimacha, Atakapa, and Tunica. It is a good source for comparing cognates and elements of grammatical structure among the three languages and with other LMV languages. After analyzing the vocabulary and phonology of "Tunican, Chitimachan, and Atakapan stocks," Swanton concluded that these three languages were "merely widely divergent dialects of one stock" (56). Haas later supported Swanton's conclusion by proposing the cover term "Gulf languages" for these languages, considering them a single stock. This hypothesis remains at best unproven and was largely abandoned by linguists in later years. Part of this thesis will attempt to show that the similarities among these languages are due to areal convergence rather than to genetic affiliation.

Swadesh published "Chitimacha Verbs of Derogatory or Abusive Connotation with Parallels from European Languages" (1933), an article about the use of positional verbs in Chitimacha; "The Phonemes of Chitimacha" (1934), an article on phonology; and "Phonologic Formulas for Atakapa-Chitimacha" (1946). His 1950 *Chitimacha Grammar, Texts, and Vocabulary* remains unpublished but is available from the Franz Boas Collection of Materials for American Linguistics, MSS. 497.3.B63C.G6.5 at the American Philosophical Society in Philadelphia, Pennsylvania. This unpublished material contains an eighty-eight-page Chitimacha-English unidirectional dictionary, a 238-page grammar, and about 110 texts. These manuscripts offer a wealth of material on the language and culture and are in the process of being reedited and transcribed for eventual publication. A DVD course was published by Rosetta Stone Limited in 2011 for use as a learning tool. It is currently available only to members of the Chitimacha Tribe of Louisiana.

### CHOCTAWS AND CHICKASAWS

Choctaws and Chickasaws, who call themselves *Čahta* (Byington and Swanton 1915) and *Chikashsha* (Munro and Willmond 1994) respectively, are Western Muskogean groups that came to inhabit modern Mississippi and Alabama and peripheral areas. Haas noted that "Choctaw and Chickasaw are only slightly differing dialects" (1975, 261); for this reason, I treat the two languages as a unit.

De Soto first encountered Muskogean groups in 1539, when they lived in what became modern South Carolina, Tennessee, Kentucky, Mississippi, Alabama, Georgia, Florida, and Louisiana. Muskogean groups were forced to move westward under the Great Indian Removal Act, called the *Nowa*

*Falaya* 'Long Walk' by Choctaws and the 'Trail of Tears' by Cherokees, in 1836–40 (Mithun 1999, 461).

Galloway (1994) has argued that a late sixteenth- or seventeenth-century confederation of refugees or remnant populations united to form the Choctaws, from whom the Chickasaws later separated, though this is at odds with Swanton's assertion that de Soto encountered the Chickasaws in December 1540 during his entrada (1946, 116), indicating that they were already separated by this time. Most Choctaws immigrated into what is now Oklahoma in 1831–33, though some remain in Mississippi to this day (122). The Choctaws, during the eighteenth century, had settled in a swath of territory bordered by the Pearl River on the west and the Tombigbee River on the east, from what is now central Mississippi to western Alabama (Galloway and Kidwell 2004, 500). The Chickasaws, from the sixteenth to the eighteenth centuries, had settled in territory north of the Choctaws, bounded by the Mississippi River on the west up to the Ohio River and along the Duck River to the east, occupying modern northern Mississippi, western Tennessee, southern Illinois, and northwestern Alabama. The Chakchiumas lived in northern Mississippi from ca. 1540 to the 1750s, before being "amalgamated with the Chickasaw" (Galloway and Kidwell 2004, 496). Choctaws, in the eighteenth century, came to venerate a mound they named *Nanih Waiya* 'Bent Hill' as their point of origin and emergence (see Choctaw text in appendix). The mound is located 15 miles (22 km) northeast of Philadelphia, Mississippi. The mound is a 25 foot (7.62 m) high platform mound, and an earthen embankment once enclosed the complex (Little 2009, 135). Ceramics found in the area date to between 100 BCE and 400 CE, indicating that the mound is contemporaneous with Hopewell culture (Little 2009, 135). The site's original builders and inhabitants, however, are unknown.

There were reportedly between 3,000 and 3,500 Chickasaws in 1700 (Swanton 1946, 119). As Swanton notes, "The Choctaw population seems always to have fluctuated between 15,000 and 20,000"; the census of 1930 gave "17,757, of whom 16,641 were in Oklahoma, 624 in Mississippi, 190 in Louisiana, and the rest scattered over more than 12 other states" (123). The Chakchiumas were situated between the Choctaws and Chickasaws and were reported to speak the same language as the Chickasaws, but the language is now extinct and was not documented. It is thought that the Houmas, who were found in 1682 on the east bank of the Mississippi south of the Natchez, were probably an amalgam of Chakchiuma, Bayogoula, and Colapissa, but their nation ceased to exist by ca. 1805 (Goddard 2005, 11, 40).

### Migrations

The origin of Muskogean peoples remains a point of controversy among academics. Based on the Muskogee (Creek) creation and migration stories gathered by Gatschet in 1886, there is the possibility that the Muskogeans originated from points farther west, perhaps west of the Mississippi River and possibly even Mexico. The migration of part of the Muskogean language family during this time period appears to have resulted in the development, by ca. 1600 CE, of two major Muskogean language varieties, Eastern and Western. Western Muskogean includes the peoples now called Choctaws and Chickasaws, and may have formerly included the Chakchiumas and Houmas.

There is a Choctaw "migration legend recounting travel from the west of the Mississippi River together with the Chickasaw and perhaps Chakchiuma" (Galloway and Kidwell 2004, 511). Native sources cite northwestern Mexico, or just generally Mexico, as the origin of this migration, an indigenous claim that has been discounted by some scholars such as Galloway, who asserts that such a claim is "highly romanticized and indeed fictionalized" (1995, 329). Such a claim certainly does not counter the migration story (above) of an eastward migration from "west of the Mississippi River." Haas noted a date supposedly given by one of her indigenous consultants of a Muskogean migration from "Mexico" in the ninth century (Haas, unpublished notes).[14] Today, many Choctaw and Chickasaw descendants inhabit Alabama, Mississippi, and Oklahoma.

### Language

Muskogean is the only language family (see fig. 11) whose ancestral roots lie wholly within the southeastern U.S. geographical region (Hardy 2005, 69). Muskogean has generally been divided into Western, Central, Eastern, and sometimes Southwestern branches (461), although "subgrouping is problematic" due to "crosscutting resemblances" from borrowing (462),

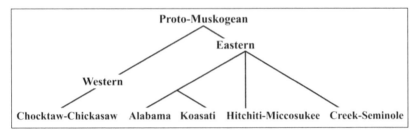

Fig. 11. Muskogean language family (after Haas 1941, in Martin 1994, 19). Created by author.

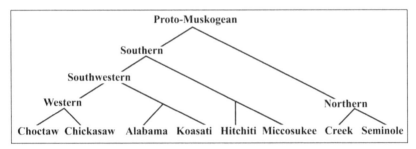

Fig. 12. Muskogean language family (after Munro 1987, in Martin 1994, 19). Created by author.

that is, from language contact. Eastern Muskogean languages spoken to the east of the LMV include Alabama, Apalachee, Koasati (Coushatta), Mikasuki, and Muskogee (Creek). Hitchiti and Mikasuki diverged early; later, ca. 1600 CE, Southwestern Muskogean emerged. This subbranch includes Alabama and Koasati (Coushatta). Around 1600 CE Choctaw and Chickasaw diverged sufficiently to constitute another subbranch, Western Muskogean. The Western Muskogean branch also includes Chakchiuma and possibly Houma, both of which are now extinct and were largely undocumented. The Muskogean family has been linked to the isolates Atakapa, Chitimacha, Natchez, and Tunica under the rubric *Gulf*, but, as mentioned earlier, such "relationships are not considered demonstrated" (Mithun 1999, 462).

A majority of Choctaws were forcibly relocated to Oklahoma between 1831 and 1833, though "a substantial number resisted removal and remained in Mississippi" (Broadwell 2006, 1). Choctaw is still spoken by approximately nine thousand people in Alabama, Mississippi, and Oklahoma

(Broadwell 2006, 1) and "children are still learning the language" (Mithun 1999, 461). Chickasaw is spoken by approximately a thousand people in Oklahoma (Munro and Willmond 1987), though most are over the age of forty (Mithun 1999, 461).

Choctaw and Chickasaw are head-marking, moderately polysynthetic languages. Although the two languages are considered dialects, minor differences between them exist. For example, a Choctaw verb must include the suffix -*h*, a marker of unspecified tense, which is no longer present in Chickasaw (Broadwell 2006, 198). Choctaw-Chickasaw vowels are /i/, /a/, and /o/, with contrastive length and nasalization. Consonants are /b/, /p/, /t/, /č/, /k/, /f/, /ɬ/, /s/, /š/, /h/, /m/, /n/, /l/, /w/, and /y/. Choctaw-Chickasaw *b* is a reflex of Proto-Muskogean (PM) *\*kʷ* (Mithun 1999, 464) and *f* is a reflex of PM *\*xʷ* (Haas 1969b, 36). Chickasaw developed a preconsonantal glottal stop, perhaps influenced by a Siouan language, either Biloxi or Dhegiha. Western Muskogean demonstratives follow the noun, as in Siouan, though this feature does not appear in other languages of the greater Gulf-Atlantic (GA) sprachbund. As in Biloxi, Muskogean languages, including Choctaw-Chickasaw, show reference-tracking.

The following is an example of Choctaw:

(5)   *ilipisalitok*
       ili-pisa-li-tok
       RFL-see-1-PST
       'I saw myself.'
       (Broadwell 2006, 177)

There is lexical and grammatical pitch accent. Contributing to vowel length, nasalization, and pitch accent is a system of verb ablaut. The shape of a verb stem can be altered depending on aspect, tense, and modality. Verb ablaut, or grades, is triggered by certain affixes, but sometimes the choice of grade is semantic (Mithun 1999, 464).

Muskogean verb morphology is elaborate. Some verb roots have suppletive forms for different numbers of participants. Verbs take pronominal affixes for agent and patient. As in Siouan, there are forms for first- and second-person agents and patients but not for third person. While Central and Eastern Muskogean languages maintain only agent and patient suffixes, in Choctaw-Chickasaw all agent and patient affixes are prefixed except for first person singular, which is suffixed. As in Siouan, some verbal prefixes function as locatives, instrumentals, and comitatives.

The only published dictionary on Choctaw is Byington and Swanton (1915), which is a 611-page, bidirectional Choctaw-English dictionary with some sample sentences but with no grammatical overview of the language. However, a useful grammar of Choctaw is Broadwell (2006), which provides an exhaustive, 375-page discussion of phonology, syntax, and morphology, as well as pragmatic features like focality, evidentiality, and switch reference. The grammar serves as a useful co-reference to Munro and Willmond's (1994) 539-page, analytical, bidirectional Chickasaw-English dictionary, which includes approximately twelve thousand main entries. The dictionary also includes an overview of Chickasaw-Choctaw grammar and many cultural annotations, making it a valuable cultural reference as well.

A useful source on Eastern Muskogean employed in this thesis for comparative purposes is a 357-page, bidirectional Creek (Muskogee)-English dictionary (Martin and Mauldin 2000). The dictionary includes an introduction to Muskogee language and history, and cultural photos and drawings, such as of ball sticks (used in indigenous stickball games) and burial houses.

## NATCHEZ

The Natchez (autonym *Nače* [Van Tuyl 1980]) are perhaps the best known of the LMV groups due to their being the longest surviving members of Mississippian Culture and the prolific European documentation of their heavily stratified caste-like society, ranging from the "Great Sun," or ruler, down to the "Stinkards," the lowest class. The Natchez were first described by La Salle's expedition of 1682, when Natchez occupied towns south and east of modern Natchez, Mississippi (Mithun 1999, 467). In 1722 wars involving the Natchez and French broke out that were "put down with considerable severity by Bienville" (Swanton 1946, 159). In 1730 French troops and their Choctaw allies attacked the Natchez, and, in 1731, the French sent four hundred Natchez into slavery in Saint-Domingue in the Caribbean. Some Natchez escaped to reside with the Cherokee, Creek, and Chickasaw nations, some coming to reside in South Carolina.

During the Mississippian-Plaquemine period, "material and geographical continuities" (Beasley 2007, 127) suggest that the Anna Mounds (22-AD-500) site was likely once occupied by Proto-Natchez. Later, in the late seventeenth and early eighteenth centuries, Natchez inhabited the mound settlement of the Grand Village of the Natchez (Fatherland site). As of 1980 a Natchez ceremonial dance ground was still located at Medicine Spring near Gore, Oklahoma, at which several hundred people of Natchez ancestry still gather (Van Tuyl 1980, 62).

Taensas were likely also Natchesan, apparently speaking the same language (Swanton 1911, 22; Goddard 2005, 13). There is also evidence that Colapissas, who lived on the lower Pearl River at the end of the seventeenth century, may also have been Natchesan (Goddard 2005, 13).

## Migrations

As with the Atakapas and Chitimachas, there are no known ancient migration stories among the Natchez, except for a passing reference to "evidence that [Natchez] had formerly extended higher up the Mississippi though hardly to the Wabash as they are said to have claimed" (Swanton 1946, 23; Swanton 1911, 182–86). Whether they actually extended that far north is open to debate, although, as just seen, Swanton often tends to dismiss Native oral history claims. Many Natchez were forced, with the Cherokees and others, to migrate, as part of the 1830s Indian Relocation Act, from the Southeast to the midwestern part of the continent to Indian Territory, what is now the state of Oklahoma.

## Language

Natchez is an isolate, a head-marking, highly polysynthetic language spoken until the early twentieth century in the LMV. Natchez was part of a broader language family, Natchesan,[15] possibly including Taensa and Avoyel, though "the evidence stops short of being conclusive" as to whether these latter really were Natchesan (Goddard 2005, 39). Unfortunately, little or no data were obtained on these latter languages before their disappearance. A previous example showed that Natchez is highly polysynthetic, incorporating a high degree of affixation to a nominal or verbal root. Another example exemplifies this further:

(6)  *tama·Lnisica*          *hikaL*             *to·ʔa·wipsik*
     *tama·L-nis·ic-a*        *hikaL-Ø*           *to·-ʔa·-wi-p-si-k*
     wife-1POSS-ERG-ART       corn.drink-ABS      pound-3OPT-AUX-2DAT-DAT-CONN
     'My wife will pound corn drink for you.'
     (Kimball 2005, 387)

Stress falls on the penultimate syllable if that vowel is long; otherwise it falls on the antepenultimate syllable (Mithun 1999, 467). Vowels are /i/, /e/, /a/, /o/, and /u/. Consonants are stops /p/, /t/, /č/, /k/, /kʷ/, and /ʔ/; fricatives /š/ and /h/; voiced sonorants /m/, /n/, /l/, /w/, and /y/; and voiceless sonorants /M/, /N/, /L/, /W/, and /Y/. There is pitch accent with four pitch contours: high, mid, rising, and falling (Kimball 2005, 396). Like Muskogean languages, Natchez displays vowel harmony; regressive harmony is optional, but progressive is obligatory (Mithun 1999, 467).

Natchez displays lexical and phonological variants, such as "the replacement of *ʔa* 'first person optative' with *ka-*" (Kimball 2005, 393), due to their supposedly being uttered by a mythological group of cannibals in Natchez stories. This may reflect multiple speech registers due to the caste-like social system (Mithun 1999, 467). Natchez, like Atakapa, does not appear to distinguish between alienable and inalienable possession. Unlike other LMV languages, in Natchez "nominalization is a fairly powerful process, while verbalization is weak and of limited productivity" (Kimball 2005, 401). Natchez shows a case system in which nouns are inflected for instrumental *-(yi)c*, comitative *-ʔa*, allative *-ku·š*, and locative *-k*. There is a form of declarative marking in which a phrase terminates with vowel nasalization; this is the only time nasal vowels occur in Natchez, thus they are always phrase-final. Singular, dual, and plural number is distinguished for all persons. Verbal roots may show ablaut or change shape with different inflections. For example, the root form of 'drink' appears in the infinitive form *hahkuši'iš* '(for one) to drink,' but with a reduced form in participles, as *ʔihkuši* 'drinking' (Mithun 1999, 468).

Natchez was one of a family of languages called Natchesan. Natchez was the sole survivor and the only Natchesan language to be extensively documented. However, as with Chitimacha, much of the extant data for Natchez is as yet unpublished, and I have had to rely heavily on copies of handwritten field notes produced by Haas. Natchez may be related to Proto-Muskogean (Haas 1970, 50), but this proposal remains inconclusive.

A purported grammar of the Taensa language (which may have been related to Natchez) was published in 1888 by a French seminary student, Jean Parisot. However, after careful linguistic analysis and scrutiny, including by Swanton (1908), this grammar was pronounced inauthentic. Swanton stated that the language of Parisot's grammar "was probably never spoken by any people whatsoever" (32) and the study was dismissed as a hoax. Swanton (1924) and Haas (1956) posited a linguistic relationship between Natchez and Muskogean, but Haas later concluded that the relationship between them was no closer than that between any other pair of languages within her proposed "Gulf" family (Galloway and Baird Jackson 2004, 598; Haas 1969, 62; Haas 1979, 318).

Swanton visited some Natchez in 1907 (Kimball 2005, 385). In 1909 he worked with the native speaker Watt Sam (born ca. 1857). From this consultation he prepared a grammatical sketch of the language, which was edited in 1991 by T. Dale Nicklas but only privately printed (Kimball 2005).

The only published dictionary of Natchez is a short 127-page, unidirectional Natchez-English lexicon by Charles Van Tuyl (1980). This lexicon follows an English translation of Antoine Simon Le Page Du Pratz's French ethnography (1751). (Du Pratz lived among the Natchez and learned the Natchez language.) In Van Tuyl's words, "This dictionary does not include listings from Dr. Haas' extensive unpublished Natchez materials, parts of which she has kindly shared with us" (1980, 65). Unfortunately, his expectations of seeing "a complete description" of the Natchez language with the publishing of Haas's materials (65) has, over thirty years later, still not been realized.

The first and only publicly published grammar of the Natchez language is Kimball (2005), a grammatical sketch based on Haas's field notes. The sixty-eight-page grammatical sketch packs in much of the phonetics and phonology, syntax, morphology, and even some suprasegmental features of the language. It also includes a Natchez text with English gloss, translation, and linguistic analysis. By far the best Natchez language data are contained in the already mentioned unpublished Haas field notes, which she took over the course of several months in 1934 while a graduate student. She consulted with the native speakers Watt Sam and Nancy Raven. Haas gathered over two thousand pages of field notes that included a bilingual Natchez-English lexicon, many Native stories in the Natchez language with inserted interlinear English glosses, and vocabulary and verbal paradigms. Haas's notebooks contain almost everything that can now be known about the Natchez language and culture; her field notes are a treasure for this reason. Her careful and articulate notes and clear writing are essential to further publication and to our further understanding of Natchez language and culture. Unfortunately, the majority of her Natchez material was never published, although it is archived at the American Philosophical Society (APS) in Philadelphia.[16]

### OFOS (MOSOPELEAS)

The Ofos, a Siouan group closely related to the Biloxis, appear under the names Ofogoula (a Western Muskogean or MTL term meaning 'dog-people') and Mosopelea. The latter term occurs on French maps indicating that "some years before 1673 they lived in 8 villages in or near southern Ohio. They are said to have been driven from this country by the Iroquois and in 1673 Marquette found them on the east bank of the Mississippi below the mouth of the Ohio" (Sapir 1946, 165–66). This would indicate that the Ofos were relatively late migrants from the Ohio Valley to the Mississippi Valley, where they eventually came to live with Tunicas, Koroas, Yazoos, and Avoyels at the Haynes Bluff mound settlement (Brain 1988). Remaining Ofos then migrated up the Red River and assimilated into the Tunica-Biloxi Tribe in present-day Marksville, Louisiana. The group is now thought extinct, with the last known Ofo, Rosa Pierette, having died ca. 1915 (Sapir 1946, 166).

Ofos, like their relatives the Biloxis, may have been salt producers and traders in the western Appalachian region before their migration to the west and south. Like the Biloxis, the Ofos apparently received maize from the Caddoans. Ofos may have produced the Old Town Red pottery that showed up in the Yazoo River basin (see below).

## Migrations

Ofos are said to have been driven from the Ohio Valley by the Haudenosau-
nees (Iroquois); in 1673 the French explorer Marquette found them living
"on the east bank of the Mississippi below the mouth of the Ohio" (Swanton 1946, 165–66). According to French documents, shortly after the European invasion the Mosopeleas moved from "some point on the upper Ohio
River to the Cumberland, and thence successively to Arkansas River, to the
Taensa at Lake St. Joseph, Louisiana, and finally to the Yazoo, where they
were known as Ofogoula (Ofo) and established their settlements near the
Tunica on the Yazoo [at Haynes Bluff]" (31).

## Language

Ofo is an Ohio Valley (also called Southeastern) Siouan language, closely
related to Biloxi, that was spoken in the upper end of the LMV, near present-
day Vicksburg, Mississippi. (Ceramic evidence places the Ofos at the Lake
George [Holly Bluff] site along with the Tunicas ca. 1600–1700.) The Ofos
likely originated in the same region as the Biloxis, in the Cumberland Plateau region of the western Appalachian highlands near modern Knoxville,
Tennessee.

Ofo, like Biloxi, is a mildly synthetic, head-marking language:

(7)   *b-aphuska*       *a-tci-tp-abe*
      my-fist          I-you-hit-IRR
      'I will hit you with my fist'
      (Rankin 2002, 66)

Vowels are /i/, /e/, /a/, /o/, and /u/ and nasalized vowels are /į/, /ą/, and
/ų/. Stops are aspirated and unaspirated /p/, /t/, /č/, /k/, /b/, and /d/; plain
fricatives /f/, /s/, /š/, /x/, and /h/; aspirated fricatives /fh/ and /sh/; sonorants /w/, /l/, and /y/; and nasals /m/ and /n/. Ofo is the only Siouan language to have the /f/ phoneme, a probable borrowing from contact with
Muskogean languages.

As in all the languages of the LMV, with the exception of MTL, the verb
is the most complex element of a clause. Nouns are relatively uninflected.
Other lexical classes include adverbs, pronouns, and postpositions. Adjec-

tives are nonexistent in Siouan languages; words translated by adjectives in English are stative verbs in Siouan. Unlike in Biloxi, deictics precede the nouns they modify. As Rankin observes, "The active-stative distinction in Ofo is not obvious, if it exists at all" (2002, 17). It appears that, like Biloxi, Ofo lost the agent-patient distinction typical of other Siouan languages, which may be either a subgroup development or independent development in each Ohio Valley Siouan language (Tutelo, the third major member of this subgroup once spoken in modern Virginia, has been insufficiently investigated in this regard).

Several instrumental prefixes are used to signify how or by what means something is done, as 'by heat,' 'pull by hand,' 'by mouth,' 'by pushing,' 'by foot,' 'by striking,' 'by pressure,' or 'by blowing or shooting.' As in Biloxi, negation is optionally periphrastic (incorporating both prefix and suffix), but one could simply suffix a negative enclitic to the element being negated, usually the verb. Like Biloxi, Ofo loses word-initial labial resonants, usually reflexes of Proto-Siouan *$w$ and *$m$. Future tense or irrealis is marked with a suffix -*abe* (Rankin 2002, 20). Ofo, like other LMV languages, used positional auxiliary verbs to express continuative or ongoing aspect.

The only material currently available on Ofo is an Ofo-English dictionary of about six hundred words and a few phrases, published along with the Dorsey and Swanton (1912) Biloxi-English dictionary. The Ofo vocabulary was elicited in 1908 by Swanton in consultation with the last known speaker, Rosa Pierette, in Marksville, Louisiana. Rankin researched Swanton's original card file at the National Anthropological Archives in the Smithsonian Institution and discovered that Swanton "marked vowel length in Ofo, but before the file went to the printer, he scratched the macrons [showing vowel length] out in each case. The reason for this is not clear" (2002, 2). Rankin then reproduced Swanton's original transcription in a grammar based on Swanton's dictionary, with original notations.

## TUNICAS

The documented history of the Tunicas begins with the final leg of Hernando de Soto's ill-fated entrada into North America in the early sixteenth century (Brain 1988, 21). Their conquests in Central and South America gave the Spaniards confidence that their desire for gold and for expanding their empire would be as easily accommodated in North America. However, not only did they find no gold in North America (only copper), but they met fierce opposition from indigenous North Americans just about everywhere they went. Their quest ended in miserable failure, including the death of de Soto. The Spanish army that had landed in Florida in 1539 was reduced "to a tattered band" by 1541 (21). Those who survived went down the Mississippi River, which took them to the Gulf and back to Mexico.

At the time of de Soto's entrada, Tunicas, who called themselves *Táyoroniku* (from *tá-* 'def. article' + *yóroni* 'Tunica' + *-ku* masculine singular suffix [Brain and Phillips 2004, 595; Haas 1950, 19n2]) were located in the region of the confluence of the Arkansas and Mississippi Rivers. It was when the Spanish reached the Mississippi River that they entered "the native 'province' of Quizquiz," where the name "Tanco" or "Tanico" appears on their maps of the Upper Sunflower region (Brain 1988, 21). The French subsequently called them *Tonicas*. Quizquiz has been theoretically identified as the Tunica ancestral homeland (Brain 1988; Hoffman 1992, 67).

Grigras, Koroas, Tioux, and Yazoos may have been Tunican, but nothing else is now known of these groups (Goddard 2005, 12). Tunica legends describe a battle between themselves and the Avoyels, a conflict that may have largely annihilated the Avoyels, leading Tunicas to absorb some Avoyel survivors into their settlement (Brain and Phillips 2004, 589).

## Migrations

Nothing is known of the Proto-Tunicas prior to their supposed encounter with the de Soto expedition in the early sixteenth century. Unfortunately, Tunica oral history is of little help in identifying their origins. There is only the mention of emergence from a mountain near which they settled (Haas 1950, 19, 141; Brain 1988, 22). (Note similarity to the Choctaw *Nanih Waiya* origin story in appendix). Brain speculates that the mountain reference could refer to the Ouachita Mountains, citing "a possible Tunican connection with that topography" (1988, 22). However, linguistic evidence may provide another clue to this supposed mountain habitat, one that points to the Rocky Mountains or mountains farther west. Tunicas have an analyzable native term for 'moose' (*yámuhtit'e*, from *yá* 'deer' + *muhti* 'hairy' + *t'e* 'big,' thus 'great hairy deer'). While moose are generally animals of the far north, moose did migrate down the Rocky Mountain range as far south as modern Colorado. Similarly, Tunicas share a word for 'wild goose' (*lá-lahki*)[17] with western and southwestern North American indigenous languages, again suggesting origins to the west. Since they were first documented in the Arkansas River region (the "Quizquiz" province), they may have migrated down the Arkansas River from farther west (this river has its headwaters in the Rockies).

The Tunicas inhabited the "Quizquiz-Tunica Oldfields" (Brain 1988, 25) near the Arkansas River before they moved southward down the Mississippi River to a point near the mouth of the lower Yazoo River near the Mississippi. This is where the first recorded French visit to the Tunicas occurred in 1698. The Tunicas settled at various points in the Yazoo River basin, along with the Ofos, who later migrated into this area. A mound settlement in modern Mississippi, now designated by archaeologists as Haynes Bluff (22-M-5) (see fig. 6), was likely the main Tunica site. Then, apparently fearing a Chickasaw raid, the Tunicas and their allies moved downriver from the Yazoo Basin ca. 1706 (25) to the confluence of the Red and Mississippi Rivers, where a French map, completed ca. 1774, records them (along with Biloxis, Ofos, and Pascagoulas, among others) resettled at what was formerly a Houma village. This region was named Portage de la Croix by Iberville, and to this day is known as Tunica Hills (31). After a Natchez raid in 1731, in which a number of Tunicas were killed, Tunica survivors relocated to a small tributary on the southern edge of the Tunica Hills still known as Tunica Bayou (33). Following raids, Tunicas moved from the Mississippi River to Mobile but were then granted permission by the French Louisiana governor to resettle on the Mississippi at Bayou Lafourche and then nearby Pointe Coupée. Tunicas then appear to have moved ca. 1786–88 up the Red River to reestablish themselves at present-day Marksville, Louisiana (42–44). In 1974 the Tunicas were incorporated along with the Biloxis and Ofos as the Tunica-Biloxi Tribe; they were federally acknowledged in 1981 (589). Many Tunica descendants today inhabit the Marksville region.

## Language

Tunica is an isolate language that was previously spoken in the Central and Lower Mississippi Valley until the early twentieth century. Tunica was once part of a broader language family, Tunican, which likely included the languages Grigra, Koroa, Tiou, and Yazoo (Swanton 1919, 7). Unfortunately, these latter languages were not recorded before their extinction, so their affiliation is tenuous, depending primarily on the hearsay of European colonists who found various groups able to intercommunicate. Tunica is a moderately polysynthetic language:

(8)  *hinya'tĭhč   ta'-yanɛra   rɔ'hpănt   se'hihtɛ'păn   yu'kʔunăhč   ši'mihk        ʔuna'nì.*
     now          DEF-ocean    near        every.        when.          DU.would.   they.say
                                           morning       DU.arrived     play

    'Now every morning when they came they would play, it is said.'

    (Haas 1940, 135)

Tunica vowels are /i/, /e/, /ɛ/, /a/, /ɔ/, /o/, and /u/. Consonants are stops /p/, /t/, /č/, /k/, and /ʔ/; fricatives /s/, /š/, and /h/; nasals /m/ and /n/; liquids /l/ and /r/; and glides /w/ and /y/.

Unlike any other LMV language, but like Indo-European languages such as Spanish and French, Tunica has a masculine-feminine gender classification system for both animate and inanimate nouns. Nouns with an article appear with a suffix marking the gender and number of the referent: masculine singular, masculine dual, masculine plural, feminine singular, or feminine dual-plural (Mithun 1999, 533). Nouns may occur alone, as in *čɔha* 'chief,' or with the definite article prefix *ta-* 'the/some' and a gender suffix *-ku* 'masculine' or *-hč* 'feminine.' Thus, *ta-čɔha-ku* 'DEF-chief-M.SG' is 'the (male) chief.' An example of a non-human noun with gender is *ta-wiši-hč* 'DEF-water-F.SG,' since 'water' is feminine.

Tunica is unique in the LMV in having the /r/ phoneme, and it is one of only two known eastern North American languages (the other being Timucua, part of the GA sprachbund) that has "both *l* and *r* in phonemic contrast" (Goddard 2005, 12). Unlike other LMV languages, Tunica transformed from a subject-object to an agent-patient type language (Nicklas n.d.).

The first work on Tunica was done in 1886 near Lecompte, Louisiana, by Albert Gatschet of the Bureau of American Ethnology (BAE). His consultant was William Ely Johnson (Haas 1953, 179). Johnson's father was Tunica, his mother Biloxi; he spoke Biloxi, Tunica, and Choctaw. Then, in 1907–10, Swanton, also of the BAE, visited the Tunicas. Swanton worked with Gatschet's consultant but also obtained information from another, Volsine Chiki. Haas did fieldwork on Tunica during several visits between 1933 and 1939. Her consultant was Sesostrie Youchigant (born ca. 1870), who was maternally related to Chiki and Johnson and was the last known speaker of the language. Members of the Tunica-Biloxi nation in Marksville, Louisiana, are currently working to revitalize the Tunica language (Haas 1953; Donna Pierite and Jean Luc Pierite, pers. comm., 2011). Although Tunica and Biloxi are unrelated and structurally different languages, the close relationship between the two groups dates back to at least the late eighteenth century, when there was a settlement at Bayou Boeuf, Rapides Parish, Louisiana, which included Tunica, Biloxi, and Choctaw settlers. Tunicas and Biloxis were incorporated as the Tunica-Biloxi Tribe in 1974; they became federally recognized in 1981 (Brain and Phillips 2004, 589).

There are two grammatical sources for Tunica: a Swanton article (1921), which gives an overview of the language, including a detailed outline of affixes and their meanings, and Haas's grammar, written as a dissertation (1940). Swanton's material was based on data collected by Gatschet. Although we are grateful to have any sources at all, I concur with Haas's assessment of the weaknesses of Gatschet's material as published in Swanton: "His material is particularly weak in that he failed to record glottal stops. Hence a better understanding of the phonetics of the language coupled with the great amount of new grammatical and text material obtained from [Haas's consultant] Youchigant has contributed much toward making possible a fuller and more adequate analysis of the language" (1940, 9). Haas's 143-page grammar covers phonology, morphology, and syntax, and a sample text with grammatical analysis. Her grammar is the best we currently have of the Tunica language.

The sole published dictionary of Tunica (Haas 1953) contains about 2,800 entries, with some examples and many etymological notes and special comments by her consultant, Sesotrie Youchigant. It contains a brief grammar section based on her earlier grammar. The dictionary is useful for comparative work as it incorporates aspects of Haas's vast knowledge of other Southeastern languages, including copying among them.

A compendium of Tunica narratives was published (Haas 1950). These were stories told to Haas by her consultant, Youchigant. These texts are invaluable as the only extant narratives of Tunica oral history.

**OTHER PEOPLES AND LANGUAGES**

Peoples and languages of the LMV region that are too poorly documented to be dealt with in this book include Akokisa, Avoyel, Bayogoula, Bidai, Houma, Mobila,[18] Moctobi (Capinan), Naniaba, Okelousa, Opelousa, Pascagoula, Quinipissa, Tawasa, Tohomé, and others mentioned above. Of these, the Mobila, Naniaba, and Tohomé were classified as Muskogean speakers under the name *Mobile* in Goddard (1996), but they were more likely using the MTL rather than a Muskogean language (Goddard 2005, 40).

The Moctobis were "evidently the Capinans" whose language may have been Siouan (Waselkov and Gums 2000, 23), like that of the Biloxis and Ofos. The Moctobis (Capinans) had a village on the Pascagoula River, as did the Biloxis and Pascagoulas (26). The Tawasas and Tohomés were apparently prosperous tribes, along with the Estananis (Biloxis), whom the Mobilians perceived as threats (26).

### Mobilian Trade Language (or Mobilian Jargon)

The one language in the LMV not associated with a single group but rather spoken as a second (or third or fourth) language by several is the Mobilian Trade Language (MTL), also called Mobilian (Trade) Jargon and Choctaw-Chickasaw Pidgin. (MTL should not be confused with the Mobilian language of the Mobilians [Mobila] once spoken in the Mobile Bay area, which is unclassified and went extinct before it could be documented.) MTL was also known by the autonyms *Yama* (the MTL word for 'yes') and *Anōpa Ela* (MTL for 'different language'). The French called it *Mobilienne* (Haas 1975, 258). The last semi-speakers of MTL were found in the 1960s, living in Louisiana and Texas, and were interviewed in the 1970s by Crawford and Drechsel (Sturtevant 2005, 33), upon referral by the indigenous basketmaker Claude Medford.

MTL was one of the trade languages spoken in Native North America at least from the seventeenth well into the twentieth century (Drechsel 1997). Other trade, or pidgin, languages of North America include Eskimo Jargon in the Arctic region, Chinook Jargon in the Northwest, and Unami, or Delaware, Jargon on the East Coast. A pidgin "is a form of natural language that has a limited vocabulary and simplified phonological and grammatical structures. The vocabulary of a pidgin consists of those words necessary for carrying on conversations restricted to particular contexts, for example, trade or work" (Silver and Miller 1997, 225).

By the eighteenth century, the MTL was the lingua franca of much of the entire North American Southeast (the Creek lingua franca spoken in the Creek Confederacy during the eighteenth century may have been an eastern variant of MTL that incorporated more Eastern Muskogean vocabulary) (Drechsel 1996, 250). MTL "appears to be a mixture of Choctaw and Alabama" (Haas 1975, 258) but, primarily due to its simplified morphology, MTL is not mutually intelligible to speakers of other Muskogean languages.

Unlike other Muskogean and LMV languages, MTL is what linguists call an *isolating*, or *analytic*, language, meaning that there is little morphology such as affixation for changing the meaning of words. Instead, independent words are used to express concepts (similar to, for example, Mandarin Chinese). For example, comparing MTL with Choctaw, we can see that the polysynthetic Choctaw sentence using affixes for patient and active pronominals attached to the verb becomes isolating in MTL:

(9)   Choctaw
      *chibashlilitok*

| chi- | bashli | -li | -tok |
|------|--------|-----|------|
| 2s | cut | 1s | PAST |
| accusative | V | nominative | |
| (patient) | | (active) | |

'I cut you.'

(10) MTL

| ešno | eno | bašle | taha |
|------|-----|-------|------|
| you | I | cut | finish |

'I cut you.'

(Drechsel 1997, 302)

The two pronouns affixed to the verb in Choctaw (creating one long word) are independent pronouns in MTL (using separate words). Similarly, the past tense suffix *-tok* in Choctaw is replaced by an independent particle, *taha*, in MTL, based on the Choctaw verb 'finish.' There is no agent-patient distinction in MTL; independent pronouns are used for both subject and object. Thus, word order is much more crucial in MTL for deducing the meaning of a phrase than it is in Choctaw-Chickasaw.

MTL has predominant object-subject-verb (OSV) word order. "The vocabulary shows considerable lexical richness with a diversity of semantic domains, confirming multiple usages and manifold social contexts for the pidgin" (Drechsel 1996, 248), evidenced by the fact that MTL served several groups, including the Alabamas, Apalachees, Biloxis, Choctaws, Pascagoulas, Taensas, and Tunicas, each having its own particular language, yet all "speak the Mobilian, which was formerly the court language amongst the Indian nations of Lower Louisiana" (Brackenridge 1814, 151). Oglethorpe in 1734 observed, "As for their Language they have two kinds, One which is a vulgar Dialect, different in each Town, the other a general Language common to the Creek Nations [,] the Choctaws, and the Blew Mouths [Biloxis] ... In this Language are the Songs which contain their History and sacred Ceremonies ...." (in Crawford 1978, 6–7).[19] There is a line of an "old Tunica song" that states *Tali hata pisa achokma*, translated as 'white rock, or silver, looks good' (Kniffen, Gregory, and Stokes 1987, 181). However, these words are not Tunica but MTL (*tali* 'rock' or 'metal' + *hata* 'white' + *pisa-achokma* 'good-looking'), the words clearly Western Muskogean in origin. But the fact that this "old Tunica song" was at least partially sung in MTL is a good indicator of MTL's widespread use not only as an intercultural but also as an *intra*cultural form of communication.

The time of MTL origin is unknown and a matter of dispute between those who posit its development before European contact, perhaps even as early as the Mississippian period (ca. 900–1500 CE) (Drechsel 1996, 1997) and those who posit its origin after European contact (Crawford 1978; Galloway 1995, 321; Sturtevant 2005, 33). The primary arguments in favor of post-European origin are based on the fact that the "earliest sources do not mention any trade language" (Sturtevant 2005, 33) and on the hearsay evidence of European chroniclers who supposedly witnessed interpreters being used, including "chain interpretation, a burdensome arrangement in which European explorers depended on several translators lined up according to their ability to speak with each other, as apparently attested for de Soto's exploration of 1539 to 1543" (Drechsel 1997, 279). This arrangement supposedly made the use of a pidgin redundant and unlikely. However, two particulars to consider are that de Soto "took a route considerably farther east and north than previously believed, and paid visits to the Cherokee and their neighbors, including speakers of Muskogean, Siouan, and other languages such as Yuchi. De Soto thus travelled into present-day North Carolina and Tennessee, beyond the historically attested range of Mobilian Jargon" (Booker, Hudson, and Rankin 1992). Thus the range of languages spoken would have been considerably broader, perhaps enough to require a chain of interpreters for various languages. There is also the possibility, often not considered by historians and anthropologists, that "chain interpretation may have served Southeastern Indians as a form of passive resistance" (Drechsel 1997, 279), making it all the more difficult for Europeans to gain inroads into indigenous cultures by requiring them to have a complex chain of interpreters acting as intermediaries.

Galloway states that "the behavior" of French newcomers and the indigenous peoples they encountered "clearly indicates that Mobilian [Jargon] was not used," at least not in "formal or important situations" (1995, 321). Contra Galloway, Drechsel notes MTL's broad range of indigenous uses and its geographic distribution across "much of the Mississippian Complex" as testament to the pidgin's pre-European origin (2001, 176). I agree with Drechsel's assessment, since the linguistic evidence against its post-European origin includes its verb-final word order, like all other indigenous languages in the LMV but unlike English, French, or Spanish verb-medial (SVO) order, and the fact that there are "few direct and indirect loans from European languages" (Drechsel 1996, 251; Drechsel 1997, 130).

Even if MTL were a post-European development, the language structure implies that it was clearly developed by indigenous populations themselves without much, if any, input from European language sources (a situation similar to that of Chinook Jargon in the Northwest).

Although Choctaw and Alabama are the predominant sources of MTL vocabulary, there are also words copied into MTL from other Native American languages and families. These include borrowings from Algonquian, some of which are recognizable to modern English speakers, such as *papo(s)* 'papoose' (baby), *nešken* 'eye,' *šešekowa* 'rattle, gourd, drum,' *māgasin* 'moccasin, shoe,' and *pakan* 'pecan nut' (Drechsel 1997, 92). Several words may have spread through the Southeast and LMV via the MTL. (Partly for this reason, borrowed grammatical elements are of more value than borrowed words in assessing the LMV as a sprachbund.)

MTL has a three-vowel system: *e a o*. These vowels "vary considerably in their phonetic realizations" (Drechsel 1996, 261), with non-phonemicized nasal variants thereof. Consonants are /p/, /b/, /t/, /k/, /č/, /f/, /ł/, /s/, /š/, /h/, /m/, /n/, /w/, /l/, /y/, and /r/ (rare). The voiceless fricatives /s/ and /š/ often appear as variants of each other as well as "with the intermediate alveolar and apical-alveolar variants" showing some degree of retroflexion (Drechsel 1997, 279).

Extant data on MTL are sparse. Crawford (1978) is a 142-page book on MTL containing a unidirectional vocabulary (English-MTL) of about 170 words gathered from semi-speakers of MTL. Drechsel (1996) is a 108-page article that is the only known published dictionary of MTL. The dictionary is unidirectional English-Mobilian with 1,250 entries and a Mobilian-English index. Drechsel's (1997) 392-page book is a much more in-depth study of MTL history, structure, and vocabulary. There is perhaps more data on MTL "to be discovered in archives, especially in France and Quebec" (Sturtevant 2005, 33).

The current author has published a learner's book (Kaufman 2017), based on data primarily gathered by Crawford and Drechsel, designed to promote revitalization of this pidgin language through the learning of common phrases. The book also includes a bidirectional (MTL-English and English-MTL) lexicon for reference and to aid in increasing vocabulary.

### Sign Language

Although somewhat peripheral to the LMV, another means of intergroup communication was the non-verbal Plains Sign Language (PSL), also known as Hand Talk, which, in addition to being used by Native American deaf communities, was used as an auxiliary form of communication for trade, hunting, and to augment verbal communication.

It is unknown just where PSL began, but evidence suggests that it spread northward from the south. Some of the earliest Europeans reported the use of PSL in the Plains, so it was likely pre-European and was probably a tool used among various groups for communication along the Gulf Coast between modern Louisiana and northern Mexico, due to the broad linguistic diversity in that region (Silver and Miller 1997, 181).

PSL reached its apex during the nineteenth century, when it was used by different groups speaking over three dozen languages from about a dozen linguistic groups (Silver and Miller 1997, 181). PSL was used by Karankawas and Tonkawas on the western periphery of the LMV as well as probably among the Atakapas.

It should be noted that the Mayan-, Nahuatl-, and Chichimec-language speakers of Mexico also used sign language(s) to augment spoken communication, as is evidenced by signs appearing on ancient Maya ceramic vessels. Fox Tree reports that, according to statistical analyses, some 38.9 percent of Cheyenne sign language, a form of PSL, is cognate with what he calls Meemul Tziij, a sign language complex of Mesoamerica (2009, 351). Thus, it is possible that what became PSL originated in Mesoamerica and spread north through the Rio Grande Valley and into the Plains via the Tonkawas and other southern Plains groups.

Now that we have some idea of the peoples and languages of the LMV, we can look at contact among these peoples and languages and get a better idea of how this sprachbund developed.

# 2

## Language Contact

# FOUR

# Language Contact

Since we now have a more complete picture of the LMV—of its geography, history, peoples, and languages—we can begin the process of analyzing the LMV as a language area, or sprachbund. A sprachbund arises when languages come into close contact, thereby encouraging "diffusion of linguistic features across geographically adjacent languages" (Winford 2003, 70). This linguistic diffusion gives us clues about past intergroup social contacts and relationships.

Often when communities speaking different languages come into contact, the speakers accommodate to each other by learning each other's languages and becoming either bilingual (speaking two languages) or multilingual (speaking three or more languages), a situation that often develops through intermarriage, alliances, intergroup gatherings, and intensive trade. Bilingual and multilingual people often *codeswitch*, that is, they use "two or more languages in the same utterance or conversation" (Winford 2003, 102; Grosjean 1982, 145). There is very little consensus on the boundary between codeswitching—it can range from a single word within a clause to an entire clause within an utterance—and borrowing, except perhaps as to the degree that monolingual speakers of the receiving language employ such phenomena, thereby interfering in the native language (Winford 2003, 107).

One might wonder why a sprachbund should arise in the first place: why would one language not become dominant in contact situations and displace others? The answer lies in the sociolinguistic and sociocultural attitudes among the groups coming into contact. Unless there is a colonialist situation, as has happened all too often with the forced imposition of, for instance, English, French, Portuguese, or Spanish on subjugated Asian, African, and American indigenous populations, language contact among peoples with relatively equal power and status often leads to language as a "salient marker of group identity," with language acting as a "boundary-marking device" (Kulick 1992, 2–3). Relatively equal status means certain norms and values "require strict separation between public and private" (kin and non-kin) activities (Gumperz and Wilson 1971, 153) and thus the maintenance of individual languages. In these relatively egalitarian situations, if one language is allowed to predominate, it is often a trade language, or pidgin, such as MTL, that is not the first language of any group, used largely for purposes of trade and other intergroup activities between or among peoples with differing mother tongues.

One of the primary results of language contact, even when such contact is minimal, is word borrowing, resulting in *loanwords*. Often such loanwords between languages come about, for example, when speakers of a language enter a new environment and encounter new flora and fauna for which they previously had no names. Loanwords also arise through contact with different cultures with, to give another example, unfamiliar foods (like our English words *pizza* and *tortilla*, names for foods with which English-speakers formerly had no familiarity and thus borrowed, or copied, once these foods became familiar to our culture). In more intensive contact situations, such as we have in the LMV, language change can go beyond the borrowing of mere words to the borrowing of sounds (phonetics and phonology) and grammatical structures (morphology).

We have seen that the LMV languages represent several linguistic families: Atakapan, Chitimachan, Muskogean, Natchesan, Siouan, and Tunican. It is likely that many speakers of these languages were bilingual or multilingual, some having maintained a degree of contact with each other for at least several centuries, made all the easier by a multitude of waterways and trails, the ancient highway networks that linked them. We have seen another manifestation of this contact in the LMV with the use of MTL as a pidgin.

Language change has been analyzed as due either to genetic (internal) or contact (external) origins. While I discussed genetic origins of language change in my dissertation (Kaufman 2014a), in this book I focus primarily on contact origins of language change.

## METHODOLOGY

Important to this discussion is the definition of a sprachbund. There are several definitions according to the parameters set by individual authors. I will repeat here my definition of a sprachbund as I defined it in Kaufman (2014): (1) there must be at least three languages demonstrating evidence of contact; (2) there must be genealogical diversity among languages forming part of a sprachbund (see, for example, Emeneau 1956; Schaller 1975; Cristofaro 2000); (3) similarities should not be restricted to one level of grammar/lexicon alone (Schaller 1975); (4) there should be a solid extralinguistic (i.e., sociohistorical) explanation for the emergence of similarities (see, for example, Sherzer 1976; Sarhimaa 1991; Cristofaro 2000); and (5) there should be evidence of diversity and differentiation of contact languages (Matras 2009). Such a definition leads to the weighting of LMV sprachbund features, as discussed below.

Sherzer (1976) was the first to present and discuss phonological and morphological traits among the languages of Native North America and to determine linguistic areas north of Mexico. I have thus used Sherzer as a framework in which to place LMV language traits, or features. I have also partially modeled the current analysis on Masica (1976) and his study of the South Asia (India) sprachbund.

I use two approaches to assess a language area: the *circumstantialist* and the *historicist* (Campbell 2002). The historicist method involves seeking concrete evidence showing that shared traits are diffused. The historicist method is useful for examining the reasons for the development of the LMV sprachbund, because we can correlate certain linguistic evidence—for example, words for cultigens—with archaeological samples—for example, of those particular cultigens—that are adequately dated to a certain region and time period. I will apply the historicist approach by examining the historical trajectory in the LMV, by, for example, examining trade and farming from an early time period. The circumstantialist approach, on the other hand, lists similarities found in the languages of a geographic area without seeking concrete material evidence demonstrating that the traits are actually diffused. In essence the circumstantialist approach involves a "laundry list" approach and, as such, does not seek to investigate the historical or archaeological background of a certain geographical area as a means of verifying how certain language features may have come about through contact. While the historicist approach is more rigorous in this regard, in an area such as the LMV, where archaeological evidence is particularly difficult to correlate with language evidence, the circumstantialist approach is the only viable option for much of this analysis, at least until more archaeological evidence comes to light to support the language evidence.

The methodology for this book comprises two primary sections. First is Phonetics/Phonology and Morphology, in which the circumstantialist approach is used. Second is Words and Calques, in which I employ the historicist approach.

## Method of Data Collection

The primary method used to collect data for this book has been the perusal and sifting through of many written sources, both published and unpublished. Since most of the languages in the LMV are extinct, there is an overall paucity of extant data on several of the languages. I have analyzed what materials are available—primarily dictionaries, lexicons, grammars, and texts, even phrase books for examples of still spoken languages—in order to extract what data exist for historical and comparative purposes.

## Phonetics/Phonology and Morphology

I use two preexisting lists of North American Southeast phonetic and grammatical features by Sherzer (1976) and Campbell (1997), adding features I have found through my own research:

(1) ejective stop
(2) vowel alternation i ~ u
(3) vowel alternation o ~ u
(4) word-initial h ~ Ø
(5) phoneme /tl/
(6) definite article
(7) plural preverb with noun meaning 'people'
(8) direct object preverb with noun meaning 'thing'

In the eight languages of the LMV, each feature is either present or absent. I then count the number of features that occur in each language. The generalized measures of conformity to a given norm thus obtained naturally break into ranges. This gives us the isoglosses, or boundary lines, between linguistic features for the proposed LMV sprachbund. In an effort to establish a more precise areal-typological boundary, I also apply this measure to languages progressively farther away from the LMV convergence area (e.g., Eastern Muskogean, Caddoan, Coahuiltec), which, following Campbell, Kaufman, and Smith-Stark (1986, 536), I term *control languages*, in order to assess the extent of a particular feature. In addition, English is also used as a control language, since it came to be a major second language (along with French and Spanish) and then the dominant language of this sprachbund. Said features are then scored on a tripartite weighting scale—0, 1, 2—and include three primary axes—existence of the feature in a language, universality of the feature, and weighted significance of the feature. This scoring scale takes into account that the most salient features of a language, such as phonemes, are easier to copy than a feature that is well embedded and relatively hidden in the language, such as a grammatical feature. A score of 0 indicates that the feature in question does not exist in the area I have delimited as the LMV and is thus not relevant, or non-significant, to the present discussion. A score of 1 indicates that the feature exists but is relatively easy to borrow (since words and sounds are easily recognizable in languages and are thus easier to copy than more obscure grammatical paradigms) and/or extends well beyond the LMV and/or is crosslinguistically common. Such a feature is thus non-significant to the LMV as a sprachbund. A score of 2, the highest weighting, indicates that the feature is either geographically limited to the LMV and its immediate periphery and/or is crosslinguistically unusual and thus very relevant to the LMV as a sprachbund. The number of LMV languages containing a particular feature is then tallied in the rightmost column, while the total number of features occurring in an LMV language is tabulated at the bottom. This bottom row then reflects the number of proposed LMV features occurring in each particular language, thus giving a numerical range of how closely or distantly the language falls from the LMV norm.

As stated in my definition of a sprachbund, a feature must occur in at least three LMV languages, not just in one or two, to make it a valid sprachbund feature. (Two languages may come into close contact and share features without being part of a broader sprachbund.) Thus, in chapters 4 and 5, only features occurring in at least three LMV languages are included in the phonetic and morphological databases.

## Weighting Features

While the concept of quantifying features is necessary and useful in delimiting and analyzing the LMV, it is also necessary to evaluate the significance of features in order to gauge the overall strength of the area as a sprachbund. I have based my weighting criteria on my working definition of a sprachbund. I also use the method employed by Campbell, Kaufman, and Smith-Stark (1986) in their analysis of Mesoamerica as a sprachbund, such that a highly marked feature would be weighted more heavily than a less marked one. For example, Campbell et al. find a vigesimal counting system to be a strong Mesoamerican language feature since it is found in virtually every Mesoamerican language but is largely absent beyond Mesoamerica, with the exception of only a few languages on its periphery (546). To this end only certain morphological features are evaluated, or "weighted," more highly than others.

In the LMV, all languages, with the possible exception of MTL, have subject-object-verb (SOV) word order. This means that SOV order is a very strong LMV areal feature. However, although SOV order is an ubiquitous feature in the LMV, it is ultimately of little to no significance since many Native American languages outside the LMV also have SOV order. On the other hand, the employment of positional verbs as aspectuals indicating incomplete or ongoing action is of much greater significance, since this occurs more rarely among Native American languages yet is a grammatical component of each language in the LMV. This indicates this feature's probable diffusion in the area through intimate contact and multilingualism; it must thus be ranked higher than SOV word order as an areal feature. Areal features must be evaluated on a case-by-case basis to gauge their overall impact and significance in relation to the broader surrounding region not judged to be part of the LMV.

## Words and Calques

The second section of this analysis concerns words and calques, or semantic borrowings, shared among LMV languages. Word and semantic borrowings help in the historicist sense of determining the intensity of contact between groups and their possible migration patterns. Data for this section of the analysis were gathered through the perusal of several dictionaries and lexicons. At least one dictionary or lexicon was chosen as representative of each language, although in cases where more than one lexicon is available (e.g., Choctaw), others were used and the source of a particular word was noted.

## Method of Data Organization

Data for the first section of this analysis were gathered and put into a comprehensive database categorized by type of feature (phonetic/phonological, morphological) sorted by individual language.

Following Masica (1976), I test against one another the distribution of several features that can be used to define the LMV as a sprachbund. The establishment of proposed sprachbund boundaries depends on the establishment of proposed sprachbund criteria; it is possible to test only a selection of criteria. It is necessary to ascertain the viability of a proposed feature and trace it outward until the farthest limits of continuous distribution are reached.

There is no easy way of measuring or characterizing the total impact of one language on another (Weinreich 1953, 63), and, despite recent advances in grammatical theory and linguistic typology, there is no rational method for ranking grammatical structures between languages (Southworth 2005). However, in defining a sprachbund, it is necessary to establish parameters that will define the region as a language area. To this end the significance of the LMV as a sprachbund can be tested by using the "trait complex" as a point of departure and assigning a numerical value to each trait, or feature, identified as part of the complex (Masica 1976, 170). For example, based on Masica's analysis, it was found that the "Indian norm" for word order is predominantly (subject)-object-verb, or (s)ov (195). We also find that the South Asian or Indian trait complex scores a fairly high

24–30 among Hindi, Telugu, Bengali, Sinhalese, Japanese, Burmese, Amharic, and Turkish, indicating an exceptionally broad extension of the "Indian norm" all the way from Ethiopia (Africa) to Japan (East Asia). However, a significant drop-off of "Indian norm" traits occurs with Tibetan, which scores only 18 out of 30; other languages, including Chinese, most Indo-European languages (including Persian), Swahili, Arabic, and Thai score even lower, indicating their relative remoteness from the "Indian norm" (195). (And this considering that at least one of the above-mentioned languages, Thai, is geographically quite close to the supposed Indian language area, yet scores the lowest at 1.)

Data for the second part of this analysis consist of words sorted by language into a lexicon representing a large cross-section of varying parts of speech and semantic categories in each language. Further, I produced another database with the lexicon of each language placed side by side for greater ease of lexical comparison across languages. I also produced a list of *basic* versus *non-basic* vocabulary in order to determine the intensity of borrowing among languages and their level of contact.

**METHOD OF ANALYSIS**

Phonetics/Phonology and Morphology

I evaluate the feature norm—the features that are typical—for the LMV. Depending on the presence or absence of any feature, a language will yield a total, the sum of the numerical values of the complex features that it possesses, which expresses its nearness to or distance from this characteristic norm. Using this method, languages with the highest totals in this case will be the "most LMV" (closest to the LMV norm), while those with the lowest totals will be the "least LMV" (furthest from the LMV norm). For example, four LMV languages have nasalized vowel sounds, while only one has ejective stops. Thus, nasalized vowels are more characteristic of the LMV and closer to the LMV norm than ejective stops. This has been called the *top-down* approach, involving less bias than the *bottom-up* approach, wherein one postulates "one to one correspondences of very specific features between individual languages" then generalizing "the resulting list to all languages in the area." An advantage of the top-down approach is "the possibility of establishing significance across linguistic areas." A disadvantage of this approach "might be that there is interference from typological patterning" (Muysken 2008, 7).

For the Phonetics/Phonology and Morphology chapters, the original database has been reduced to two smaller databases for each chapter, the first focusing specifically on phonetics and phonology (chapter 5), the second specifically on morphology (chapter 6). Features more heavily weighted in the phonetic/phonological and morphological databases are given a score of 2 instead of 1.

### Basic vs. Non-basic Vocabulary

I assess the copied vocabulary between LMV languages to identify how many *basic* words there are and between which languages. So-called basic vocabulary is supposed to be universal to human languages and unlikely to be borrowed, words such as 'mother,' 'hand,' 'run,' 'sleep,' 'one,' 'five,' 'sun,' and 'water,' so that it would be more unlikely for a language to copy such words as opposed to more culture-specific vocabulary such as 'tamale' or 'karaoke.' Basic vocabulary for the LMV is analyzed in accordance with the Leipzig-Jakarta 100 basic word list rather than from the more commonly used, but older and slightly more subjective, Swadesh list. The distinction between basic and non-basic vocabulary is relevant to the application of Thomason's (2001) borrowing scale, since, again, so-called basic vocabulary is supposedly least likely to be copied between languages.

Assessing copied lexemes between languages as either basic or non-basic allows me to use Thomason's scale to posit the intensity of contact between any two or more LMV languages. For example, a language that has copied basic vocabulary would indicate more intense contact with the source language than between two languages with only non-basic vocabulary copied between them, suggesting only casual contact.

### Degree of Language Convergence

In order to assess the degree of language convergence in the LMV, I use the Thomason scale. It must be emphasized that any borrowing scale is a matter of probabilities, not possibilities. The predictions it makes can be violated, in principle and sometimes in fact. But since these predictions are robust—that is, they are valid in the great majority of cases that have been described in the literature—any violation should provide interesting insights into social and, to a lesser extent, linguistic determinants of contact-induced change. (Thomason 2001, 71)

This chapter has covered my methodology and analysis. In the next two chapters, I will focus on the phonetic, phonemic, and morphological features of the LMV sprachbund.

# FIVE

# Phonetic and Phonological Features

In this chapter I examine the phonetic and phonological elements of the
LMV sprachbund. While phonological features are generally more difficult
to borrow than phonetic features, there are cases where phonological rules
are borrowed "under conditions of close typological fit" (Winford 2003,
55). Since LMV languages are typologically close (most having SOV constituent order), I consider the possible copying of phonological as well as phonetic features.

I begin with an analysis of vowel phonemes followed by consonant phonemes that occur in at least three LMV languages. After this I list phonemes
that occur in two or fewer LMV languages, thus not playing a significant
role in the LMV as sprachbund and listed only for informational purposes.

The presence of four language isolates makes an analysis of phonetic
and phonological copying in the LMV difficult, since we cannot determine if
the ancestral languages of the isolates contained certain features and thus
involved internal (genetic) rather than external (contact) change. Thus, by
necessity, certain possible phonetic and phonological borrowings involving these languages must remain uncertain, as there is no longer a means
of determining internal or external impetus.

## INVENTORY OF LMV PHONEMES

### Vowel Phonemes

A compilation of LMV vowel phonemes is shown in figure 13.

Nasalized variants of *a*, *i*, and *o* occur in Biloxi and Ofo, as in most other
Siouan languages. Nasalized variants of *a*, *e*, *i*, and *o* occur in Atakapa, while
nasalized variants of all five vowels occur in Natchez, but only in phrase-
final position as the result of phonological rather than phonemic rules.

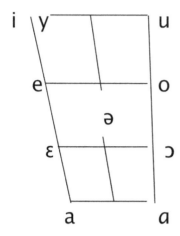

Fig. 13. IPA chart of LMV vowel phonemes. Created by author.

Nasalized variants of *a*, *i*, and *o* occur in Choctaw-Chickasaw as well as in the MTL.

All LMV languages, except those of the Muskogean language family, have at least a five-vowel system. Muskogean (including MTL) languages have only a three-vowel system (*a, i, o*), as does the peripheral Caddoan.

### Consonant Phonemes

The cumulative LMV consonantal phonemes are shown in table 3.

The voiced labiovelar approximate *w* occurs in all LMV languages. A labialized form of *k* (*kʷ*) occurs only in Natchez. The double articulated consonant *tl* occurs only in Atakapa. Voiceless variants of *m, l,* and *j* occur only in Natchez, although devoicing of sonorants also occurs in Chitimacha and Tunica. Chitimacha appears to have had a /kʷ/ phoneme at an earlier period of its existence (Swadesh 1939, 34).

### MOST RELEVANT PHONETIC AND PHONOLOGICAL FEATURES OF THE LMV SPRACHBUND

Features are ranked along a tripartite weighting scale: 0, 1, 2. A score of 0 indicates that the feature in question does not exist in the area I have delimited as the LMV. A rank of 1 indicates that the feature exists but extends well beyond the LMV and/or is so common crosslinguistically as to be non-

Table 3. The cumulative LMV consonantal phonemes

| | BILABIAL | LABIO-DENTAL | ALVEOLAR | PALATO-ALVEOLAR | RETROFLEX | PALATAL | VELAR | GLOTTAL |
|---|---|---|---|---|---|---|---|---|
| NASAL | m | | n | | | | ŋ | |
| PLOSIVE | p b | | t d | | | | k g | ʔ |
| FRICATIVE | | f | s | ʃ ʒ | ʂ | | x | h |
| APPROXIMANT | | | | | | j | | |
| TAP, FLAP | | | | ɾ | | | | |
| LATERAL FRICATIVE | | | ɬ | | | | | |
| LATERAL APPROXIMANT | | | l | | | | | |

significant in supporting the LMV as a sprachbund. A rank of 2, the highest weighting, indicates that the feature is either geographically limited to the LMV and its immediate periphery and/or is so crosslinguistically unusual as to be very relevant in supporting the LMV as a sprachbund.

## More Highly Weighted Phonetic and Phonological Features

The features that are weighted more highly, scoring 2 points instead of 1, are nasalized vowels, the voiceless labiodental fricative /f/, the lateral fricative /ɬ/, the retroflex sibilant /ʂ/, alternation of /i/ and /u/, alternation of word-initial /h/ ~ /Ø/, and vowel harmony—all features that are relatively rare around the LMV periphery and thus most representative of the LMV sprachbund.

## Nasalized Vowels

As stated earlier, nasalized vowels are a feature of Siouan and Muskogean, occurring in several LMV languages: Atakapa, Biloxi, Choctaw-Chickasaw, MTL, Natchez, and Ofo. In Natchez, however, nasal vowels occur only in phrase- or sentence-final position and are thought to be based on underlying final /n/, which acts as a type of declarative marker (Geoffrey Kimball, pers. comm., 2013). Vowel nasalization in Atakapa is at times uncertain, perhaps being an allophone of the phoneme /ŋ/. Vowel nasalization in Atakapa and Natchez may be due to contact with the Siouan and Muskogean languages of the LMV.

Vowel nasalization occurs in the following peripheral languages: Eastern Muskogean; the Plains Siouan languages Dakota, Mandan, Ioway-Otoe, and Dhegiha (including Quapaw); Yuchi, Karankawa, Kiowa, Apache, and Cherokee. Nasalized vowels do not occur in the Great Basin Uto-Aztecan and Washo languages. Outside of North America vowel nasalization is especially prominent in West Africa and in several South American languages.

Vowel nasalization is an internal Siouan development in Quapaw and possibly also in Yuchi, which may be a remote relative of Siouan. It is possible that nasalized vowels diffused from Siouan and Muskogean into the peripheral languages. The relative scarcity of nasalized vowels among languages beyond the LMV in North America and universally warrants a more highly weighted score of 2.

### Bilabial Fricative /f/

All Muskogean languages, including MTL, have the labiodental fricative /f/ phoneme. Haas postulated Muskogean /f/ as the modern reflex of Proto-Muskogean /$x^w$/ (1969b, 36). This phoneme is also found in Atakapa and Ofo, and at least as a dialectal reflex of Biloxi /$x^w$/, as evidenced by Mrs. Jackson's pronunciation of *nixuxwi* (*nišofeʾ*) 'ear' (Haas and Swadesh 1968, 79). Timucua and Yuchi, on the periphery of the LMV, also have this phoneme.

Labial fricatives, both /f/[1] and /v/, are a feature of the Southwest, including southern California and the Great Basin, and the Tanoan region (Sherzer 1976, 138). Bilabial fricatives also occur in Comanche (173). These phonemes do not occur in the upper Plains or in the Northeast. Since it appears that /f/ was an internal change from /$x^w$/ within Muskogean, it is likely that Atakapa, Ofo, Timucua, and Yuchi borrowed this phoneme from contact with Muskogean languages. The last known speaker of Biloxi, Emma Jackson, pronounced /$x^w$/ as *f*, a pronunciation that correlates with the probable change of Proto-Muskogean /$x^w$/ to *f*. (It is unclear whether this was a dialectal feature of Biloxi at the time data were elicited or whether this was an idiosyncratic pronunciation based on possible personal influence of Choctaw-Chickasaw.)

Since labiodental-bilabial fricatives are relatively scarce among languages beyond the LMV in North America (with the notable exception of the U.S. Southwest), they have been more highly weighted with a score of 2.

### Lateral Fricative /ɬ/

The voiceless lateral fricative /ɬ/ occurs in Atakapa, though rarely, and in Muskogean languages. This phoneme occurs in MTL, though variations arose (e.g., *ɬaɬo* > *šlašo* and *nani* 'fish'; Drechsel 1996, 282), presumably due to its difficulty of articulation in speakers of the pidgin unfamiliar with it in their own languages (e.g., English, French, Spanish). The fact that the phoneme /ɬ/ is rare in Atakapa may indicate that it was not originally a feature of Atakapa and was likely borrowed, probably through contact with Tonkawa, Karankawa, or Muskogean languages. The Atakapa phoneme /tl/ may be a variant of the /ɬ/ phoneme.

This phoneme occurs on the periphery of the LMV in Apache, Karankawa, Tonkawa, and Yuchi. The Mesoamerican language Totonac also has the /ɬ/ phoneme. The relative scarcity of /ɬ/ among languages beyond the LMV in North America and universally warrants a more highly weighted score of 2.

### Retroflex Sibilant /ʂ/

The retroflex sibilant /ʂ/ is a feature of Muskogean (including MTL), Natchez, and Tunica. This is not a typical phoneme among eastern North American languages; it is now unknown whether it could originally have been a Natchesan or Tunican feature. A "back ş" is pervasive in an area centered in California but also extending into Oregon, the Great Basin, and western Mexico (Mithun 1999, 16; Bright 1984).

The fact that Tunica has this feature may lend support to the idea that the Tunicas were once farther west and in contact with peoples of the Great Basin. However, retroflexed fricatives and affricates also occur in several Mesoamerican languages, including in some highland Mayan languages, Mixean, Yuman (Campbell, Kaufman, and Smith-Stark 1986, 544), and Totonac (MacKay 1999). Thus, there is also the possibility that this phoneme was diffused into the LMV through contact with Mesoamerican languages via overland or maritime trade.

The phoneme /ʂ/ is thus a feature of the LMV that was likely diffused via contact with Tunica (though it is unknown whether this was originally a feature of Tunican or if Tunicans copied this phoneme, perhaps from a Great Basin or other western language). The relative scarcity of retroflex sibilants among languages beyond the LMV in North America and universally warrants a more highly weighted score of 2.

### /i/ ~ /u/ Alternation

The alternation of /i/ and /u/ occurs in Biloxi, Natchez, and Tunica. This alternation appears to be a feature of Siouan languages, particularly of Biloxi but also of the Dhegihan Siouan languages. Examples include Biloxi *či* and *ču* 'put, place, plant,'; Natchez *ʔišuš* and *ʔušuš* 'back'; and Tunica *tahišini ~ tahišuni* 'sieve'; *hiši ~ hišu* 'sift.' The transition of /u/ to /i/ in Siouan is most apparent in Kansa (Kaw), wherein /u/ is pronounced like German *ü*, apparently midway in transition between /u/ and /i/. Dorsey and Swanton (1912) also note such a phoneme in Biloxi pronunciation, though it was apparently infrequent.

This feature is likely not a genetic or internally developed feature and is typologically rare crosslinguistically. The feature is possibly borrowed from Siouan (Biloxi).

### Alternation of Word-Initial /h/ ~ /Ø/

The alternation of word-initial /h/ ~ /Ø/ (zero marking) appears to be a feature of the LMV area. Examples include Atakapa *hipa ~ ipa* 'husband' (Gatschet and Swanton 1932, 42), *hikat ~ ikat* 'foot' (40), *himatol ~ imatol* 'four' (41), *huket ~ uket* 'mother' (46); Biloxi *hane ~ ane* 'find', *hamihi ~ amihi* 'heat', *hasne ~ asne* 'thief' (Dorsey and Swanton 1912); and MTL *hat(t)ak ~ atak* 'man' (Crawford 1978, 88; Drechsel 1996, 295), *hoyba ~ oyba* 'rain' (Drechsel 1996, 306). This feature appears to be crosslinguistically non-significant.

This feature appears to be a development internal to Siouan, since the "glottal stop is often inserted before word-initial vowels in Siouan sentences as a *Grenzsignal*—a boundary marker—so it is possible that the

Biloxi initial *h*- that comes and goes in these words is the local reflex of [ʔ]" (Rankin 2011, 4). In MTL, the alternation appears "to be instances of an *h*- that was present etymologically in Western Muskogean that was lost among certain users of Mobilian" (13). While this may be true, the fact that three LMV languages—Atakapa, Biloxi, and MTL—exhibit such a feature is likely indicative of diffusion through contact. Since the change from [ʔ] to *h*- appears to be an internal Siouan development, it seems likely that this feature was copied from Siouan (Biloxi) into the other two languages.

### Vowel Harmony

Vowel harmony occurs in Natchez (regressive and progressive) and Tunica. In Natchez regressive vowel harmony is optional while progressive is obligatory:

(11)  *cuku•hu•-*
     cuk-ə-•hə•-
     trot-PL
     'trot (plural subject)'
     (Kimball 2005, 400)

(12)  *ʔacpopo•noh*
     ʔacpopopoh-•nuh
     Irishman-DIM
     'little Irishman'
     (Kimball 2005, 400)

Vowel harmony is also known in Mayan and Copainalá Zoque (Campbell, Kaufman, and Smith-Stark 1986, 543). The relative scarcity of vowel harmony among languages beyond the LMV in North America and universally warrants a more highly weighted score of 2.

### Less Highly Weighted Phonetic and Phonological Features

The following features are weighted less primarily because they are cross-linguistically prominent or likely arose through internal impetus.

### Velar Fricative /x/

The velar fricative /x/ is a feature of Atakapa and of Siouan languages—it occurs in Biloxi. (This phoneme appears to have largely disappeared from Ofo [Robert Rankin, pers. comm., 2013].) Examples include Atakapa *itsix* 'above' and *sapixk* 'dead'; Biloxi *xuxwê* 'wind' and *naxê* 'hear.' It is now unknown whether Atakapa originally had this phoneme or if it was copied from Siouan.

The phoneme /x/ occurs far beyond the LMV, however. It occurs in Quapaw, Yuchi, Apache, Karankawa, Tonkawa, and Coahuiltec, spreading through the Great Basin into California and through the Algonquian languages of the Upper Plains as well as also occurring in Huastec and other Mayan languages. Its development in Quapaw and Yuchi is likely an internal development, while its occurrence in Karankawa and Coahuiltec could reflect influence from Huastec or Atakapa, or both.

I propose that the phoneme /x/ is a feature of the LMV that is likely to have spread into Atakapa from Siouan (Biloxi). However, this phoneme is found far beyond the LMV and is crosslinguistically fairly common. It is thus given a rank of 1.

### Voiced Liquid /l/

The voiced liquid /l/ is present in Atakapa, Muskogean (including MTL), Ofo, Natchez, and Tunica; it is not present in Biloxi or Chitimacha. The phoneme /l/ contrasts with /r/ in Tunica, the only LMV language to have /r/. While /l/ is a feature of the LMV, it is unlikely to have been diffused; it more likely arose in each language through internal impetus and is thus given a rank of 1.

### Glottalized Nasals

Glottalized nasals are absent from the LMV; they do occur in Apachean in the Plains (Sherzer 1976, 141). This is an example of the *absence* of a feature also being indicative of a sprachbund.

### Devoicing of Sonorants

Devoicing of the sonorants *l, r, y,* and *w* occurs in Chitimacha, Natchez, and Tunica. At least final *w* was also apparently devoiced in Atakapa. Final devoicing of sonorants is also a noted feature in Mesoamerica, including Mayan languages (primarily Quichean), Nahuatl (Uto-Aztecan), and Totonacan (Campbell, Kaufman, and Smith-Stark 1986, 537), thus also providing the possibility of diffusion through contact with Mesoamerica. While it is a feature of the LMV, there is no sure way to determine if such devoicing arose through internal impetus in each language or if it was diffused through contact. Thus, devoicing of sonorants is not indicative of the LMV being a sprachbund.

### NON-SIGNIFICANT PHONETIC AND PHONOLOGICAL FEATURES

The following features occur in only one LMV language and are thus not helpful or indicative in determining a sprachbund. They are included only for informational purposes.

### Ejective Stops

Ejectives (glottalized stops and affricates) occurs only in Chitimacha, though they "are very common in North America" (Mithun 1999, 19), appearing in Siouan (though not in Biloxi or Ofo), Kiowa-Tanoan, Caddo, Coahuiltec, many languages of California and the northwestern United States (19), Tonkawa (Campbell, Kaufman, and Smith-Stark 1986, 544), and Tepehua (Totonacan) and Mayan. Since ejectives occur in only one LMV language, this feature is non-significant to the LMV sprachbund.

### Labiovelar /kʷ/

The labiovelar /kʷ/ is a standard feature only of Natchez, although Biloxi superficially shows *kʷ*, as in *kwįhi* 'valley.' However, upon deeper examination, this Biloxi word turns out to be composed of underlying *kuwi* 'up, above' + *įhi* 'reach, arrive,' thus demonstrating /u/ vowel devoicing in the first syllable rather than a true /kʷ/ phoneme. Since this phoneme occurs in only one LMV language, it is not indicative of a sprachbund.

On the periphery, /kʷ/ occurs in Caddoan, Tonkawa, Comanche, Karankawa, Coahuiltec, and Timucua. It is possible Natchez developed this phoneme through contact with Caddoan or Timucua. Since this feature occurs in only one LMV language, it is non-significant for the LMV as a sprachbund.

### Velar Nasal /ŋ/

Atakapa is the only LMV language in which the phoneme /ŋ/ is known to occur. This phoneme occurs throughout the Great Basin into California and in the Southwest, including in Karankawa and Coahuiltec. It also occurs in Mesoamerican Totonac.

The nasalization of an immediately preceding vowel /ⁿ/ (ñ in Swanton's [1932] data) may simply reflect an allophone of /ŋ/ in Atakapa. For example, Atakapa 'house' is written in Swanton's data as both *aŋ* and *aⁿ* (Swanton 1932, 27). A variant of this phoneme is full vowel nasalization, represented by /ⁿ/ in place of final /ŋ/ in Atakapa, which may reflect influence from contact with Siouan and/or Muskogean languages, although the original Atakapan /ŋ/ may also have developed through contact with Great Basin or Southwestern North American languages (including Karankawa and Coahuiltec) in which this feature is prominent. The velar nasal /ŋ/ is also crosslinguistically quite ubiquitous and thus non-significant for the LMV sprachbund.

### Liquid /r/

The liquid /r/ occurs only in Tunica in the LMV. However, this phoneme has a broad distribution through the Great Basin into California and in the Southwest in Yuman, Hopi, Acoma, and Tanoan (Sherzer 1976), as well as in Caddoan, Karankawa, and Comanche. The phoneme also occurs in Timucua as well as in Huastec and some other Mayan languages. It is possible Tunican copied the phoneme through contact with either Caddoan or Timucua, or possibly even through contact with Southwestern or Great Basin languages, but it could also have been an original phoneme of Tunican languages.

The liquids /l/ and /r/ contrast phonemically in Tunica. Since /r/ occurs in only one LMV language and is crosslinguistically common, it is non-significant for the LMV sprachbund.

## /r/ and /l/ Opposition

The opposition between /r/ and /l/ occurs only in Tunica, which is also the only LMV language that has the /r/ phoneme.

## Lateral Affricate /tl/

The lateral affricate /tl/ occurs in the LMV only in Atakapa. In the extant Atakapa data, /tl/ occurs only in word- or syllable-initial position, for example, *tlakš* 'dirty,' *tla* 'mosquito,' *tluk* 'smoke tobacco.' It is unknowable whether this phoneme arose in Atakapa through internal impetus or through external contact. However, the apparent phonological limitation of occurring only word or syllable initially, and the fact that Nahuatl /tl/ is not limited to word-initial position, would suggest an internal impetus. This phoneme may also be an allophone of the lateral fricative /ɬ/.

   On the periphery this phoneme occurs in Apache, Kiowa, Cherokee, and Totonac. Crosslinguistically the lateral affricate /tl/ is comparatively rare, occurring most prominently in the Pacific Northwest, the Caucasus, and Central Africa (Maddieson 2013). The phoneme /tl/ occurs in the LMV only in Atakapa and is thus non-significant for the LMV sprachbund.

## Preaspirated Voiceless Stops

In the LMV preaspirated voiceless stops occur only in Muskogean languages, though they also occur in Osage, a Dhegihan Siouan language on the periphery of the LMV. Its restricted occurrence in the LMV renders it non-significant for the LMV sprachbund.

## Pitch

Pitch accent occurs in Choctaw and Natchez. In the latter, there are four pitch contours: high, mid, rising, and falling (Kimball 2005, 396). Examples include:

(13) *kúNà*      (3–1) (high-mid)
    kuN-a
    water-DEF
    'the water'
    (Kimball 2005, 396)

(14)  *ʔíꞏMšàLsìk*              (3–4–1–1) (rising-mid-mid)

      ʔiꞏM-ša-Lsi-k

      agree-QT-AUX-CONN

      'He agreed, so they say.'

      (Kimball 2005, 396)

Choctaw also has pitch accent, "but there seem to be almost no pairs which are distinguished by pitch alone" (Broadwell 2006, 17). Pitch or tonal contrast is also known in Cherokee, some Mayan languages, and in Northern Tepehuan and Cora-Huichol (both Uto-Aztecan) (Campbell, Kaufman, and Smith-Stark 1986, 544).

In this assessment, each feature occurring in three or more LMV languages and known to be relatively scarce outside of the LMV and universally receives a score of 2, while those features that are relatively ubiquitous, both within North America and universally, receive a score of 1. Features that do not occur in an LMV language receive a score of 0.

Table 4 summarizes LMV phonetic and phonological features; table 5 does the same for peripheral languages. The total number of LMV features that each LMV language contains is shown at the bottom of the chart.

## Table 4. LMV phonetic and phonological features

| | FEATURE | SOURCE | AT. | BIL. | CHIT. | MTL | NAT. | OFO | TUN. | WM |
|---|---|---|---|---|---|---|---|---|---|---|
| | *PHONETIC/ PHONOLOGICAL* | | | | | | | | | |
| 1 | nasalized vowels | Sh76 | 2 | 2 | 0 | 2 | 2 | 2 | 0 | 2 |
| 2 | ejective stop | K12 | 0 | 0 | 1 | 0 | 0 | 0 | 0 | 0 |
| 3 | vowel alternation i ~ u | K12 | 0 | 1 | 0 | 0 | 1 | n/d | 1 | 0 |
| 4 | vowel alternation o ~ u | K12 | 1 | 1 | 0 | 0 | 0 | n/d | 0 | 0 |
| 5 | word-initial h ~ Ø | K12 | 1 | 1 | 0 | 1 | 0 | n/d | 0 | 0 |
| 6 | /θ/ | Sh76 | 0 | 0 | 0 | 0 | 0 | 0 | 0 | 0 |
| 7 | /kʷ/ | Sh76 | 0 | 0 | 0 | 0 | 1 | 0 | 0 | 0 |
| 8 | /f/ | Sh76 | 2 | 2 | 0 | 2 | 0 | 2 | 0 | 2 |
| 9 | /x/ | Sh76 | 1 | 1 | 0 | 0 | 0 | 1 | 0 | 0 |
| 10 | /h/ | Sh76 | 1 | 1 | 1 | 1 | 1 | 1 | 1 | 1 |
| 11 | /l/ | Sh76 | 1 | 0 | 0 | 1 | 1 | 1 | 1 | 1 |
| 12 | /ɬ/ | Sh76 | 2 | 0 | 0 | 2 | 0 | 0 | 0 | 2 |
| 13 | glottalized nasals | Sh76 | 0 | 0 | 0 | 0 | 0 | 0 | 0 | 0 |
| 14 | /ŋ/ | Sh76 | 1 | 0 | 0 | 0 | 0 | 0 | 0 | 0 |
| 15 | /r/ | Sh76 | 0 | 0 | 0 | 0 | 0 | 0 | 1 | 0 |
| 16 | /q/ | Sh76 | 0 | 0 | 0 | 0 | 0 | 0 | 0 | 0 |
| 17 | r/l opposition | Sh76 | 0 | 0 | 0 | 0 | 0 | 0 | 1 | 0 |
| 18 | s/š opposition | Sh76 | 0 | 0 | 1 | 1 | 0 | 1 | 1 | 1 |
| 19 | /tl/ | K12 | 1 | 0 | 0 | 0 | 0 | 0 | 0 | 0 |
| 20 | glottalized semivowels | Sh76 | 0 | 0 | 0 | 0 | 0 | 0 | 0 | 0 |
| 21 | preaspirated voiceless stops | C97 | 0 | 0 | 0 | 0 | 0 | 0 | 0 | 1 |
| 22 | retroflex sibilants | C97 | 0 | 0 | 0 | 2 | 2 | 0 | 2 | 2 |
| 23 | vowel harmony | N94 | 0 | 0 | 0 | 0 | 2 | 0 | 2 | 2 |
| 24 | five-vowel system | Sh76 | 1 | 1 | 1 | 0 | 1 | 1 | 1 | 0 |
| 25 | tone | K12 | 0 | 0 | 0 | 0 | 1 | 0 | 0 | 0 |
| 26 | devoicing of sonorants (m, n, l, r, w, y) word-final and before-voice consonant | C97 | 0 | 0 | 1 | 0 | 1 | 0 | 1 | 0 |
| | Totals | | 14 | 10 | 5 | 12 | 13 | 9 | 12 | 14 |

Key: At. = Atakapa, Bil. = Biloxi, Chit. = Chitimacha, Nat. = Natchez, Tun. = Tunica,

WM = Western Muskogean

Sh76 = Sherzer 1976, K12 = Kaufman 2012, C97 = Campbell 1997, N94 = Nicklas 1994.

## Table 5. Peripheral phonetic and phonological features

| | FEATURE | SOURCE | EM | QUA. | CAD. | YU. | KAR. | TON. | KIO. | AP. |
|---|---|---|---|---|---|---|---|---|---|---|
| | *PHONETIC / PHONOLOGICAL* | | | | | | | | | |
| 1 | nasalized vowels | Sh76 | 2 | 2 | 0 | 2 | 2 | 0 | 2 | 2 |
| 2 | ejective stop | K12 | 0 | 1 | 1 | 1 | 0 | 0 | 1 | 1 |
| 3 | vowel alternation i ~ u | K12 | 0 | ? | 0 | 0 | 0 | 0 | 0 | 0 |
| 4 | vowel alternation o ~ u | K12 | 0 | ? | 0 | 0 | 0 | 0 | 0 | 0 |
| 5 | word-initial h ~ Ø | K12 | 0 | ? | 0 | 0 | 0 | 0 | 0 | 0 |
| 6 | /ɵ/ | Sh76 | 0 | 0 | 0 | 0 | 0 | 0 | 0 | 0 |
| 7 | /kʷ/ | Sh76 | 0 | 0 | 1 | 0 | 1 | 1 | 0 | 0 |
| 8 | /f/ | Sh76 | 2 | 0 | 0 | 2 | 0 | 0 | 0 | 0 |
| 9 | /x/ | Sh76 | 0 | 1 | 0 | 1 | 1 | 0 | 0 | 1 |
| 10 | /h/ | Sh76 | 1 | 1 | 1 | 1 | 1 | 1 | 1 | 1 |
| 11 | /l/ | Sh76 | 1 | 0 | 0 | 1 | 1 | 1 | 1 | 1 |
| 12 | /ɬ/ | Sh76 | 2 | 0 | 0 | 2 | 2 | 0 | 0 | 2 |
| 13 | glottalized nasals | Sh76 | 0 | 0 | 0 | 1 | 0 | 0 | 0 | 0 |
| 14 | /ŋ/ | Sh76 | 0 | 0 | 0 | 0 | 1 | 0 | 0 | 0 |
| 15 | /r/ | Sh76 | 0 | 0 | 1 | 0 | 1 | 0 | 0 | 0 |
| 16 | /q/ | Sh76 | 0 | 0 | 0 | 0 | 0 | 0 | 0 | 0 |
| 17 | r/l opposition | Sh76 | 0 | 0 | 0 | 0 | 1 | 0 | 0 | 0 |
| 18 | s/š opposition | Sh76 | 1 | 1 | 1 | 1 | 1 | 0 | 0 | 1 |
| 19 | /tl/ | K12 | 0 | 0 | 0 | 0 | 0 | 0 | 1 | 1 |
| 20 | glottalized semivowels | Sh76 | 0 | 0 | 0 | 1 | 0 | 0 | 0 | ? |
| 21 | preaspirated voiceless stops | C97 | 1 | 0 | 0 | 1 | 0 | 0 | 0 | 0 |
| 22 | retroflex sibilants | C97 | 2 | 0 | 0 | 0 | 0 | 0 | 0 | 0 |
| 23 | vowel harmony | N94 | 2 | 0 | 0 | 0 | n/d | 0 | 0 | 0 |
| 24 | five-vowel system | Sh76 | 0 | 1 | 0 | 1 | 1 | 1 | 1 | 0 |
| 25 | tone | K12 | 0 | 0 | 1 | 0 | n/d | 0 | 0 | 1 |
| 26 | devoicing of sonorants (m, n, l, r, w, y) word-final and before-voice consonant | C97 | 0 | 0 | 0 | 0 | 0 | 0 | 0 | 0 |
| | Totals | | 14 | 7 | 6 | 15 | 13 | 4 | 7 | 11 |

## Table 5. Continued

| FEATURE | SOURCE | COM. | SHAW. | COAH. | TIM. | CHER. | CAT. | NAH. | HUA. |
|---|---|---|---|---|---|---|---|---|---|
| *PHONETIC / PHONOLOGICAL* | | | | | | | | | |
| 1 nasalized vowels | Sh76 | 0 | 0 | 0 | 0 | 2 | 2 | 0 | 0 |
| 2 ejective stop | K12 | 0 | 0 | 1 | 0 | 0 | 0 | 0 | 1 |
| 3 vowel alternation i ~ u | K12 | 0 | 0 | 0 | 0 | 0 | ? | 0 | 0 |
| 4 vowel alternation o ~ u | K12 | 0 | 0 | 0 | 0 | 0 | ? | 0 | 0 |
| 5 word-initial h ~ Ø | K12 | 0 | 0 | 0 | 1 | 0 | ? | 0 | 0 |
| 6 /θ/ | Sh76 | 0 | 1 | 1 | 0 | 0 | 0 | 0 | 1 |
| 7 /kʷ/ | Sh76 | 1 | 0 | 1 | 1 | 0 | 0 | 1 | 1 |
| 8 /f/ | Sh76 | 0 | 0 | 0 | 2 | 0 | 0 | 0 | 0 |
| 9 /x/ | Sh76 | 0 | 0 | 1 | 0 | 0 | 0 | 0 | 1 |
| 10 /h/ | Sh76 | 1 | 1 | 1 | 1 | 1 | 1 | 1 | 0 |
| 11 /l/ | Sh76 | 0 | 1 | 1 | 1 | 1 | 0 | 1 | 1 |
| 12 /ɬ/ | Sh76 | 0 | 0 | 0 | 0 | 2 | 0 | 0 | 0 |
| 13 glottalized nasals | Sh76 | 0 | 0 | 0 | 0 | 0 | 0 | 0 | 0 |
| 14 /ŋ/ | Sh76 | 0 | 0 | 0 | 0 | 0 | 0 | 0 | 0 |
| 15 /r/ | Sh76 | 1 | 0 | 0 | 1 | 0 | 1 | 0 | 1 |
| 16 /q/ | Sh76 | 0 | 0 | 0 | 0 | 0 | 0 | 0 | ? |
| 17 r/l opposition | Sh76 | 0 | 0 | 0 | 1 | 0 | 0 | 0 | 1 |
| 18 s/š opposition | Sh76 | 0 | 0 | 1 | 0 | 0 | 1 | 1 | 0 |
| 19 /tl/ | K12 | 0 | 0 | 0 | 0 | 1 | 0 | 1 | 0 |
| 20 glottalized semivowels | Sh76 | 0 | 0 | 0 | 0 | 0 | 0 | 0 | 0 |
| 21 preaspirated voiceless stops | C97 | 0 | 0 | 0 | 0 | 0 | 0 | 0 | 0 |
| 22 retroflex sibilants | C97 | 0 | 0 | 0 | 0 | 0 | 0 | 0 | 0 |
| 23 vowel harmony | N94 | 0 | 0 | 2 | 0 | 0 | 0 | 0 | 0 |
| 24 five-vowel system | Sh76 | 1 | 1 | 1 | 1 | 1 | 1 | 0 | 1 |
| 25 tone | K12 | 0 | 0 | 0 | 0 | 1 | 0 | 0 | 0 |
| 26 devoicing of sonorants (m, n, l, r, w, y) word-final and before-voice consonant | C97 | 0 | 0 | 0 | 0 | 0 | 0 | 0 | ? |
| Totals | | 4 | 4 | 10 | 9 | 9 | 6 | 5 | 8 |

## Table 5. Continued

| | FEATURE | SOURCE | MAYAN (OTHER) | TOTONAC | ENGLISH |
|---|---|---|---|---|---|
| | *PHONETIC / PHONOLOGICAL* | | | | |
| 1 | nasalized vowels | Sh76 | 0 | 0 | 0 |
| 2 | ejective stop | K12 | 1 | 0 | 0 |
| 3 | vowel alternation i ~ u | K12 | 0 | 0 | 0 |
| 4 | vowel alternation o ~ u | K12 | 0 | 0 | 0 |
| 5 | word-initial h ~ Ø | K12 | 0 | 0 | 0 |
| 6 | /θ/ | Sh76 | 0 | 0 | 1 |
| 7 | /kʷ/ | Sh76 | 0 | 0 | 1 |
| 8 | /f/ | Sh76 | 0 | 0 | 2 |
| 9 | /x/ | Sh76 | 1 | 0 | 0 |
| 10 | /h/ | Sh76 | 1 | 1 | 1 |
| 11 | /l/ | Sh76 | 1 | 1 | 1 |
| 12 | /ɬ/ | Sh76 | 0 | 2 | 0 |
| 13 | glottalized nasals | Sh76 | 0 | 0 | 0 |
| 14 | /ŋ/ | Sh76 | 0 | 1 | 1 |
| 15 | /r/ | Sh76 | 1 | 0 | 0 |
| 16 | /q/ | Sh76 | 1 | 1 | 0 |
| 17 | r/l opposition | Sh76 | 1 | 0 | 0 |
| 18 | s/š opposition | Sh76 | 0 | 1 | 1 |
| 19 | /tl/ | K12 | 0 | 0 | 0 |
| 20 | glottalized semivowels | Sh76 | 0 | 0 | 0 |
| 21 | preaspirated voiceless stops | C97 | 0 | 0 | 0 |
| 22 | retroflex sibilants | C97 | 2 | 2 | 0 |
| 23 | vowel harmony | N94 | 2 | 2 | 0 |
| 24 | five-vowel system | Sh76 | 1 | 0 | 1 |
| 25 | tone | K12 | 1 | 0 | 0 |
| 26 | devoicing of sonorants (m, n, l, r, w, y) word-final and before-voice consonant | C97 | 1 | 0 | 0 |
| | Totals | | 14 | 11 | 9 |

Key: EM = Eastern Muskogean, Qua. = Quapaw (Dhegiha), Cad. = Caddoan, Yu. = Yuchi, Kar. = Karankawa, Ton. = Tonkawa, Kio. = Kiowa, Ap. = Apache.
Com. = Comanche, Shaw. = Shawnee, Coah. = Coahuiltec, Tim. = Timucua, Cher. = Cherokee, Cat. = Catawba, Nah. = Nahuatl, Hua = Huastec.
Sh76 = Sherzer 1976, K12 = Kaufman 2012, C97 = Campbell 1997, and N94 = Nicklas 1994.

# SIX

# Morphological Features

In this chapter I discuss the morphological features of the LMV. Treatment of morphological traits, or features, will be similar to that for phonetics and phonology, except that some morphological features will be weighted more heavily (i.e., given an extra point), since certain morphological features are easier to copy, or borrow, than others. I begin with a discussion of the features that are weighted followed by discussion of non-weighted features and features that are judged to be inconsequential to the LMV sprachbund.

While phonetic resemblances have long been accepted as evidence of linguistic borrowing, the notion of syntactic and morphological borrowing has met with various degrees of objection. Sapir believed that morphology was very unlikely to be borrowed. The opposite belief also took hold, that all aspects of language could be borrowed so freely that every language had "multiple roots" and that genetic classification was no longer even possible. It is possible that "Indo-Europeans" were never one people, but a group of unrelated peoples who came linguistically to resemble each other through close geographical and cultural association.

## LANGUAGE UNIVERSALS

Language universals are the set of human language characteristics or categories that may be stated as a list of "rules," according to likely typological or grammatical patterns of occurrence among the world's languages. These rules are divided among "absolute universals," or those that are without exception (such as that all languages have vowels) and tendentious universals, those that tend toward universality but with exceptions (such as that if a language has subject-object-verb [SOV] word order, it probably has *post*positions rather than *pre*positions, but not always) (see Comrie 1981,

1989). Greenberg ([1939] 1961) came up with such a set of language universal rules. For instance, his Universal 4 rule states that "with overwhelmingly greater than chance frequency, languages with normal SOV order are postpositional" (79), while his Universal 16 states that "in languages with dominant order SOV, an inflected auxiliary always follows the main verb" (85). LMV languages, which have SOV order, are indeed postpositional and have auxiliaries following the main verb, thus supporting Greenberg's language universal rules.

## MOST RELEVANT MORPHOLOGICAL FEATURES
## FOR DETERMINING A SPRACHBUND

As in the preceding chapter on phonetic and phonological features, morphological features are ranked on a tripartite weighting scale: 0, 1, 2. A score of 0 indicates that the feature in question does not exist in the area I have delimited as the LMV and is thus not relevant, or is non-significant, to the present discussion. A rank of 1 indicates that the feature exists in the area but, like SOV word order, it is so common crosslinguistically that its presence in the LMV is not distinctive and thus non-significant to the LMV as a sprachbund. A rank of 2, the highest weighting, indicates that the feature is either geographically limited to the LMV and its immediate periphery and/or is so crosslinguistically unusual as to be *very* relevant in supporting the LMV as a sprachbund.

The morphological features that are weighted more highly in this analysis:

(1) Focus and topic marking
(2) Indirect animate object prefix, valence reducer
(3) Indirect inanimate object prefix, valence reducer
(4) Positional verb auxiliaries
(5) Verb number suppletion

Table 7, at the end of the chapter, summarizes these morphological features in the LMV.

### Discourse Marking

I use the term *discourse marking* to include such speaker-centered emphatic marking often labeled *focus, topic,* and *assertion,* as well as evidentiality and reference tracking. Discourse, or pragmatic, marking is one of the most fascinating features of LMV and many other Native American languages. Much of this linguistic marking is a matter of letting a speaker interject more of his or her emotions and feelings into a conversation or story via the use of certain verbal elements supplied by the language. Discourse marking in oral narrative serves a similar purpose to punctuation in writing: to simplify comprehension and to serve as a means of inserting a speaker's parenthetical comments or feelings into the narrative.

### Focus

I use the term *focus* to refer to newly given information (what Prague School linguists call *rheme*) (Payne 1997, 271). LMV focus-marking suffixes can occur with both nouns and verbs.

Atakapa, Biloxi, Chitimacha, Choctaw-Chickasaw, and Natchez have focus-marking suffixation. Atakapa and Chitimacha appear to share a focus-marking suffix -*š,* or-*sh,* while Choctaw-Chickasaw and Natchez appear to share -*ook.* Peripheral languages with focus-marking suffixes are Yuchi and Cherokee.

Atakapa and Chitimacha both have a focus-marking suffix -*š* (Campbell 1997, 344). Atakapa -*š* appears affixed to nouns and acts as a type of definiteness marker:

(15)  *ti-š*
       go-DEF
       'the going' ?
       (Gatschet and Swanton 1932, 17)


(16)  *neš hišom-š-kin*
       tree small-DEF-LOC
       'in the small trees (bushes)'
       (Gatschet and Swanton 1932, 11)

(17) *yul-š*

writing-DEF

'the letter'

(Gatschet and Swanton 1932, 12)

The Chitimacha focus-marking suffix -*š* is also affixed to the noun:

(18) *we*          *ʔasi-š*       *ha·nk*     *ʔap*     *ne-n-iʔi*

that man-FOC   this-LOC    here     come    water-out-3s

'That is how man came over here out of the water.'

(Daniel Hieber, pers. comm., 2013)

(19) *ha*      *še·ni-š*       *nenču·*     *ʔati-i*        *ni-n-šwi-čuki*

this    pond-FOC    too large   AOR.INDF.3s   to.water-out-move.up-1s.FUT

'Man came out of this large pond.'

(Daniel Hieber, pers. comm., 2013)

A Choctaw focus marker is -*ook*, which Broadwell describes as "poorly understood" and tentatively glosses as "comparison" (2006, 80):

(20) *ofi-(h)ook-ano*     *isht*     *iya-l-aachi̱-h*

dog-FOC-ACC   INST   go-1p-IRR-TNS

'the dogs I'll take'

(Broadwell 2006, 81)

Natchez shares an identical focus marker *o·k*, which is either due to borrowing or to the possibility that Natchez may be genetically distantly related to the Muskogean languages:

(21) *toMičo·k*            *ʔele·he·ʔi-lu-ha·t*

*toM-ič-o·k*           *ʔel-ə·hə·ʔi-lu-ha·t*

person-ERG-FOC   see.PL/PL-PRT-AUX-NEG

'As for the people, they did not see them.'

(Kimball 2005, 448)

In Choctaw-Chickasaw, the suffix -*oosh* acts as a focus marker:

(22) *hattak-**oosh***
     man-FOC
     'the man (focus)'
     (Broadwell 2006, 77)

(23) *wak-**oosh** woha*
     cow-FOC sound
     'It's a cow that's lowing.'
     (Haag and Willis 2001, 191)

In Biloxi the marker *-di* is often affixed to nouns in texts, particularly with nouns newly introduced into the narrative or discourse (Kaufman 2011). The suffix *-di* descends directly from Proto-Siouan *-ri*, a focus marker also found in the northern Siouan languages Hidatsa and Mandan (John Boyle, pers. comm., 2007). This suffix is sometimes used at first mention, when objects or characters are first introduced into a story, thus signaling new information, or FOCUS.

(24) *Skakana-**di***           *ewite-xti*       *eyąhi*    *yuhi*    *yohi-yą*
     Ancient.of.Opposums-FOC     early-INTENS     3s-arrive  3s-think  pond-TOP
     'The Ancient of Opossums thought he would reach a certain pond very early in the morning.'
     (Dorsey and Swanton 1912, 26)

(25) *Ayaa-**di***       *wax*    *ni*     *yukê*
     person-FOC     hunt    walk    move
     'Some people were hunting . . .'
     (Dorsey and Swanton 1912, 65)

## Topic

In this book the term *topic* refers to old, previously mentioned, or known information (what Prague School linguists call *theme*) (Payne 1997, 271). For instance, *-yą* is a form of definite article that tends to occur most frequently when the noun to which it is affixed has already been introduced into a story, thus marking old or already given information, or TOPIC, as the following Biloxi examples show:

(26)  *ątatka-yą* *khu-ni*      *ǫǫni*          *e-tu*      *xa*
      child-TOP            3.give-NEG    PST      3.say-PL always
      'always she did not give him the child' ('she never gave him the child'?)
      (Dorsey and Swanton 1912, 43)


(27)  *"Yamą na,"*    *e-di*                    *ąyaa-xohi-yą*
      no            DECL.M 3s.say-ASRT    person-old-TOP
      '"No," the old woman said.'
      (Dorsey and Swanton 1912, 67)

In the above examples, 'child' and 'old woman' were previously mentioned in the discourse.

The Choctaw-Chickasaw suffix *-aash* also indicates previous mention, in essence acting as a type of definite article, as discussed earlier.

(28)  *Hattak-Ø-**aash**-at*        *chaaha-h*
      man-COP-PREV-NOM      tall-TNS
      'The previously mentioned man is tall.'
      (Broadwell 2006, 89)

### Assertive Marking

Atakapa, Biloxi, Chitimacha, and Natchez have assertive markers, with which a speaker may choose to add particular emphasis or sense of immediacy to a verb. The following examples show the Atakapa assertive suffix *-š*:

(29)  *šak-yon-š-ul-it*
      person-call-ASRT-3SUBJ.PL-PERF
      'they called (him/them)'
      (Gatschet and Swanton 1932, 10)

(30)  *ini*          *šak-naw-š*

search   PL-let-ASRT
'let them search'
(Gatschet and Swanton 1932, 13)

(31) *šoxmon*      *iš-yam-š-ehe*
everything   1OBJ.PL-gather-ASRT-FUT
'we will (indeed) gather everything'
(Gatschet and Swanton 1932, 13)

Chitimacha has similar assertive marking, which could suggest either common genetic ancestry with Atakapa or borrowing:

(32) *Kun*     *čuw-k'-š*        *šeni-nk*      *hup*     *hi*      *ni-čw-iʔi.*
INDF    go-PRT-ASRT    pond-LOC    to      there    water-move.up-3s
'Going and going some, he came there to a pond.'
(Daniel Hieber, pers. comm., 2012)

The Chitimacha particle *ne* is primarily used as the conjunction 'and' in Chitimacha (Daniel Hieber, pers. comm., 2013), but it also occurs as a type of emphatic:

(33) *we*      *huyu*     *kamčin*     **ne'**[1]
DEF    turtle    deer      and
'the turtle and the deer'
(Swadesh 1939, 127)

(34) *na·kšbu*    **ne'**    *kaš*    *ni*    *kušminaʔa'*
child    also    clam    PVB    eat
'The children, too, ate clams.'
(Swadesh 1939, 128)

(35) *susbink*    *pa·limičuy*    **ne'**    *himks*    *keti*    *ka·han*
gun      shoot       even    3s      kill    unable
'Even if you shot it with a gun, you could not kill it.'
(Swadesh 1939, 129)

The Chitimacha particle carries "emphatic reference 'just, precisely'" (Swadesh 1939, 127). However,

> in the emphatic sense, the reason for the use of *ne* is not always clear. It is very common in negative sentences even where there is no strong reason for emphasis. Similarly, the use in positive sentences, though less common, is also not obviously called for. It seems that the degree of emphasis implied is rather mild and that the usage is largely "stylistic." (Swadesh 1939, 128)

We have seen the Biloxi focus marker *-di* attached to nouns, but *-di* also attaches to verbs. With verbs, *-di* shows more emphasis or immediacy and has been glossed as an assertive marker (Kaufman 2011), as the following examples demonstrate:

(36) *Sǫǫnitǫǫni-k*   *ǫha*   *ąyaa*   *ǫǫni*   *ustax*   *kanê-di*
      tar-ACC      with     man     make     stand.up     EVID2-ASRT
      'He made a tar baby [person] and stood it up there.'
      (Dorsey and Swanton 1912, 13)

(37) *Kąkǫǫni*   *dǫhi*   *tê*   *dê-di*   *ê-tu-xa*
      trap       see     want     go-ASRT     they-say-always
      'They say that he departed, as he wished to see the trap.'
      (Dorsey and Swanton 1912, 184)

Natchez has three marked degrees of emphasis: *ya·* 'that,' *ka·* 'this,' and *ma·* 'that there,' the last appearing to be the least emphatic of the three. These are based on the deictics *ya·na*, *ka·na*, and *ma·na*. Kimball calls these "exclamatory postverbs" (Kimball 2005, 422). Each of these is exemplified below:

(38) *ča·wiNčiya*         *ʔi·Minu·k*                     **ya·na**
      *ča·wiNči-ya-O*      *ʔi·m-ʔ-ni-w-k*                *ya·na*
      deer-meat-ART-ABS     be.tired.of-3PT-1STAT-AUX-CONN     EMPH
      'I am tired of deer meat!'
      (Kimball 2005, 422–23)

(39) *mâ·h*   *tama·Lho-La*          *toMa katitani·sa·t* **ka·na**

     *mâ·h*   *tama·L-ho-L-a-n*      *toM-a-O*

     lo      woman-virgin-ART-ABS   man-ART-ABS

     *kat-ʾi-tani-··-O-sa·t*          *ka·na*

     lack-PRT-DU-AUX-3DAT-DAT-NEG   EMPH

     'Lo! The two girls never lack a man!'

     (Kimball 2005, 423)

(40) *ʔeLhalawi.ta.N*         *tama.L ʔawiti. kačassitanki*     **ma.na**

     *ʔeLhalawi.ta.N*         *tama.L ʔawiti.-O ka-čas-si-tan-ki-Ṽ*   *ma.na*

     split-QT-AUX-MOD identical   PVB-stand-QT-DU-AUX-PHR.TRM   EMPH

     woman two-ABS

     'Two identical women stood there.'

     (Kimball 2005, 423)

Tunica has an emphatic suffix *-pa* translated as 'too, also, even' (Haas 1946, 122):

(41) *taʾ-ya-ku-**păn***       *ʾuh-kaʾli-n-ʾun-keʾnì*

     *taʾ-ya-ku-**pă-n***     *ʾuh-kaʾli-n-ʾuhki-anì*

     DEF-deer-MASC-also-PAUS   3s.MASC.OBJ-create-CAUS-3s.M-QT

     'He created the deer, too.'

     (Haas 1946, 122)

(42) *koʾtyuki-**pă-n***     *saʾm-ʔahă-n*

     hominy-also-PAUS   cook-NEG-INTER

     'Hominy, also, is it not cooked?'

     (Haas 1946, 122)

Focus and topic marking are weighted more heavily than certain other morphological features since discursive/pragmatic features are more embedded in the grammar of a language and are thus more difficult to borrow. Also, since focus and topic marking do not extend far into the LMV periphery, this is a strongly defining feature of the LMV sprachbund.

Prefix for Indefinite Animate Subject- or Object-Marking, Valence Reducer

A preverb or prefix meaning 'person' or 'people' is used in Atakapa, Choctaw-Chickasaw, and Natchez as a type of indefinite person or animate subject or object marker.

In Atakapa, the prefix is *šak-*:

(43)  *yul-š*        **šak-***in*          *ok*
      letter-DEF     INDF.ANIM-ask       come
      'the letter of invitation'
      (Gatschet and Swanton 1932, 12)

The Choctaw word *oklah* 'people' is sometimes used for plural animate subjects:

(44)  *Hitokoosh*     *chokf*     **oklah**     *falaama-tok*
      And.then        rabbit      INDF.PL      meet-PST
      'And then they met a rabbit.'
      (Broadwell 2006, 41)

The Natchez indefinite animate prefix is *tah-*:

(45)  **tah-***le·le·nal-ʔiš*
      INDF.ANIM-burn.repeatedly-INF
      'buckmoth caterpillar'[2]
      (Kimball 2005, 434)

Peripherally, Nahuatl has a similar prefix for indefinite animate objects:

(46)  *ni-**te**-tla-maka*
      1s-INDF.ANIM-INDF.INAN-give
      'I give it to someone'
      (Lockhart 2001, 26)

Due to the relative scarcity of this feature in Native North American languages outside of the LMV, this is a strongly defining feature of the LMV as a sprachbund.

### Prefix for Indefinite Inanimate Object, Valence Reducer

All languages have operations that adjust the relationship of semantic roles and grammatical relations, using a range of structures for accomplishing this (Payne 1997, 169). In the LMV, a preverb or prefix is used as a valence-reducing operation. Atakapa, Biloxi, Choctaw-Chickasaw, Natchez, and Ofo have valence-reducing prefixation. All of these languages, except Biloxi and Ofo, use a lexeme meaning 'thing, something' as a valence-reducing prefix. In Biloxi and Ofo, a non-lexical prefix *(w)a-* is used. On the periphery, Quapaw, Yuchi, Apache, Coahuiltec, Nahuatl, and Totonac have similar affixation.

In Atakapa, the valence-reducing prefix is *šok-*:

(47)  *šok-šil-kit*
      INDF.OBJ-sew-CONT
      'she was sewing (things)'
      (Gatschet and Swanton 1932, 15)

(48)  *šok-koy*
      INDF.OBJ-speak
      'chief' ('speaking things')
      (Gatschet and Swanton 1932, 9)

The Choctaw valence-reducing prefix is **naa-** or **nąn-**:

(49)  **nąn-**-*óffo-'*
      INDF.OBJ-plant-NZR
      'plant'
      (Broadwell 2006, 53)

(50)  **naa-**-*hóoyo-'*
      INDF.OBJ (SUBJ)-hunt-NZR
      'hunter' or 'prey'
      (Broadwell 2006, 53)

Example 50 demonstrates that Choctaw *nan-* or *naa-* can be ambivalent, since the preverb *naa-*can represent either the agent (hunter) or the patient (prey) (Broadwell 2006, 53). The Western Muskogean prefixes *nan-* and *naa-* likely derive from the word *nanta* 'what, something, someone.' The Natchez valence-reducing prefix is *kin-*:

(51)  *nokkinhantawąą*
      nok-**kin**-han-ta-w-aa-n
      PVB-INDF.OBJ-make-1s-AUX-INC-PHR.TRM
      'I can work.'
      (Kimball 2005, 405)

As stated earlier, Siouan languages have a non-lexical prefix *wa-* (reduced to *a-* in Biloxi and Ofo), whose actual translation is murky, though it often can be translated as 'thing' or 'something' (i.e., an indefinite object prefix) and acts as a type of valence reducer (Robert Rankin, pers. comm., 2013):

(52)  ***a-****duska*
      something-bite
      'rat'
      (Dorsey and Swanton 1912, 186)

Peripherally, Nahuatl and Totonac have indefinite inanimate object affixation. In Nahuatl the prefix is *tla-*:

(53)  *ni-k-**tla**-maka*
      1s-3s-INDF.OBJ-give
      'I give him/her something.'
      (Lockhart 2001, 26–27)

In Totonac, an affix *-nan* appears identical to Choctaw-Chickasaw *nan-*, except that the Totonac form is suffixed rather than prefixed:

(54)  *čana**nan**kał*
      *čan-nan-kan-la(ł)*
      SOW-INDF.OBJ-INDF.SUBJ-PERF
      'someone planted (habitually), planting was done'
      (MacKay 1999, 195)

It remains to be determined if borrowing of this form between the Muskogean and Totonacan languages is indicated, but the correlation is intriguing, particularly in light of other such similarities discussed in this book. Since the Choctaw-Chickasaw affix appears to have an internal motivation from the lexeme for 'what' or 'thing' (see examples 49–50 above), if borrowing is indicated, it would likely be from Western Muskogean into Totonacan.

Due to the relative scarcity of this feature in the periphery of the LMV, the use of a valance-reducing prefix based on the word 'thing' or 'something' is a strongly defining feature of the LMV sprachbund.

### Reference Tracking

A reference-tracking device, often referred to as a switch reference (SR) system, is used, at least in part, to track the subject of consecutive clauses, primarily to determine whether the subject of a new clause is the same (same-subject [SS]) or different from the subject (different-subject [DS]) of an immediately preceding clause (Whaley 1997, 276).

Biloxi, Choctaw-Chickasaw, and Natchez have SR marking. Atakapa, Chitimacha, and MTL show no SR marking. Tunica allows two or more active verbs having the same subject to be linked together, the events expressed being either simultaneous or consecutive. Tunica also has a type of switch-topic marking to indicate the dependence of one sentence on a prior one. Data are insufficient for determining the existence of reference tracking in Ofo.

Peripheral languages with forms of reference tracking are Tonkawa, Kiowa, Comanche, and Coahuiltec. Three other Siouan languages of the northern Plains—Crow, Hidatsa, and Mandan—also have SR marking, although the markers are not cognate with those in Biloxi nor with each other.

An SR system is particularly useful in languages with no third-person marking (i.e., third person is Ø [zero-marked or null]). Biloxi and Chickasaw-Choctaw, both with zero-marked third-person pronouns, have SR marking. The Biloxi markers are SS *hą* and DS *ką*:

(55) *ąsu-di*      *čį-xti*          **ką**  *ąk-učučati*   *ąk-pačo*   *ąk-paxa*    **hą**    *ąktąhį*
     pine-TOP   fat-INTENS  DS  1s-split     my-nose   1s-stick.in  SS  1s-run
     'That fat pine (branch), I will split it and put it in my nose and run (with it).'
     (Dorsey and Swanton 1912, 67)

In example 55, the pine tree is the subject of the first clause, then in the next clause the subject changes to the Old Woman, who sticks the pine branch into her nose and runs with it.

It is likely that the Biloxi ss marker *hą* evolved from this particle's use as a phrasal coordinator meaning 'and.' The origin of the Biloxi DS marker is uncertain, though it exactly corresponds to the Choctaw DS marker *-ką*, suggesting borrowing between them.

Choctaw markers for third-person SR are *-kat* (ss) and *-ką* (DS):

(56)  *John-at      anokfilli-h    pisachokma-**kat***
　　　John-NOM     think-TNS      good.looking-ss
　　　'John thinks that he (himself) is good-looking.'
　　　(Broadwell 2006, 269)

(57)  *John-at      anokfilli-h    pisachokma-**ką***
　　　John-NOM     think-TNS      good.looking-DS
　　　'John thinks that he/she is good-looking.'
　　　(Broadwell 2006, 269)

In example 56, John thinks that he himself is good-looking, indicating use of the ss marker. In 57, however, John thinks someone else is good-looking, indicating use of the DS marker. When other than third person reference is involved (i.e., either first or second person), the Choctaw markers are *-ooš* (ss) and *-ǫ* (DS):

(58)  *Kaah    sa-nna-haatok-**oosh**,    iskali'     ittahobli-li-tok*
　　　car     1s-want-because-ss         money      save-1s-PST
　　　'Because I wanted a car, I saved money.'
　　　(Broadwell 2006, 263)

(59)  *kaah    banna-haatok-**ǫ**,    iskali'     ittahobli-li-tok*
　　　car     want-because-DS         money      save-1s-PST
　　　'Because he wanted a car, I saved money.'
　　　(Broadwell 2006, 263)

Choctaw has a second type of ss reference marking, using the suffix *-t* as a serial verb linker when each verb has the same subject or agent:

(60) *holisso'*   *hokmi-t*   *ammohmichi-li-tok*
     paper   burn-SS   complete-1s-PST
     'I completely burned all the papers.'
     (Broadwell 2006, 207)

(61) *Bill-at*   *itti'*   *chạ-t*   *aya-h*
     Bill-SUBJ   tree   chop-SS   go.along-TNS
     'Bill went along chopping (down) trees.'
     (Broadwell 2006, 219)

Contra Watkins (1976, 36), the fact that SR systems are generally lacking in Siouan languages (with the exception of the northern Siouan Mandan, Crow, and Hidatsa) suggests that the borrowing likely was from Muskogean into Biloxi rather than in the opposite direction.

Natchez employs three reference-tracking devices: first is the suffix *-k*, which "indicates that one phrase has ended and another is to follow" (Kimball 2005, 445), in essence marking the continuance of subject, theme, or topic:

(62) *ma·na*   *toM-piš-ič-a*   *čop-a-p-ku-k*
     that.one   man-2POSS-ERG-ART   pluck-1OPT-2OBJ-AUX-CONN
     'That one, your husband said to me, I will pluck you . . . .'
     (Kimball 2005, 445)

Second is the suffix *-Ṽ*, indicating "that a sentence, which can be made up of many phrases, has come to an end, that there may or may not be a further sentence, and that if there is, there will be a shift in tone or focus from the previous sentence" (445), thus acting as a type of DS and/or different-topic marker:

(63) *makte*   *ce·kihan*   *ka·kinšuškụ*
     *ma·kte*   *ce·kih-a-n*   *ka·–kin-šu-šk<sup>w</sup>-Ṽ*
     then.after   Jack-PRT-ABS   PST-something-QT-eat-PHR.TRM
     'Then after that, Jack ate.'
     (Kimball 2005, 447)

Third is a new-topic marker *-šu·*, which simultaneously occurs with the modal affix *-ne* 'when' (415):

(64)  *toM*      *heMkup*      *še-n-či-**šu·**-ne*
    person    widowed    QT-IMPF-dwell-NEW.TOP-MOD
    'Now, it is said that there was once a widowed person dwelling there, and . . .'
    (Kimball 2005, 415)

Tunica also has a suffix *-k* that acts as a "future subjunctive" (Haas 1946, 120), or irrealis marker. It thus acts as a type of subordination marker, similar to Chitimacha and Natchez *-k*, indicating a non-final sentence:

(65)  *honu-wi-k*                *ʾu-ni-sin-ani*
    come.down-3s.M-FUT    3s.M-tell-QT
    'They told him to come down' (that he should come down).
    (Haas 1946, 120)

(66)  *hihč-ʾaka-wi-k*        *ʾu-ni-koni*
    there-enter-3s.M-FUT    3s.M-tell-?
    'He told him to go in there' (that he should go in there).
    (Haas 1946, 120)

Due to the relative scarcity of reference tracking in Native North American languages and in the periphery of the LMV, this is a strongly defining feature of the LMV sprachbund.

### Positional Verb Auxiliaries

Classificatory verbs of the LMV signal position classification of nouns: SIT, STAND, LIE, and MOVE. Positional verbs have been grammaticized in the Siouan languages as continuative aspect markers and proximal demonstrative determiners (Mithun 1999, 116). The positionals SIT, STAND, LIE, and MOVE occur as markers of continuative aspect in the Siouan languages. Atakapa, Biloxi, Choctaw, Ofo, and Tunica all use positionals in a similar manner, indicating possible borrowing among them. Similar positional verb usage also occurs in Nahuatl and Totonac.

The following are examples of positional auxiliary verb usage in the LMV languages:

(67)  Atakapa

    *kew*    *kam-š-kin-tu*

    sit    protrusion-DEF-LOC-sit?

    'I am (seated) paddling.'

    (Gatschet and Swanton 1932, 61; Watkins 1976, 27)[3]

(68)  Biloxi

    *nihǫ*    *ani*    *dêxtowê*    *nê*

    cup    water    full    STAND

    'The cup is full of water.'

    (Dorsey and Swanton 1912, 166)

(69)  Chitimacha

    *wetk*    *kas*    *tuYti:k'*    *pe'anki*

    *we-t-k*    *kas*    *tuYti-k'*    *pe-'e-nk-i*

    DEM-RFL-LOC    back (PREV)    stoop.down-PRTP    be (horizontal)-3s-LOC-NZR

    'when he had stooped down'

    (Swadesh, unpublished notes)

(70)  Choctaw

    *Bill-at*    *ma*    *biniḽi*

    SUBJ    there    sit (ANIM)

    'Bill is (sitting) over there.'

    (Watkins 1976, 21)

(71)  Ofo

    *b-ašě*    *nąki*

    1-sit    SIT

    'I am sitting down.'

    (Rankin 2002, 20)

(72) Natchez

| ya· | potkop | ka'ašup ka'epe·nakiyaku·š | |
|---|---|---|---|
| ya· | potkop | ka'ašup-Ø | ka·'epe·-na-ki-ya-ku·š |
| that | mountain | blue-ABS | PVB-lie-3P-AUX-ART-ALL |

'towards where that blue mountain is lying'

(Kimball 2005, 438)

(73) Tunica

t-uruna-t'e-ku          'u-na

DEF-frog-large-M.SG      3s.M-sit

'There is the bullfrog.'

(Haas 1940, 110)

In many languages of the world the same lexical item can express actual physical stance as well as being used as an auxiliary. In Biloxi, however, physical stance and locative-existential predicates or verbal auxiliaries generally form two different sets of words. The stance verbs used as independent verbs in Biloxi are *toho* ('lie'), *xêhê* ('sit'), *sįhį* ('stand'), and *hine* and *ni* ('move'). Their grammaticized auxiliary counterparts are *mąki* ('lie'), *nąki* ('sit'), *nê* ('stand'), and *ąde* and *hine* ('move'). The form *hine* is used for both singular and plural, while *ąde* has a suppletive plural form, *yuke*. *Ąde* is used for general movement and running while *hine* is for walking only. These auxiliary verbs SIT, STAND, LIE, and MOVE form a discrete set of auxiliary verbs that often no longer specify actual physical position or movement but, rather, are used to express nuanced aspectual meanings. *Mąki*, *nąki*, and *nê* are used for both animates and inanimates, while *ąde* and *hine* are confined to use only with animates. *Mąki*, *nąki*, and *nê* share a common plural form *(h)amąki*, apparently a form of *mąki*, 'lie.' The origin of these positionals is uncertain, but it appears that *mąki* may be related to the word *(a)mą*, 'land' or 'earth,' and *ąde* seems to incorporate the word for 'go' (*ą* ? + *de* [perhaps *dêê*] 'go').

The Chitimacha positional verbs are *hi(h)* 'neutral/sitting,' *ci(h)* 'standing/vertical,' and *pe(h)* 'lying/horizontal' (Swadesh 1939, 230). What is unique about the Chitimacha positional system is that the connotation of a positional is more important than the denotation. The horizontal positional *pe* connotes disrespect while *ci* connotes respect (Watkins 1976, 28).

In Tunica nouns are also classified into three positions: standing (*ka'l'ura* < *ka'li* 'to stand' + *'ura* 'lies' [literally, stand-lie]), sitting (*'u'na*), and lying (*'u'ra*) (Haas 1946, 111). As Haas observes, "Although the choice of auxiliary is in certain cases apparently arbitrary, it is found to depend in large part on a combination of the features of gender and position" (112). Human or non-human animate nouns can take any of these positions as their characteristic form of embodiment allows:

(74)  *t-o'nĭ-ku*          *'u-rá*
      DEF-man-M.SG    3S.M-lie
      'There is the (lying/reclining) man.'
      (Haas 1946, 110)

(75)  *ta'-să-ku*          *'u-ná*
      DEF-dog-M.SG    3S.M.-sit
      'There is the (sitting) dog.'
      (Haas 1946, 110)

Certain non-human elongated animates, as fish, snakes, and alligators, are always classified in the horizontal position:

(76)  *ta'-nară-ku*          *'u-rá*
      DEF-snake-M.SG    3S.M.-lie
      'There is the (lying/reclining) snake.'
      (Haas 1946, 110)

Certain other non-human animates, as frogs, birds, and insects, are always classified in sitting position:

(77)  *t-e'hkuna-ku*          *'u-ná*
      DEF-mosquito-M.SG    3S.M-sit
      'There is the (sitting) mosquito.'
      (Haas 1946, 110)

Inanimate nouns that have a characteristic erect position use the 'standing' classifier:

(78) *ta'-hkă-ku*            *ka'l-'u-rá*
DEF-corn.plant-M.SG     stand.3s.M-lie
'There is the (standing) corn plant.'
(Haas 1946, 111)

Atakapa appears to have a correlation to the Tunica 'stand.lie' positional form, which may be due to contact:

(79)
| *yil* | *lat* | *himatol* | *u* | *ta-tixi* | *ăn* | *ta-at* | *ha* | *išat* | *pam-lik-š* | *mon* |
|---|---|---|---|---|---|---|---|---|---|---|
| day | three | four | or | stand. lie | and | stand- PST | his | head | beat- mash- ASRT | all |

'For three or four days he lay there with his head all beaten and mashed in.'
(Gatschet and Swanton 1932, 11)

Tunica abstract nouns are classified as supine, or 'lying':

(80)
| *hi'nahkŭn* | *la'hon* | *sa'hkŭn* | *'ará* | *ha'tikàn* |
|---|---|---|---|---|
| thus-PL | early.one-PL | 3F | lie | once.more |

'Thus there is one early (morning) (left) once more'
(Haas 1946, 111)

The following example is from the peripheral Nahuatl:

(81) *wetska-tikak*
laugh-stand
's/he is (standing) laughing'
(Lockhart 2001, 39)

(82) *ti-koč-tok*
2 sleep-lie
'you are (lying) sleeping'
(Lockhart 2001, 39)

And from the peripheral Totonac:

(83)  *ut*                          *ɬtata-ta-wila*
      3                           sleep-INC-seated
      's/he sleeps (sitting)'
      (MacKay 1999, 225)

(84)  *hun-čiwiš*     *ta-nuu-maa-la(ɬ)*
      DET-stone      INC-inside-lie-PERF
      'the stone is (lying) inside'
      (MacKay 1999, 225)

It is worth noting that the positionals in both Nahuatl and Totonac indicate a progressive or ongoing state or action, just as positionals do in the LMV. The ubiquitous occurrence of positional auxiliaries in the LMV and their relative absence in the periphery makes this a strong determining feature of the LMV sprachbund.

### Verbal Number Suppletion

The verbal suppletion treated here relates to nominal arguments of the verb, and the verb agrees with its arguments. All languages of the LMV, except MTL and Natchez, have verbal number suppletion in relation to nominal arguments. This feature is further limited in the region by being primarily used in relation to the positional auxiliaries STAND, SIT, LIE, and MOVE. In languages like Tunica, only these auxiliary verbs show suppletion, while other verbs in the language do not (Haas 1946, 40). In Atakapa, on the other hand, suppletion also occurs in certain verbs other than positionals.

The Atakapa singular positional verb forms and their suppletive plural equivalents are (Gatschet and Swanton 1932):

|        | singular     | plural |
|--------|--------------|--------|
| STAND  | *to* or *ta* | *cot*  |
| SIT    | *ke*         | *nul*  |
| LIE    | *tixt*       | *yoxt* |

The Biloxi forms are (Dorsey and Swanton 1912):

|        | singular | plural    |
|--------|----------|-----------|
| STAND  | *nê*     |           |
| SIT    | *nąki*   | *(h)amąki* |
| LIE    | *mąki*   |           |
| MOVING | *ąde*    | *yuke*    |

In Chitimacha, the conjugations of auxiliary (positional) verbs "are complicated and irregular, so that the simplest account is a list of the forms" (Swadesh 1939, 32). These forms are:

|        | singular | plural  |
|--------|----------|---------|
| STAND  | *ci(h)*  |         |
| SIT    | *hi(h)*  | *na(h)* |
| LIE    | *pe(h)*  |         |

Chitimacha, like Biloxi, neutralizes the singular auxiliary forms to a single plural form, *na(h)*.

The Choctaw-Chickasaw forms include a dual as well as a plural form and animate and inanimate forms of SIT:

|               | singular | dual    | plural    |
|---------------|----------|---------|-----------|
| STAND         | *hikiya* | *hiili* | *(hi)yoh-* |
| SIT (anim.)   | *binili* | *chiiya* | *binoh-*  |
| SIT (inanim.) | *talaya* | *taloha* | *taloh-*  |
| LIE           | *ittola* | *kaha*  | *kah-*    |

Choctaw-Chickasaw has both animate and inanimate forms for SIT. In Tunica, suppletion is "a process not used by any other word-class of the language" (Haas 1946, 40). The forms:

|       | singular | dual     | plural   |
|-------|----------|----------|----------|
| STAND | *kali*   | ?        | ?        |
| SIT   | *ʾuna*   | *ʾunana* | *ʾukʾɛra* |
| LIE   | *ʾura*   | *ʾurana* | *naʾara* |

No such suppletion is evident in MTL. Verb number suppletion does not occur in Natchez; unfortunately, we have insufficient data to make any determination about verb number suppletion in Ofo.

Other languages of North America that have similar suppletion are Ute, Cahuilla, Northern Tepehuan (Uto-Aztecan), Passamaquoddy-Maliseet (Algonquian), and Slave (Athapaskan).

Since nominal verbal suppletion does not extend far into the LMV periphery, and is, in fact, quite rare crosslinguistically, this is a strongly defining feature of the LMV sprachbund.

## LEAST RELEVANT MORPHOLOGICAL FEATURES TO THE LMV SPRACHBUND

These features are weighted less than other features since they (1) extend geographically well beyond the LMV, and/or (2) occur in only one or two languages of the LMV and are thus not pervasive enough within the LMV (as here delineated) to be considered an LMV feature, and/or (3) are universal enough crosslinguistically that they are of little value in defining the LMV as a sprachbund.

These features are:

- evidentiality
- overtly marked case system
- definite article
- demonstrative precedes noun
- circumfixed negative construction
- reduplication in nominal stems for plurality
- reduplication in verbal stems for plurality
- plurality in pronouns
- duality in pronouns
- plurality in nouns
- duality in nouns
- locative-directional affixes
- subject person prefixes
- SOV constituent order
- quinary number marking
- masculine/feminine gender distinction
- inclusive/exclusive plural pronouns

These less heavily weighted features will be addressed in the order given above.

### Evidentiality

Evidential marking, also called *verificational* and *validational* marking, indicates source of information, that is, whether the information relayed by a speaker was gained from personal (firsthand) experience or from secondary (non-firsthand) reporting or inference. While every language has some lexical means of referring to information source (e.g., the English words *reportedly* or *allegedly*), not all languages grammatically *require* a speaker to indicate source of information (Aikhenvald and Dixon 2006, 320). While many of the most familiar IE languages such as English and French, lack required evidential marking, evidentials appear in many non-IE languages, including those of the Caucasus and Central Asia, as well as in many indigenous American languages such as those of the LMV.

Omitting an evidential marker among languages that employ them can result in an ungrammatical and even "highly unnatural" sentence. "Languages with evidentials fall into a number of subtypes, depending on how many information sources acquire distinct grammatical marking" (Aikhenvald and Dixon 2006, 320) so that, for instance, some languages have just two choices: *firsthand* versus *nonfirsthand and everything else*. Other languages may have three or more choices, including an *inferred* evidential, in which case an event is inferred based on physical evidence (e.g., 'it [must have] rained, since the ground is wet').

Biloxi and Choctaw-Chickasaw have at least three subtypes of evidential marking: firsthand, nonfirsthand, and inferred. No other LMV languages show evidential marking per se, although quotative markers, often subsumed under evidentiality, appear in Biloxi, Chitimacha, Choctaw-Chickasaw, Natchez, and Tunica. Such marking appears to be absent from Atakapa and MTL. The Biloxi evidentiality system may have been influenced by contact with Choctaw.

Evidential marking is fairly widespread among Native American languages and occurs peripherally in Quapaw (Siouan), Yuchi (isolate), Caddoan, Tonkawa (isolate), Apache (Athapaskan), Comanche (Uto-Aztecan), Cherokee (Iroquoian), the Plains (Algonquian, Siouan), the Great Basin

(Northern and Southern Paiute, Washo), and the Southwest (Papago, Apachean, Taos) (Sherzer 1976). It also occurs in Totonac (Totonacan).

The LMV would not be the first language area to share the concept of evidentiality marking. Some languages in the Balkan sprachbund of eastern Europe likely received evidential marking from Turkish, the only non-IE language to participate in that sprachbund.

Due to the pervasive nature of evidential marking in Native North America, including in the periphery of the LMV, it has not been weighted more heavily than certain other morphological features. Evidentiality cannot be considered a defining characteristic of the LMV as a sprachbund.

### Overtly Marked Case System

All languages of the LMV, except for MTL, have case-marking suffixes. These suffixes, however, unlike those of case-marking languages like Latin or Russian, are not consistently overtly marked, indicating that these systems are *differential*, being more discursive or pragmatic in nature. For example, speakers of Choctaw tend to interpret noun phrases "with overt accusative marking as topical" (Broadwell 2006, 74).

Case systems also occur in Comanche (Uto-Aztecan), Tonkawa (isolate), in the Great Basin (Uto-Aztecan and Washo), in the Southwest (Yuman and Hopi), and in California. Tonkawa's case system is the most elaborate in the Plains, with suffixes marking nominative, accusative, genitive, instrumental, conjunctive, and two dative cases (Sherzer 1976, 177). Case systems do not occur in Iroquoian; Algonquian languages have a locational suffix marker, but lack any other type of case marking. Due to this feature's crosslinguistic commonality, it is non-significant for the LMV sprachbund.

### Definite Article

Atakapa, Biloxi, Chitimacha, Choctaw-Chickasaw, Natchez, and Tunica all have forms of definite article. There is no definite article in MTL and no data for articles in Ofo. In Atakapa, Biloxi, Choctaw-Chickasaw, and Natchez the definite article is a suffix, whereas in Tunica it is a prefix. Peripheral languages with definite articles are Quapaw, Yuchi, Timucua, Totonac, and Mayan.

Definite articles may, at times, overlap with focus and topic marking. As

Gundel notes, "A number of researchers ... have observed that in various languages expressions referring to topics are necessarily definite" (1988, 213). Due to this feature being crosslinguistically common, it is a non-significant feature of the LMV sprachbund.

### Demonstrative Precedes Noun

Demonstratives precede the noun in all LMV languages with the exception of Biloxi, Choctaw-Chickasaw, and MTL. Since, for the most part, other Siouan languages have demonstratives preceding nouns, it is possible that Biloxi borrowed this demonstrative order from Choctaw-Chickasaw or MTL. Due to this feature being crosslinguistically common, it is a non-significant feature of the LMV sprachbund.

### Circumfixed Negative Construction

Biloxi, Ofo, and Choctaw-Chickasaw have a periphrastic, or circumfixed, negative construction. In both the Biloxi and Ofo negative constructions, the prefixed element (*ka-* and *ki-* respectively) appears to be stylistic or speaker-centered and is not required.

A circumfixed negative construction also occurs in Tutelo, another Ohio Valley Siouan (OVS) language, indicating that this negation paradigm is an internal development within the OVS branch of Siouan. Given the rather complex structure of Choctaw-Chickasaw circumfixed negation, this feature most likely arose internally in both language families (OVS and Muskogean) and is thus not indicative of borrowing.

Double marking of negation is not common; nor is it rare (Whaley 1997, 228). Standard French, for example, has the negative circumfix *ne ... pas*, as in *Je ne suis pas seul* 'I am not alone.'

Given the relative non-rarity of negative circumfixation crosslinguistically, this feature is not a strong determining feature of the LMV sprachbund.

### Reduplication in Nominal Stems for Plurality

Reduplication, both nominal and verbal, is "a widely used morphological device in a number of the world's languages" (Rubino 2013). Nominal reduplication for the plural or distributive occurs in the LMV in Atakapa, Biloxi, and Natchez. Reduplication of nominal stems also occurs in the Great Basin (Uto-Aztecan, Washo), the Plains (Siouan, Comanche, Tonkawa), and the Southwest (but only in Uto-Aztecan Tohono O'odham [Papago], Hopi, and Taos), thus being particularly rare in the Southwest (Sherzer 1976, 144).

Contra Rubino, who indicates that "no productive reduplication" occurs in Totonac (2013), MacKay provides several examples of reduplication, both nominal and verbal, in Totonac (1999, 374). This feature also occurs in Nahuatl and Mayan. Due to this feature extending well beyond the LMV, it is non-significant for the LMV sprachbund.

### Reduplication in Verbal Stems

Verbal reduplication often indicates iterative (repetitive) actions. Verbal reduplication occurs as such in Atakapa, Biloxi, Choctaw-Chickasaw, and Natchez. In Tunica reduplication is employed only in auxiliary verbs and is not used elsewhere in the language (Haas 1946). Limited use of verbal reduplication is noted to occur in Chitimacha.

Peripherally, verbal reduplication occurs in Eastern Muskogean, Comanche (Uto-Aztecan), Yuchi (isolate), Nahuatl (Uto-Aztecan), and Mayan. Due to this feature extending well beyond the LMV and being crosslinguistically common, it is non-significant for the LMV sprachbund.

### Plurality in Pronouns

Atakapa, Biloxi, Chitimacha, Choctaw-Chickasaw, Natchez, and Ofo have plural pronouns. Tunica has both dual and plural pronouns. Pronominal plurals occur in all Northeast languages and are "a family trait of Algonquian, Iroquoian, and Siouan" (Sherzer 1976, 196). Given the ubiquitous nature of pronominal plurality marking throughout North American languages, this feature is irrelevant to the LMV sprachbund.

### Duality in Pronouns

Tunica is the only LMV language to have dual as well as plural pronouns, thus following Greenberg's Universal 34: "No language has a dual unless it has a plural" ([1939] 1961, 94). Dual pronouns occur in the Great Basin (Uto-Aztecan and Washo) and in the Southwest (Apachean, Zuñi, Acoma, Taos) (Sherzer 1976). This is a family trait of Iroquoian (Sherzer 1976, 196), and it occurs in Cherokee. It is possible that Tunica developed this feature through contact with Great Basin or Southwestern languages. Since Tunica is the only LMV language to have a pronominal dual, this feature is irrelevant to the LMV sprachbund.

### Plurality Marking in Nouns

Biloxi, Chitimacha, and Tunica have nominal plural marking. Atakapa sometimes employs the prefix *šak-* as a form of plural marking, and a few animate nouns change form for plural. MTL and Natchez do not show plural marking on nouns. Data are insufficient to determine nominal plurality in Ofo. Choctaw-Chickasaw generally does not show plural marking on nouns, but, at least in Chickasaw, "[a] few complex nouns that include verb stems that change depending on the number of their subject do have singular and plural forms" (Munro and Willmond 1994, lv).

The nominal plural occurs ubiquitously in the Southwest, and "all Algonquian and Iroquoian languages of the Northeast have an overtly marked nominal plural" (Sherzer 1976, 196). Given the ubiquitous nature of nominal plurality marking crosslinguistically, this feature is irrelevant to the LMV sprachbund.

### Duality in Nouns

Tunica is the only LMV language to show a dual form for nouns. Dual noun marking occurs peripherally in Kiowa and in the Uto-Aztecan languages Comanche, Northern Paiute, Shoshone, and Hopi. Tunica may have developed this feature through contact with Plains or Southwestern languages. Since this feature occurs in only one LMV language, this feature is non-significant for the LMV sprachbund.

### Locative and Directional Affixes

All LMV languages, with the exception of MTL, have locative and directional affixation. Locative and directional affixation also occur in the Great Basin and in the Southwest (Yuman, Tohono O'odham [Papago], and Apachean). Since locative and directional marking through affixation is ubiquitous throughout North American languages, this feature is non-significant for the LMV as a sprachbund.

## Subject Person Prefixes

All LMV languages, like the majority of North American languages, again with the exception of MTL (which has only independent pronouns), have subject-person affixation. However, both Atakapa and Tunica suffix subject (agentive) pronouns while object (patientive) pronouns are prefixed. In Choctaw-Chickasaw, only the first-person agentive pronoun is suffixed, while all other person pronouns are prefixed.[4] Agent-subject affixes precede patient-object affixes except in Atakapa and Tunica.

Chitimacha has subject-agent pronouns only for first person, while second and third persons (i.e., non-first persons) are unmarked. This runs counter to Greenberg's Universal 42, which states that "all languages have pronominal categories involving at least three persons and two numbers" ([1939] 1961, 96). Both the Muskogean and Siouan language families share zero-marking of third-person singular pronoun prefixes, a feature that also occurs in Nahuatl (Uto-Aztecan). Since subject prefix marking is ubiquitous among Native North American languages, this feature is non-significant for the LMV sprachbund.

## Subject-Object-Verb (SOV) Word Order

All languages in the LMV, with the sole exception of MTL, are of SOV constituent order. While this is an areal feature, it is by no means unique to the area. Many languages of the eastern United States, particularly those of the Siouan, Iroquoian, Caddoan, and Muskogean families, have SOV word order. For this reason, this feature is non-significant for the LMV as a sprachbund.

## Quinary Number Marking

All but one of the LMV languages have number systems that are semi-quinary (based on 5) in nature. Atakapa is the only LMV language to have a semi-dual (based on 2) number system.

Biloxi-Ofo and Choctaw-Chickasaw well demonstrate the quinary (base 5) system. Biloxi and Choctaw-Chickasaw repeat the stems for 'two' and 'three' in the numbers for 'seven' and 'eight.' (Calques, or semantic borrowings, seem apparent between Biloxi and Choctaw-Chickasaw in the numbers for 'seven' and 'eight.') Ofo repeats the stem for 'three' in 'eight' but, unlike Biloxi, does not show repetition in 'seven.'

These systems are termed semi-quinary in nature since they are not fully quinary. A fully quinary number system is clearly expressed, for example, in Khmer (Austroasiatic), in which numbers run 1, 2, 3, 4, 5, 5+1, 5+2, 5+3, 5+4, 10 (Huffman 1970, 15). As seen above only remnants of this fully quinary system remain in Biloxi and Choctaw-Chickasaw, in which only certain numbers (i.e., seven and eight) retain quinary features. This is because the tendency of quinary number systems is toward the establishment of another and larger base with the formation of a number system in which both systems are used (Conant 1896). The peripheral Nahuatl distinctly shows a combination of two number systems, the quinary and vigesimal (base 20), the latter system kicking in after the number 20.[5]

Atakapa shows a type of dual (base 2) system, since the word for 'six' is composed of the numbers 'three' and 'two' (3 x 2 = 6) and the number 'eight' is composed of the numbers 'four' and 'two' (4 x 2 = 8). Atakapa shows two sets of numbers from purportedly two main dialects, Western Dialect (WD) and Eastern Dialect (ED) (Gatschet and Swanton 1932, 21) (in table 6a, the left side of Atakapa is WD, the right side is ED). Oddly, however, the numbers appear drastically different for ED and WD supposedly being mere dialects of each other. The Atakapa number 'nine' is literally 'hand(s) little finger minus.' This matches the PSL finger-counting system, where both hands are shown with all fingers but one pinky extended.

Tunica likewise seems to correlate the number nine, which is literally 'strike together one,' with a type of sign language, but apparently not the PSL, as was used by the Atakapas. To my knowledge there has not been a comprehensive examination of the connection between oral counting systems or other spoken-language patterns and visual sign language systems such as the PSL. Such a correlation awaits further study. Numbers will be further examined in chapter 7, in regard to word and semantic borrowing.

### Masculine/Feminine Noun Gender Distinction

Tunica is the only LMV language to have a nominal gender distinction in inanimate as well as animate nouns. Among peripheral languages, Comanche, Yuchi, and Cherokee show systems of gender differentiation. Since Tu-

Table 6a. Numbers in the LMV

| # | BILOXI | OFO | TUNICA | ATAKAPA |
|---|--------|-----|--------|---------|
| 1 | sǫsa | nufha | sa'hku | tanuk / hanik |
| 2 | nǫpa | nųųpha | i'li | cik / hapalst |
| 3 | dani | taani | e'nihku | lat |
| 4 | topa | toopa | ma'nku | himatol / cec |
| 5 | ksani, ksą | kifą | si'nku* | nit |
| 6 | akaxe | akape | ma'sahki | lacik / lact, talst |
| 7 | nǫpahudi | fakumi | ta'yihki | pax(e) / pako |
| 8 | dąhudi | patani | ti'sihku | himatol cik / cikhuyaw |
| 9 | ckanê | kištateška | to'hkusa'hku** | woš išol han / tekhuyaw |
| 10 | ohi | iftaptą | mi'ču sa'hku | wošpe / hisiŋ |
| 11 | ohisǫsaxêhe | iftaptą nufha | mi'ču sa'hteya sa'hku | woš pe ha(l) tanuk / halk hanik |
| 12 | ohinǫpaxêhe | n/a | mi'ču sa'htey 'i'li | woš pe ha(l) cik / halk hapalst |
| 13 | ohidanaxêhe | n/a | mi'ču sa'htey 'e'nihku | woš pe ha(l) lat / halk lat |
| 14 | ohitopaxêhe | n/a | mi'ču sa'hteya ma'nku | woš pe ha(l) / halk cec |
| 15 | ohiksanaxêhe | n/a | mi'ču sa'hteya si'nku | woš pe ha(l) himatol, halk nit |
| 16 | ohiakaxpaxêhe | n/a | mi'ču sa'hteya ma'sahki | woš pe ha(l) nit / halk lact (talst) |
| 17 | ohinǫpahuxêhe | n/a | mi'ču sa'hteya ta'yihku | woš pe ha(l) lacik / halk pako |
| 18 | ohidąhuxêhe | n/a | mi'ču sa'hteya ti'sihku | woš pe ha(l) cikhuyaw, halk cikhuyaw |
| 19 | ohickanaxêhe | n/a | mi'ču sa'hteya to'hkusa'hku | woš pe ha(l) himatol cik / halk tekhuyaw |
| 20 | ohi nǫpa | iftaptą nupha | mi'ču 'i'li | woš pe cik / halk hisiŋ |
| 30 | ohi dani | iftaptą taani | mi'ču e'nihku | woš pe lat / hisiŋ lat |
| 40 | ohi topa | iftaptą toopa | mi'ču ma'nku | woš pe himatol / hisiŋ cec |

## Table 6a. Continued

| # | BILOXI | OFO | TUNICA | ATAKAPA |
|---|--------|-----|--------|---------|
| 50 | ohi ksą | iftaptą kifą | mi'ču si'nku | woš pe nit / hisiŋ nit |
| 60 | ohi akaxpê | iftaptą akape | mi'ču ma'sahki | woš pe lacik / hisiŋ lact |
| 70 | ohi nǫpahudi | iftaptą fakumi | mi'ču ta'yihku | woš pe pax(e) / hisiŋ pako |
| 80 | ohi dąhudi | iftaptą patani | mi'ču ti'sihku | woš pe himatol cik / hisiŋ cikhuyaw |
| 90 | ohi ckane | iftaptą kištateška | mi'ču to'hkusa'hku | woš pe woš išol han / hisiŋ tekhuyaw |
| 100 | tsipa | iftapta nufha | po'lun sa'hku | hiyen pon / hehin pon |
| 1000 | tsipa įcya | ącaaki keehi | po'lunt'e sa'hku | hiyen pon cakop / hehin pon ioliš |

* Although Tunica *si'nku* looks like a borrowing from Spanish *cinco*, it may not be; note *-ku* ending of other numbers.

** Tunica 'nine' = 'strike-together one' / Atakapa 'hands minus little finger' (matches Plains Sign).

## Table 6b. Numbers in the LMV

| # | CHITIMACHA | NATCHEZ | WESTERN MUSKOGEAN | MTL |
|---|------------|---------|-------------------|-----|
| 1 | unk'u | wiitąą | ačafa | ačofa |
| 2 | (h)upa, (h)upkamiig | awitii | tuklo | tokolo |
| 3 | kaayči | neetii | tučina | točena |
| 4 | meša | kinawatii | ušta | ošta |
| 5 | husa, huskamiig | išpitii | tałapi | tałape |
| 6 | hatka(m), hatkamiig | lahanah | hannali | hanale |
| 7 | kišta, kištkamiig | ąkwah | untuklo | ontokolo |
| 8 | keeta | apkatupiš | untočena | ontočena |
| 9 | mišta | witipkatupiš | čakali | čakale |
| 10 | heytši | ooko | pokoli | pokole |
| 11 | heytši unk'u patniš | ooko wiitanišiiwic | pokoli auah ačafa | pokole awa čafa |
| 12 | heytši hupa patniš | ooko awitišiiwic | pokoli auah tuklo | pokol(e) awa tokolo |
| 13 | heytši kaayči patniš | ooko neetišiiwic | pokoli auah tučina | pokol(e) awa točena |

nica is the only LMV language to have masculine-feminine gender marking on all nouns, this feature is non-significant for the LMV sprachbund.

### Inclusive/Exclusive Plural Pronouns

Only Choctaw-Chickasaw shows separate inclusive and exclusive plural pronouns, that is, plural pronouns that either include or exclude the person spoken to. On the periphery, this feature occurs in Yuchi, Caddoan, Comanche, Shawnee, and Cherokee. Since Choctaw-Chickasaw is the only LMV language to have inclusive-exclusive plural pronominal markings, this feature is non-significant for the LMV sprachbund.

Table 7 summarizes LMV morphological features, while table 8 shows the same for peripheral languages. Italicized features in the tables are those considered most significant to the LMV sprachbund (scoring 2).

## Table 7. LMV morphological features

| | FEATURE | SOURCE | AT. | BIL. | CHIT. | MTL | NAT. | OFO | TUN. | WM | LMV TOTAL |
|---|---|---|---|---|---|---|---|---|---|---|---|
| | NOMINALS | | | | | | | | | | |
| 27 | *focus particle* | C97 | 2 | 2 | 2 | 0 | 2 | n/d | 0 | 2 | 10 |
| 28 | overtly marked case system | Sh76 | 0 | 1 | 0 | 0 | 1 | 0 | 1 | 1 | 8 |
| 29 | reduplication in stems (for nominal distribution/plurality) | Sh76 | 1 | 1 | 0 | 0 | 1 | n/d | 0 | 0 | 3 |
| 30 | masculine/feminine gender distinction | Sh76 | 0 | 0 | 0 | 0 | 0 | 0 | 1 | 0 | 1 |
| 31 | animate/inanimate gender | Sh76 | 0 | 0 | 0 | 0 | 0 | 0 | 0 | 0 | 0 |
| 32 | plurality in pronouns | Sh76 | 1 | 1 | 1 | 0 | 1 | 1 | 1 | 1 | 7 |
| 33 | plurality in nouns | Sh76 | 1 | 1 | 1 | 0 | 1 | 1 | 0 | 1 | 6 |
| 34 | inclusive/exclusive plural in pronouns | Sh76 | 0 | 0 | 0 | 0 | 0 | 0 | 0 | 1 | 1 |
| 35 | dual in pronouns | Sh76 | 0 | 0 | 0 | 0 | 1 | 0 | 1 | 1 | 3 |
| 36 | dual in nouns | Sh76 | 0 | 0 | 0 | 0 | 0 | 0 | 1 | 0 | 1 |

## Table 7. Continued

| | FEATURE | SOURCE | AT. | BIL. | CHIT. | MTL | NAT. | OFO | TUN. | WM | LMV TOTAL |
|---|---|---|---|---|---|---|---|---|---|---|---|
| 37 | locative suffixes | Sh76 | 1 | 1 | 1 | 0 | 1 | 1 | 1 | 1 | 7 |
| 38 | *definite article* | K12 | 0 | 2 | 0 | 0 | 2 | n/d | 2 | 0 | 6 |
| 39 | demonstrative follows noun | C97 | 0 | 2 | 0 | 2 | 0 | 2 | 0 | 2 | 8 |
| | VERBALS | | | | | | | | | | |
| 40 | subject person prefixes | Sh76 | 1 | 1 | 1 | 0 | 1 | 1 | 1 | 1 | 7 |
| 41 | reduplication in stems | Sh76 | 1 | 0 | 1 | 0 | 1 | 0 | 1 | 1 | 4 |
| 42 | instrumental markers | Sh76 | 1 | 1 | 1 | 0 | 1 | 1 | 1 | 1 | 7 |
| 43 | evidentiality marking | Sh76 | 0 | 1 | 1 | 0 | 1 | n/d | 1 | 1 | 10 |
| 44 | *indir anim obj pref/valence reducer* | K12 | 2 | 0 | 0 | 0 | 2 | 0 | 0 | 2 | 6 |
| 45 | *indir inanim obj pref/ valence reducer* | K12 | 2 | 0 | 0 | 0 | 2 | 0 | 0 | 2 | 6 |
| 46 | *reference tracking* | Sh76 | 2 | 0 | 0 | 0 | 2 | n/d | 2 | 2 | 8 |
| 47 | sov word order | Sh76 | 1 | 1 | 1 | 0 | 1 | 1 | 1 | 1 | 7 |
| 48 | quinary number system (base 5) | C97 | 0 | 1 | 1 | 1 | 1 | 1 | 1 | 1 | 3 |
| 49 | vigesimal number system (base 20) | K12 | 0 | 0 | 0 | 0 | 0 | 0 | 0 | 0 | 0 |
| 50 | *positional verb auxiliaries* | C97 | 2 | 2 | 2 | 0 | 2 | 2 | 2 | 2 | 14 |
| 51 | circumfixed negative construction | C97 | 0 | 1 | 0 | 0 | 0 | 1 | 0 | 1 | 3 |
| 52 | *number suppletion/verbal arguments* | K12 | 0 | 2 | 0 | 0 | 0 | 0 | 2 | 2 | 3 |
| | LMV MORPHOLOGY TOTALS | | 18 | 21 | 13 | 3 | 24 | 12 | 20 | 27 | |
| | LMV PHONETIC / PHONOLOGY TOTALS | | 14 | 10 | 5 | 12 | 13 | 9 | 12 | 14 | |
| | FEATURE GRAND TOTAL | | 32 | 31 | 18 | 15 | 37 | 21 | 32 | 41 | |

Key: At. = Atakapa, Bil. = Biloxi, Chit. = Chitimacha, Nat. = Natchez, Tun. = Tunica, WM = Western Muskogean.

Sh76 = Sherzer 1976, K12 = Kaufman 2012, C97 = Campbell 1997.

Table 8a. Peripheral morphological features

| | FEATURE | SOURCE | EM | QUA. | CAD. | KAR. | YU. | SHAW. | COAH. | COM. | AP. | TON. |
|---|---|---|---|---|---|---|---|---|---|---|---|---|
| | **NOMINALS** | | | | | | | | | | | |
| 27 | *focus particle* | C97 | 2 | ? | 0 | n/d | 2 | 0 | 0 | 0 | 0 | 0 |
| 28 | overtly marked case system | Sh76 | 1 | 1 | 1 | n/d | 0 | 0 | 1 | 1 | 0 | 1 |
| 29 | reduplication in stems (for nominal distribution / plurality) | Sh76 | 1 | ? | 0 | n/d | 1 | 0 | 0 | 1 | 0 | 1 |
| 30 | masculine/feminine gender distinction | Sh76 | 0 | 0 | 0 | 1 | 1 | 0 | 0 | 0 | 0 | 0 |
| 31 | animate/inanimate gender | Sh76 | 0 | 0 | 0 | 0 | 1 | 1 | 0 | 1 | 0 | 0 |
| 32 | plurality in pronouns | Sh76 | 1 | 1 | 1 | n/d | 1 | 1 | 1 | 1 | 0 | 1 |
| 33 | plurality in nouns | Sh76 | 1 | 0 | 1 | n/d | 1 | 1 | 1 | 1 | 0 | 1 |
| 34 | inclusive/exclusive plural in pronouns | Sh76 | 0 | 0 | 1 | n/d | 1 | 1 | 0 | 1 | 0 | 0 |
| 35 | dual in pronouns | Sh76 | 0 | 1 | 1 | n/d | ? | 0 | 0 | 1 | 1 | 1 |
| 36 | dual in nouns | Sh76 | 0 | 0 | 0 | n/d | 0 | 0 | 0 | 1 | 0 | 0 |
| 37 | locative suffixes | Sh76 | 1 | 1 | 1 | n/d | 1 | 1 | 1 | 1 | 1 | 1 |
| 38 | *definite article* | K12 | 0 | 1 | 0 | 0 | 2 | ? | 0 | ? | ? | 0 |
| 39 | demonstrative follows noun | C97 | 0 | 0 | 0 | n/d | 0 | 0 | 0 | 0 | 0 | 0 |
| | **VERBALS** | | | | | | | | | | | |
| 40 | subject person prefixes | Sh76 | 0 | 1 | 1 | 0 | 1 | 1 | 1 | 1 | 1 | 0 |
| 41 | reduplication in stems | Sh76 | 1 | 1 | 1 | n/d | 1 | 1 | ? | 1 | 0 | 1 |
| 42 | instrumental markers | Sh76 | 1 | 1 | 1 | n/d | 1 | 1 | ? | 1 | 0 | 1 |
| 43 | evidentiality marking | Sh76 | 1 | 1 | 1 | n/d | 1 | ? | ? | 1 | 1 | 1 |
| 44 | *indir anim obj pref/ valence reducer* | K12 | ? | 0 | 0 | n/d | 2 | ? | ? | ? | ? | 0 |
| 45 | *indir inanim obj pref/ valence reducer* | K12 | 2 | 2 | 0 | n/d | 0 | ? | 2 | ? | ? | 0 |
| 46 | *reference tracking* | Sh76 | 2 | 0 | 0 | n/d | ? | 0 | 2 | 2 | ? | 2 |
| 47 | sov word order | Sh76 | 1 | 1 | 1 | n/d | 1 | 0 | 1 | 1 | 1 | 1 |

## Table 8a. Continued

| FEATURE | SOURCE | EM | QUA. | CAD. | KAR. | YU. | SHAW. | COAH. | COM. | AP. | TON. |
|---|---|---|---|---|---|---|---|---|---|---|---|
| 48 quinary number system (base 5) | C97 | 1 | 1 | 1 | n/d | 1 | 1 | 0 | 1 | 1 | 1 |
| 49 vigesimal number system (base 20) | K12 | 0 | 0 | 0 | n/d | 0 | 0 | 1 | 0 | 0 | 0 |
| 50 *positional verb auxiliaries* | C97 | 2 | 2 | 2 | n/d | 2 | 0 | ? | 0 | 0 | 0 |
| 51 circumfixed negative construction | C97 | 1 | 1 | 0 | n/d | 0 | 0 | 0 | 0 | 0 | 0 |
| 52 *number suppletion/verbal arguments* | K12 | 2 | 2 | 0 | n/d | 0 | 0 | 0 | 0 | 0 | 0 |
| PERIPHERAL MORPHOLOGY TOTALS | | 21 | 18 | 14 | 1 | 21 | 9 | 11 | 17 | 6 | 13 |
| PERIPHERAL PHONETIC / PHONOLOGY TOTALS | | 14 | 7 | 6 | 13 | 15 | 4 | 10 | 4 | 11 | 4 |
| PERIPHERAL FEATURE GRAND TOTAL | | 35 | 25 | 20 | 14 | 36 | 13 | 21 | 21 | 17 | 17 |

Key: EM = Eastern Muskogean, Qua. = Quapaw (Dhegiha), Cad. = Caddoan, Kar. = Karankawa, Yu. = Yuchi, Shaw. = Shawnee, Coah. = Coahuiltec, Com. = Comanche, Ap. = Apache, Ton. = Tonkawa.

## Table 8b. Peripheral morphological features

| FEATURE | SOURCE | KIO. | TIM. | CHER. | CAT. | NAH. | TOT. | HUA. | OM | ENG. | PT |
|---|---|---|---|---|---|---|---|---|---|---|---|
| **NOMINALS** | | | | | | | | | | | |
| 27 *focus particle* | C97 | ? | 0 | 2 | 0 | ? | 0 | ? | 0 | 0 | 6 |
| 28 overtly marked case system | Sh76 | 0 | 0 | 0 | 0 | ? | 0 | 0 | 0 | 0 | 6 |
| 29 reduplication in stems (for nominal distribution / plurality) | Sh76 | 0 | 0 | 0 | 1 | 1 | 1 | 0 | 0 | 0 | 7 |
| 30 masculine/feminine gender distinction | Sh76 | 0 | 0 | 1 | 0 | 0 | 0 | 0 | 0 | 0 | 3 |
| 31 animate/inanimate gender | Sh76 | 1 | 0 | 0 | 0 | 0 | 0 | 0 | 0 | 0 | 4 |
| 32 plurality in pronouns | Sh76 | 1 | 1 | 1 | 1 | 1 | 1 | 1 | 1 | 1 | 17 |
| 33 plurality in nouns | Sh76 | 1 | 1 | 1 | ? | 1 | 1 | 0 | 1 | 1 | 14 |
| 34 inclusive/exclusive plural in pronouns | Sh76 | 1 | 0 | 1 | 0 | ? | 0 | ? | 0 | 0 | 6 |
| 35 dual in pronouns | Sh76 | 1 | 0 | 1 | 0 | 0 | 0 | 0 | 0 | 0 | 7 |
| 36 dual in nouns | Sh76 | 1 | 0 | 0 | 0 | 0 | 0 | 0 | 0 | 0 | 2 |
| 37 locative suffixes | Sh76 | 1 | 1 | 1 | 1 | 1 | 1 | ? | 1 | 0 | 16 |
| 38 *definite article* | K12 | ? | 1 | ? | 1 | 0 | 1 | ? | 1 | 1 | 8 |
| 39 demonstrative follows noun | C97 | 0 | 0 | 0 | 1 | ? | 0 | ? | ? | 0 | 1 |
| **VERBALS** | | | | | | | | | | | |
| 40 subject person prefixes | Sh76 | 1 | 1 | 1 | 1 | 1 | 1 | 1 | 1 | 0 | 15 |
| 41 reduplication in stems | Sh76 | 0 | 1 | 0 | 1 | ? | ? | ? | ? | 0 | 9 |
| 42 instrumental markers | Sh76 | 0 | 1 | 1 | 1 | ? | 1 | 0 | 0 | 0 | 11 |
| 43 evidentiality marking | Sh76 | 1 | ? | 1 | 1 | ? | 1 | 0 | 0 | 0 | 11 |
| 44 *indir anim obj pref/ valence reducer* | K12 | ? | ? | ? | ? | 1 | 0 | 0 | 0 | 0 | 3 |
| 45 *indir inanim obj pref/ valence reducer* | K12 | ? | 0 | 0 | 2 | 2 | 2 | 0 | 0 | 0 | 12 |
| 46 *reference tracking* | Sh76 | 2 | 0 | ? | 0 | 0 | 0 | 0 | 0 | 0 | 10 |
| 47 sov word order | Sh76 | ? | 1 | 1 | ? | ? | 0 | 0 | 0 | 0 | 10 |

## Table 8b. Continued

| FEATURE | SOURCE | KIO. | TIM. | CHER. | CAT. | NAH. | TOT. | HUA. | OM | ENG. | PT |
|---|---|---|---|---|---|---|---|---|---|---|---|
| 48  quinary number system (base 5) | C97 | 1 | ? | 0 | 1 | 0 | 0 | 0 | 0 | 0 | 10 |
| 49  vigesimal number system (base 20) | K12 | 0 | 0 | 0 | 0 | 1 | 1 | 1 | 1 | 0 | 5 |
| 50  *positional verb auxiliaries* | C97 | ? | 0 | 2 | 2 | 0 | 2 | 0 | 0 | 0 | 14 |
| 51  circumfixed negative construction | C97 | ? | 0 | 1 | 0 | ? | 0 | 0 | 1 | 0 | 4 |
| 52  *number suppletion/verbal arguments* | K12 | 0 | 0 | 0 | 2 | 0 | 2 | 0 | 0 | 0 | 8 |
| PERIPHERAL MORPHOLOGY TOTALS | | 12 | 8 | 15 | 16 | 9 | 15 | 3 | 7 | 3 | |
| PERIPHERAL PHONETIC / PHONOLOGY TOTALS | | 7 | 8 | 9 | 6 | 5 | 11 | 8 | 14 | 9 | |
| PERIPHERAL FEATURE GRAND TOTAL | | 19 | 16 | 24 | 22 | 14 | 26 | 11 | 21 | 12 | |

Key: Kio. = Kiowa, Tim. = Timucua, Cher. = Cherokee, Cat. = Catawba, Nah. = Nahuatl, Tot. = Totonac, Hua = Huastec, OM = other Mayan, Eng. = English, PT = periphery total.

# SEVEN

## Word Borrowings and Calques

In this chapter I examine word and semantic copying, or calques, among the languages of the LMV. Word borrowing has been considered less important than phonetic, phonological, and morphological borrowing, and also for establishing the LMV as a sprachbund (see Kaufman 2014a), partly because MTL may have been the primary catalyst for several lexical borrowings. (Drechsel hypothesizes that the words for 'bison/buffalo,' 'goose,' and 'milk' likely spread via the MTL [1997, 316].) But the degree of word borrowing between languages and the semantic categories of such borrowings can help us infer something about migration patterns and items of cultural importance at such a distant time period.

I first examine individual words that appear to be shared between two or more languages, according to the Leipzig-Jakarta 100 basic word list. I also try to determine the direction of borrowing and the semantic classes of borrowings, which may help us infer something about cultural practices and encounters.

After an examination of word and semantic data, I examine word borrowing and calques in the context of oral histories and certain aspects of the archaeological data. Then I make tentative conclusions about the historical and cultural patterns of the LMV based on the extant word-borrowing data.

### WORD BORROWING

Word borrowings operate according to a certain set of probabilities. For instance, languages are more likely to borrow nouns than verbs. Adjectives and adverbs are almost as unlikely to be borrowed as verbs, and words with grammatical meanings (function words) are less likely still than verbs to be borrowed (Tadmor, Haspelmath, and Taylor 2010, 231). Basic vocabulary is borrowed before structural elements and is indicative of more intense contact, while non-basic vocabulary is most easily borrowed (Thomason 2001, 69) and is borrowed under conditions of casual contact. Intensity of contact is, however, a vague concept that is impossible to determine precisely since such things as speakers' attitudes and fluency level of the borrowers necessarily come into play (Tadmor, Haspelmath, and Taylor 2010, 231).

## Basic Vocabulary

The concept of basic vocabulary is important to the analysis of word borrowings in the LMV. Several lists have been created to reflect basic concepts that are considered to be universal and culturally independent, such as basic kinship (e.g., mother, father), general animal terms (e.g., fish, bird), and basic verbs (e.g., make, go). The first of these lists was the Swadesh 100 basic word list, assembled by the linguist Morris Swadesh (1971), who "determined a priori what constituted basic vocabulary" from intuition and then further refined the list through trial and error (Tadmor, Haspelmath, and Taylor 2010, 230).

A newer list, the Leipzig-Jakarta (L-J) 100 word list (2009), is based on systematic empirical data from forty different languages, but it is not yet as widely known and used as the Swadesh list. Some sixty-two items overlap between the L-J and Swadesh lists (Tadmor, Haspelmath, and Taylor 2010, 242); these differences will be noted where appropriate. The L-J list "has a strong empirical foundation"; for this reason, I have chosen it for this analysis. However, as with any word list, certain questions remain unaddressed, such as why black is considered a basic color but not white.

## Semantic Classes of Borrowings

As may be seen in table 10 several semantic classes are reflected in the copied lexemes of the LMV, including body parts, animals, food, colors, trees, and numbers. Several of these borrowings include basic vocabulary found in the L-J word list: arm/hand, bird, black, blow, breast (female), rope, cry, die, dog, eat, to fall, fish, to hear, house, knee, soil, to laugh, mouth, to speak, to suck, tooth, water, wind, and wood.

The number of borrowings between LMV languages can tell us something about the prior location and migration patterns of LMV groups. For example, the sheer volume of borrowings between Atakapa and Biloxi sug-

Table 9. Leipzig-Jakarta 100 basic word list

| | | |
|---|---|---|
| ant | good | to run |
| arm/hand | hair | salt |
| ash | hard | sand |
| back | he/she/it/him/her | to say |
| big | to hear | to see |
| bird | heavy | shade/shadow |
| to bite | to hide | skin/hide |
| bitter | to hit/to beat | small |
| black | horn | smoke |
| blood | house | soil |
| to blow | I/me | to stand |
| bone | in | star |
| breast | knee | stone/rock |
| to burn (intransitive) | to know | to suck |
| to carry | to laugh | sweet |
| child (reciprocal of parent) | leaf | tail |
| to come | leg/foot | to take |
| to crush/to grind | liver | thick |
| to cry/to weep | long | thigh |
| to do/to make | louse | this |
| dog | mouth | to tie |
| drink | name | tongue |
| ear | navel | tooth |
| to eat | neck | water |
| egg | new | what? |
| eye | night | who? |
| to fall | nose | wide |
| far | not | wind |
| fire | old | wing |
| fish | one | wood |
| flesh/meat | rain | yesterday |
| fly | red | you (singular) |
| to give | root | |
| to go | rope | |

gests that these languages were heavily in contact at one time. This seems extraordinary given the post-contact geographic locations of these groups, on opposite sides of the Mississippi River. It is also notable that there are fewer borrowings between Chitimacha and Biloxi than between Atakapa and Biloxi, even though the Chitimachas, at least according to their post-contact location, were in between the other two groups. This could indicate, however, that Atakapas and Biloxis were geographically much closer to each other at one time. Biloxis may once have been located west of the Mississippi River before migrating eastward to the Pascagoula River region along the Gulf of Mexico, where they encountered the French in 1699. Another possibility is that the Biloxis may have established a merchant colony in the region, perhaps due to the salt trade with Caddoans.

The following table is a list of LMV borrowings by semantic category (L-J basic vocabulary is shown in bold):

Table 10. List of LMV borrowings by semantic category

| | |
|---|---|
| AGRICULTURE | seed, turn (soil?) |
| BODY PARTS | anus/back, arm/hand, belly, breast, elbow, face, knee, mouth, tooth |
| BOTANY | berry, cedar, corn, cotton, cypress, oak, peach, pepper, pumpkin/turnip |
| COLOR | black |
| FOOD | tortilla, bread |
| KINSHIP | brother |
| TRANSPORT | canoe |
| WEAPONRY | bow |
| ZOOLOGY | bee, bird, bison/buffalo, blackbird, bullfrog, buzzard, cow/calf, crane, deer, dog, duck, fish, flying squirrel, raccoon, robin, skunk, snake, wildcat, woodpecker |

A total of nine basic words have been shared among LMV languages.

Table 11 lists the basic vocabulary that has been copied among LMV languages. Atakapa, Chitimacha, and Biloxi have the largest number of shared basic vocabulary items, with nine, eight, and eight respectively. Tunica and Natchez have seven and six respectively. Ofo and Choctaw-Chickasaw rank the lowest with only one and zero respectively. In addition Atakapa and

Table 11. Basic words copied among LMV languages

| | |
|---|---|
| ATAKAPA-BILOXI | hear, laugh |
| ATAKAPA-CHITIMACHA | house, soil |
| ATAKAPA-CHITIMACHA-NATCHEZ-CADDO-KARANKAWA | water |
| ATAKAPA-NATCHEZ | bird |
| BILOXI, ATAKAPA, CHITIMACHA, NATCHEZ | blow |
| BILOXI-TUNICA | cry, rope |
| BILOXI-TUNICA-ATAKAPA | knee |
| BILOXI-OFO-NATCHEZ | mouth |
| BILOXI-TUNICA-CHITIMACHA | wind |
| CHITIMACHA-NATCHEZ | arm/hand, wood |
| TUNICA-ATAKAPA-CHITIMACHA | breast |
| TUNICA-CHOCTAW | fish |

Table 12. Basic words shared between Atakapa-Chitimacha and peripheral languages

| | |
|---|---|
| ATAKAPA-TONKAWA | eat |
| ATAKAPA-KARANKAWA | fall |
| CHITIMACHA-KARANKAWA-COTONAME | dog |
| CHITIMACHA-KARANKAWA-COMECRUDO | tooth |

Chitimacha share basic words with the following languages on the periphery of the LMV: Comecrudo, Cotoname, Karankawa, and Tonkawa (see table 12).

### Widespread Borrowings in the LMV

Certain nouns, and at least three verbs, are fairly widespread in their diffusion: 'bison/buffalo,' 'bullfrog,' 'cardinal,' 'cut,' 'deer,' 'goose,' 'metal,' 'robin,' 'split,' 'town,' 'turn,' 'water,' and 'woodpecker.' These terms are here explained in more detail:

(1) 'Bison/buffalo': Similar terms for 'bison/buffalo' based on *yanas* or *yanaš* are particularly widespread, ranging from Caddoan in the western Plains to Catawba near the Eastern Seaboard. (The Ofo term *naf* 'cow' is

likely also derived from this widespread bison term.) The source of the borrowing is unknown. Totonac has the word *tiyaná* for 'ox,' raising the possibility of borrowing between this Mexican Gulf coastal language and the LMV, which would indicate a possible semantic shift in Totonac from its original meaning of 'bison' to the other bovine later introduced by the Spanish.

(2) 'Bullfrog': Atakapa, Biloxi, Choctaw-Chickasaw, MTL, and Natchez have similar terms for 'bullfrog'; the term also extends into Eastern Muskogean and Cherokee. The source language of the borrowing is unknown.

(3) 'Cut': Similar terms for 'cut' based on a form *kuts* appear to be fairly widespread in the LMV and into the Plains. Atakapa, Biloxi, Natchez, and Tunica in the LMV all share a similar term while the Plains languages Comanche, Tonkawa, and possibly Caddoan share terms similar to the LMV form. Yukatek Mayan also has a similar form meaning 'separate.' The source language of the borrowing is unknown.

(4) 'Deer': Similar terms based on *ta* for 'deer' appear to have been borrowed in the LMV as well as in the Plains periphery. The Proto-Siouan form is *wi-htáa*, indicating possible borrowing from Siouan (possibly Biloxi) into Natchez (Natchesan), Pawnee (Caddoan), and Kiowa (Kiowa-Tanoan).

(5) 'Goose': Western and Eastern Muskogean languages, including MTL, Natchez, and Tunica, share a similar term based on *lala-* or *lalak* for 'goose.' The term also occurs to the west in Karankawa and all the way into California, for example, Mutsun (Costanoan) *lalak*, Nisenan (Maiduan) *la·lak'*, Pomoan *lala*, Luiseño (Uto-Aztecan) *laʔla*, and Southern Sierra Miwok (Miwokan) *laŋlaŋ* (Haas 1969a, 82). This evidence lends credence to the idea that Tunicas migrated from much farther west into the LMV.

(6) 'Metal': Several LMV languages have similar words based on the Siouan (Biloxi) term *maas(a)* for the substance.

(7) 'Robin': Similar terms for 'robin' based on *wišk-* or *bešk-* occur in the LMV, in Biloxi, Choctaw-Chickasaw, MTL, Natchez, and Tunica. The term also extends into Eastern Muskogean languages.

(8) 'Split': Similar terms for 'split' based on *ča* or *čal* occur in Atakapa, Biloxi, Chitimacha, Choctaw-Chickasaw, MTL, and Tunica. It may be significant that the semantically similar verb 'cut' also has a fairly widespread distribution.

(9) 'Town': Terms similar to MTL *tamaha* 'town' occur in Western Musko-gean (but not Eastern Muskogean) languages. The word appears to have been borrowed into Proto-Siouan as *tama*; similar terms are widespread across Siouan languages. It is possible that the term was borrowed between Siouan and Muskogean, though the direction of borrowing is uncertain.[1]

(10) 'Turn': Similar terms for 'turn' based on *mixi* or *miš* occur in Ata-kapa, Biloxi, Chitimacha, and Tunica.

(11) 'Water': Similar terms for 'water' occur in Atakapa, Chitimacha, and Natchez, extending west into Caddoan, Karankawa, Tonkawa, and Coa-huiltecan.

(12) 'Woodpecker': Similar terms for 'woodpecker' based on *pakpak-* or *bakbak* occur in the LMV in Biloxi, Choctaw-Chickasaw, Natchez, and Tu-nica, extending into Eastern Muskogean. While probably onomatopoeic in origin, borrowing between languages is perhaps indicated.

Certain of the above terms (e.g., 'goose,' 'woodpecker') may owe their form to onomatopoeia. Yet, as Haas reminds us, certain resemblances among terms appear "remarkably precise even if one allows for onomato-poeia" (1969b, 82), as in the above examples.

It might also be noted that the diffusion of certain terms may be cultural in nature, as attested by the Chickasaw text (see appendix), in which the Redheaded Woodpecker holds high cultural prominence. (The Redheaded Woodpecker has a particular association with the ball game in Chickasaw culture; the association with this sport and its nomenclature could easily have been copied by other groups through the ritual of intergroup ball games.) The widespread diffusion of the 'bison' term is likely related to the bison fur trade, while that of the 'deer' term is likely related to this animal's importance as a source of meat. The spread of the term for 'metal' may be at least partly related to the copper trade, although it may also reflect post-contact trade in such items as kettles, utensils, and tools.

The significance of the sharing of certain terms such as 'cut,' 'split,' and 'turn' is unknown. 'Cut' and 'split' may be related to such activities as com-munal hunting and feasting and the sharing of meat. 'Turn' may be related either to the turning of soil in agriculture or perhaps to communal danc-ing. But the reasons behind the copying of such words on a broad scale re-main mere speculation.

## CALQUES

Calques are loan translations, or word-for-word semantic translations, shared among languages. Rather than an individual term being copied, calques involve the copying of the concept behind the phrase rather than just the individual words.

The following table lists the calques found among LMV languages (some are also found beyond the LMV in peripheral languages):

Table 13. List of widespread calques in LMV and beyond

| | | |
|---|---|---|
| bedbug | 'flat bug' | Biloxi, Caddoan |
| butter | 'cow/milk grease' | MTL, Natchez, Atakapa, Biloxi |
| cardinal | 'red bird' | Biloxi, Chickasaw, Ofo, Koasati |
| cologne | 'smell good water' | Biloxi, Natchez |
| corn crib | 'corn house' | Biloxi, Tunica, Atakapa, Natchez |
| donkey/mule | 'long ear' | Biloxi, Natchez, Atakapa, Choctaw, MTL, Caddoan |
| door | 'house mouth' | Atakapa, Chitimacha, Natchez, Mayan |
| horse | 'big dog' | Tunica, Chitimacha, Natchez |
| jail | 'strong house' | Biloxi, Atakapa, Choctaw, MTL, Creek |
| monkey | 'raccoon man' | Choctaw, Chitimacha, Koasati |
| nostril | 'nose hole' | Biloxi, Atakapa, Natchez, Caddoan, Comanche, Kiowa, Nahuatl |
| ocean | 'big water' | Biloxi, Natchez, Comanche, Nahuatl |
| pestle | 'child of mortar' | Choctaw, Totonac |
| rattlesnake 1 | 'big snake' | Biloxi, Tunica, Tonkawa |
| rattlesnake 2 | 'chief/king snake' | Biloxi, Tunica, Natchez, Yukatek (Mayan) |
| stable (horse) | 'horse house' | Biloxi, Atakapa, Comanche, Nahuatl, Natchez |
| sugar | 'sweet salt' | Biloxi, Atakapa, Natchez, Choctaw, MTL |
| thumb | 'big/old hand' | Biloxi, Tunica, Atakapa, Natchez, Comanche |
| vein | 'blood house' | Biloxi, Atakapa |
| whisky | 'fire water' | Atakapa, Natchez, Tunica ('heated water') |

As with word borrowings, certain calques are particularly widespread such as 'long ear' for mule/donkey, 'strong house' for jail, 'nose hole' for nostril, 'chief snake' for rattlesnake, 'sweet salt' for sugar, and 'big hand' for thumb. Chitimacha and Choctaw, as well as peripheral Koasati (Coushatta), have 'raccoon man' for monkey. The calque 'red bird' for cardinal occurs in Biloxi, Ofo, and Chickasaw as well as in Eastern Muskogean (Koasati). The Koasati term seems suspiciously close to the Ofo Siouan term, suggesting borrowing between them. (Remember that Ofos and Biloxis probably inhabited the Cumberland Plateau region near Koasatis and may have participated in the Dallas Phase.)

Some of the most widespread calques — 'butter,' 'donkey,' 'jail,' 'sugar' — were likely diffused through the MTL pidgin, which shared the calques. Since extant data are limited for MTL, it is now impossible to know if other borrowings and calques were diffused via this medium, though it seems probable.

## THOMASON BORROWING SCALE

The apparent extent of contact between two or more languages is a matter of degree. Such contact can have very little effect on a particular language, or contact can be so intense that it can lead a language to assume a different structural type (Weinreich 1953; Gumperz and Wilson 1971). While it is difficult to assess the degree of contact and convergence among languages in a sprachbund, Thomason compiled a "borrowing scale," which I have used to obtain a clearer picture of the intensity of contact among languages in the LMV. Although a borrowing scale is only a matter of probabilities, not possibilities, "these predications are robust ... they are valid in the great majority of cases that have been described in the literature" (Thomason 2001, 70). Thomason's scale relies heavily on the concept of basic vocabulary in determining the degree of contact between languages:

(1) CASUAL CONTACT, in which only *non-basic vocabulary* is copied;
(2) SLIGHTLY MORE INTENSE CONTACT, in which copying includes function words and slight structural borrowing;
(3) MORE INTENSE CONTACT, in which there is *copying of basic as well as of non-basic vocabulary* and moderate structural borrowing; and
(4) INTENSE CONTACT, in which there is both heavy lexical and structural copying.

(Thomason 2001; italics mine)

Using Thomason's scale, we find level (3) to be the most appropriate ranking for contact in the LMV, based on the sharing of basic vocabulary. This indicates that the level of contact in the LMV was quite intense, which correlates with the intensity of contact implied by the phonetic/phonological and morphological data.

**OTHER LINKS**

The following section is devoted to a discussion of what we can infer about agriculture, weaponry, migration, oral history, and possible LMV-Mesoamerican links based on LMV word data.

### LMV Lexicon and Agriculture

There is evidence that farming may have begun to some degree in the LMV ca. 4000 BCE. At early LMV sites, farming, where it existed, was probably done only on a very limited basis, perhaps as private garden plots. The level of farming practiced did not make it necessary for the population to be sedentary, unlike some 4,700 years later during the Mississippian-Plaquemine period, when the arrival of large-scale maize agriculture demanded a large, sedentary maintenance population.

The lack of language evidence demonstrating copying of agricultural terminology in the LMV (see table 14) indicates that LMV groups likely developed farming independently of one another, at least in some cases probably before their arrival in the LMV. Nichols's (1992) proposal that a language area may be a residual zone for groups that have been pushed into a peripheral area opens the possibility that many LMV groups may have been "pushed" into the region. One potential push factor could have been the arrival of Hopewell (Marksville) culture ca. 100 CE, or possibly the Mississippian-Plaquemine culture ca. 1200 CE. The arrival of the bow and arrow (see below) in the region would suggest a post-Hopewell migration for most groups into the LMV.

### Maize in the LMV

Maize (*Zea mays* subsp. *mays*) was first domesticated as a wild grass, called teosinte (*Zea mays* subsp. *parviglumis*) (from Nahuatl *teocintli*), which currently grows primarily in the Río Balsas region of western Mexico (Blake 2010, 45). Maize was first domesticated there between ca. 8000 and 4300 BCE (Jaenicke-Després and Smith 2010, 32).

Maize arrived in North America from Mesoamerica (Blake 2010, 45). Maize appears in southwestern North America ca. 3000 BCE, then later in eastern North America ca. 1500 BCE at Lake Shelby (Clark and Knoll 2005; Fearn and Liu 1995, 109), in modern-day coastal Alabama near Mobile Bay, and ca. 400 BCE at the north end of the Tombigbee River, a tributary of the Mobile River, in what is now northeastern Mississippi. Maize occurs in the Cumberland Plateau region ca. 200 CE, at the Icehouse Bottom site, and ca. 400 CE, at Tuskeegee Pond, both in modern-day eastern Tennessee (Fearn and Liu 1995, 110). The first securely dated evidence of maize (based on pollens) in eastern North America occurs near Mobile Bay. Genetic evidence suggests that maize in the American Northeast is most similar to southwestern maize (Blake 2010, 47), suggesting that southwestern maize "was carried eastward across the Plains." But the Southeast shows "greater genetic variability" in strains of maize, which may indicate more direct connections with Mexican maize varieties (White 2005, 16). This suggests that southeastern North American strains of maize may have arrived directly from Mexico via the Gulf.

Large-scale maize farming appears largely to have accompanied the advent of Mississippian-Plaquemine culture. An increased birth rate and reduced infant mortality led to a large increase in population density from the inception of agriculture (Bellwood and Renfrew 2002, 8). The decline of freshwater ecosystems being a good indicator of growing population worldwide, there was a decline in freshwater mussels in the Southeast beginning ca. 3000 BCE, likely related to the development of agriculture (Peacock, Haag, and Warren 2005). This time period agrees with the archaeological evidence presented above. This decline of ecosystems became even more evident ca. 1000 CE, likely with the arrival of maize agriculture (549). Further, women were the primary farmers in most of these societies; the Tunicas were an exception, as men did the majority of farming (Brain 1988). Work-related medical pathologies increased significantly among women in a manner consistent with "a model of increased labor . . . with the acquisition of maize agriculture" (Buikstra, Konigsburg, and Bullington 1986, 531).

Table 14. LMV words related to planting and agriculture

| | BILOXI | OFO | ATAKAPA |
|---|---|---|---|
| SOURCE | DS12 | DS12 | GS1932 |
| bean | tątka yįki | ąkonaki | kimat |
| crop | | | |
| cultivate (crops), to | | | |
| field | amǫǫni | | neyuc nepom |
| gourd | kôô | | kipadsu |
| grow / come up (of something planted), to | | ithǫ | |
| hoe | mąyįke / mikǫǫni | | kantsau |
| hoe, to | mąyįke / mikǫǫni | tufthahe | |
| maize | ayêêki | ačêêki | tso?ots / nešo'um |
| plant, to | ci / cu | akhe (*lit.* 'dig in certain place') | hi |
| pumpkin | (t)ąthaani | ǫtą | moyum |
| seed | su | ifhu | šo |
| sow, to | | | pam ('throw') |
| squash | (t)ąthaani | | |
| sunflower | | | texlk lak ('glittering? flower') |

Key: DS12 = Dorsey-Swanton 1912, GS32 = Gatschet and Swanton 1932, HMS = Haas ms,
H52 = Haas 1952, Swd52 = Swadesh 1952, BS15 = Byington and Swanton 1915, D96 = Drechsel 1996.

While other LMV groups became fervent maize agriculturalists during the Mississippian-Plaquemine period ca. 1200 CE, Atakapas appear largely to have remained fishermen and hunter-gatherers even during this period. There is little to no evidence of large-scale farming in southeastern Texas, for example, but there *is* evidence of an increase in population along the Texas Gulf barrier islands and more societal stratification around the time that the Mississippian-Plaquemine culture arrived to the east (Ricklis

| NATCHEZ | TUNICA | CHITIMACHA | CHOCTAW | MTL |
|---------|--------|------------|---------|-----|
| *HMS* | *H52* | *SWD52 MS* | *BS15* | *D96* |
| popkeh | šihpari | uksgasma (*lit.* snake-corn) | bala / tobi | bala tohbe |
| kimpaa'ikti | | huwo, huu | awaya / hatip | |
| | lač021u | | toksali | |
| peeLiluu 'land cleared off' | haluni | hukatsi | osaapa | osaba |
| iwi | šuhkali | kupu | isht kafa / shukshi okpulo / shukshubok | sheshekowa / sheshekoshe |
| ecale-haa'iš / mip-haakiš | šuka | huštka- | | |
| | | čaahpada | chahe | čahe |
| | | aawit- | leeli / okchali / hopochi | |
| haku | hahka | časa | tạče | čašše / tạče |
| paa-heluu'iš | | ni gast- | hokchi | hokči |
| iwišk(a-) (cf. Bi. turnip?) | šulihki | čiška | isito | (e)seto |
| iNc | tosu | kapi | nihi / atia | nihi |
| wac-hoo'iš | | witi- / witma- | fimmi, hokchi | |
| co:Y | šulihtohku | | isito | (e)seto |
| | | | hashi (same as sun) | |

2004). This suggests some cultural influence from the east, whether or not agriculture ever played a major role in Atakapan society.

### LMV Lexicon for Weaponry

Terms for weaponry in the LMV also demonstrate what we have seen with farming vocabulary: there is little to no borrowing involved (see table 15). This may tell us something about time lines. Since the bow and arrow did

Table 15. Weaponry in the LMV

| BILOXI | OFO | TUNICA | ATAKAPA | CHIT. | NATCHEZ | WM | MTL | ENGLISH |
|---|---|---|---|---|---|---|---|---|
| ąksi | ǫfhi | ala | tik / skenne | ʔakt (also flute, reed, horn, etc.) | išahkw | oski / šumo naki | oske nake šomate | arrow |
| ąksi | uʃaptąta (*lit.* ǫfhi + ?) / šleka | wiškatahi | te (cf. Maya t'e 'tree/wood,' but also At. tei 'vine' and MTL ete 'wood/tree') | ʔakt | kunahaʔeteʔikti | iti tanąpo | ete tanąbo | bow |
| aphuhǫni | | alatašuru | tikpuns (*lit.* 'arrow-blow') | puhtibak | uwaloho / uwatololkop | oski ɬupa | oske tanąbo | blowgun |
| ąpanahǫni | | roha 'stab' | tsa | zhaat- / zhama- | ęcakhal'iš | api, išt baha | | spear |

not arrive in the LMV until ca. 600–700 CE, the lack of copying suggests that speakers of LMV languages were not in contact at the time of this weapon's arrival, indicating migration for most groups to the LMV after ca. 600–700 CE.

## LANGUAGE, MIGRATION, AND ORAL HISTORY

We should take into account the migration stories of Native peoples themselves in assessing their possible origins and migrations. Scholars often minimize the importance of oral histories, perceiving such non-written histories to be largely irrelevant to serious academic consideration. For instance, Galloway dismisses as "romanticized" and "fictionalized" the migration legends gathered from indigenous Creek sources that speak of "a general 'Moskoqui' migration from northwest Mexico (!) to eastern Alabama/western Georgia" (Galloway 1995, 329; original emphasis). However, in Haas's unpublished field notes, a Creek consultant informed her of a Muskogean migration from Mexico occurring in the ninth century, specifying not only Mexico as the origin point but also an actual time period of migration. Haas was apparently less critical of this idea and felt it was important enough to include in her notes.

## POSSIBLE LMV-MESOAMERICA CONNECTIONS

As stated earlier there has been little interaction and collaboration between linguists and archaeologists. Similarly, archaeologists who focus on the southeastern United States and northern Mexico "seldom communicate with each other" (White 2005, 1). I hope that this book will be the beginning of much more cooperation and collaboration not only between linguistics and archaeology but also between archaeologists who study the North American Southeast and northern Mexico. These two regions are currently separated by a national political border that did not exist before the European invasion; furthermore, culturally and linguistically, this border did not exist for Native Americans. Researchers should not let this modern political boundary interfere with indigenous cultural and linguistic studies.

The Biloxis and Ofos copied Caddoan terms for maize, which seems reasonable given that the Caddoans' location and probable occupation of Spiro were in a good geographic position to trade with both the Southwest and the LMV and greater Southeast. That the words were likely borrowed into these two Siouan languages from Caddoan between ca. 600 and 1100 CE also suggests that Caddoans were likely present in this region (on the western border of the LMV) at an early date. And, if, as evidence seems to indicate, the Biloxis and Ofos were relative newcomers to the LMV, probably after the European invasions, these two Siouan groups, though geographically located fairly distantly from the Caddoan area, can be inferred to have been in contact with Caddoans at this early period. This may indicate two things: (1) these eastern Siouan groups (Biloxis and Ofos) had at least a trading relationship with Caddoans from an early time period, perhaps even having established colonial outposts for such trade in the region, and (2) Southwest maize may have been taken to the Appalachian region by these two Siouan groups. Interestingly the Cumberland Plateau and Appalachian regions were fairly late joining the Mississippian cultural realm (ca. 1400 CE), which is heavily associated with intensive maize farming. Perhaps maize agriculture predated the arrival of Mississippian Culture in this region.

Earlier evidence for the presence of maize, though not necessarily for maize agriculture, leads one to consider the possibility of Gulf coastal maritime trade in addition to overland trade. Linguistic evidence for a possible coastal aquatic trade route comes from several languages along the northern Gulf—Alabama, MTL, Koasati (Coushatta), Chitimacha, and Catawba—which share a possible cognate with a word for 'maize' from the Totonac language of east-central Mexico. Since Alabama and MTL were spoken in close proximity to Mobile Bay, such a potential borrowing would support this region as a Gulf coastal trading area.[2] Yet another potential borrowing for 'maize' occurring in Atakapa, possibly from Proto-Mayan or Soke (Zoque), would further support the existence of maritime Gulf trade between the LMV and Mexico.

Choctaw-Chickasaw shares calques that are also found in Mesoamerica, including 'child of mortar' for pestle and 'mother of hand' for thumb. 'House mouth' for door appears in Atakapa, Chitimacha, and Natchez, as well as in Mayan. Such calques help bolster the argument for the Meso-american origin of the Muskogean peoples.

Possible borrowings in Chitimacha and Atakapa in the LMV from languages on the western periphery into the Rio Grande Valley and Mexico include:

Table 16. Possible borrowings by Atakapa and Chitimacha from RGV and Mexico

| | |
|---|---|
| back, bad, divide-separate, whip | Atakapa-Coahuiltec |
| black | Atakapa-Tunica-Karankawa |
| dog | Chitimacha-Karankawa-Cotoname |
| (to) fall, ocean | Atakapa-Karankawa |
| now | Atakapa-Choctaw/Chickasaw-MTL-Coahuiltec |
| shell | Atakapa-Chitimacha-Huastec |
| six | Atakapa-Coahuiltec-Nahuatl |
| tooth | Chitimacha-Karankawa-Comecrudo |
| water | Atakapa-Coahuiltec-Tonkawa |

Such borrowings, including basic words, suggest a continuum of intimate language contact from the LMV over into Gulf coastal Mexico, suggesting trade routes between the LMV, the Rio Grande Valley, and the Mexican Gulf. (It also suggests a possible, much broader sprachbund, extending from the Rio Grande Valley or even northeastern Mexico all the way to the Atlantic Seaboard.) Archaeological evidence supports language contact during the Mississippian era between the LMV and the Huasteca region of Mexico (see, for example, Zaragoza-Ocaña 2005 and Cabrera 2005). This indicates that northeastern Mexico was indeed an extension of the "Southeast" cultural area traditionally considered, in line with modern political boundaries, to end at the modern U.S.-Mexico border in Texas. However, Mexican sites such as Tantoc and Tlacolula, in San Luis Potosí, and Las Flores and El Triunfo, in Tamaulipas, "have earthen mounds very different from the architecture of classic Mesoamerica" (Zaragoza-Ocaña 2005, 249), looking more like structures of the North American Southeast. Other evidence includes sculptures and artistic motifs that appear very similar to motifs found in parts of the North American Southeast (Zaragoza-Ocaña 2005).

The region of the northern part of Tamaulipas, Mexico, and the southern part of Texas has been considered to be a great barrier to trade and communication due to its hostile desert environment. This region was supposedly inhabited "only by the nomadic groups who were well adapted to those climatic conditions. For this reason interactions among the prehistoric people were more likely facilitated by the maritime and fluvial routes that we know were already very well established in the sixteenth century, such routes as the Pánuco River, the Gulf Coast shoreline, and the Mississippi River" (Zaragoza-Ocaña 2005, 248). We might also add Mobile Bay to this list of maritime routes that may have been well known to merchants.

If we extend the traditional archaeological concept of the artifact to include not only material remains but also words and grammatical structures possibly left behind as the result of language and cultural contact, then these linguistic artifacts should be treated as seriously as material remains as evidence for such contact. At the very least such language evidence should be taken into consideration by archaeologists in the evaluation of physical remains, perhaps to include the possibility of trans-Gulf contact.

# Conclusion

## SUMMARY AND SYNTHESIS

In this book we have examined the Mississippi Valley, a region of rich diversity and natural resources, the heartland of early North American civilizations, and the hub of transportation to every region of eastern North America and to Mesoamerica (Mexico). It is no wonder that the LMV became one of the world's major language areas. I have chosen to examine this sprachbund and cultural area in detail to an extent that has never before been done.

A sprachbund cannot be separated from the geography, history, peoples, and cultures of the region that came into contact with each other for such purposes as trade, marriage, intergroup gatherings, and war. In part 1, I focused heavily on the geography, archaeological history, and peoples of the region. Peoples within close geographical range of each other and who come into contact regularly find that they must accommodate each other by learning either each other's languages or a trade language, or pidgin, not native to any of them for purposes of communication. As in other parts of the world such as the Balkans of eastern Europe, South Asia, and the North American Northwest, this is what happened in the LMV.

The LMV has a lengthy history dating well back into what archaeologists call the Paleoamerican (Paleoindian) and Archaic periods. The period ca. 3500 BCE is especially important, since it is in this time period that the first known earthen monumental mound structures were built in the Americas, in what is now northeastern Louisiana. The LMV lies at the very heart of the mound-building tradition in North America, a tradition that lasted into the eighteenth century. We do not know who frequented or inhabited the first mound sites like Watson Brake and Poverty Point. Unfortunately, many mounds were destroyed with impunity in post-European times before they could be satisfactorily investigated. Their soils were employed in the building of roads and railroads or plowed over for modern agriculture and subdivisions; thereby traces were erased of the civilizations that once flourished in North America prior to the European invasion. Such destruction resulted from the U.S. government's ideology of "manifest destiny." This wanton destruction bolstered the popular myth, still prevalent today, that all Native Americans were nomadic hunter-gatherers living in an untamed wilderness who deserved to be conquered by European and Euro-American "civilization."

The histories, languages, and interactions of the groups that came to settle in the LMV—Atakapas, Biloxis, Chitimachas, Choctaw-Chickasaws, Natchez, Ofos, and Tunicas—have here been explored. Language evidence such as the lack of agricultural cognate forms, and thus the apparent independent development of agriculture, suggests that most of these peoples were already at least small-scale farmers. For various reasons, at least probably partly due to push factors from outside the region, these groups migrated into the LMV, where farming on a large scale was not practiced until ca. 1200 CE. It was around this time that large-scale agriculture, dominated by maize, developed in the LMV. Large-scale maize farming probably developed in tandem with the arrival of the politicoreligious phenomenon called the Mississippian-Plaquemine culture, which had already been spreading from the north toward the south and west for a couple hundred years before reaching its tentacles into the LMV.

While we cannot precisely date the migrations of most groups into the LMV, its languages give us a clue as to the timing of this migration: the apparent lack of cognates for agricultural and weapon terms, and the fact that Tunica and Natchez oral narratives lack the rabbit-as-trickster motif typical of most Southeastern societies (Haas 1950), suggest a shorter length of habitation in the North American Southeast. LMV words for weaponry inform us that words for such items as the bow and arrow were not borrowed among LMV languages. This suggests that the peoples mentioned above who came to inhabit the LMV likely already had this weapon, which did not arrive in the LMV until ca. 600–700 CE, and they had already independently developed terms for it. This, perhaps more than anything, suggests that several of the peoples discussed in this book who came to inhabit the LMV did so sometime after 600–700 CE, perhaps just after the Hopewell cultural phenomenon and close to the time of the emergence and dispersal of Mississippian-Plaquemine culture. Could, as Nichols (1992) has suggested, the LMV have been a "residual zone" into which peoples speaking several languages from different linguistic families were propelled in order to maintain a certain amount of both geographical and ideological distance from a spreading economic, political, and religious culture farther north?

The exact origins of the Atakapas, Chitimachas, Natchez, and Tunicas are largely unknown. The apparent lack of Atakapa migration or origin stories, while possibly representing mere omission on the part of early ethnographers, might indicate Atakapan habitation in the LMV for a long period of time, longer than any of the other LMV groups. Chitimachas may have also been in the LMV quite early, at least since ca. 600 CE. Proto-Muskogean groups may have entered the LMV ca. 900–1000 CE, with Haas's notes specifically mentioning the period ca. 900 CE for their supposed migration, possibly from Mexico. If, as Haas hypothesized, Natchez is remotely related to Muskogean languages, it would seem that the Natchez branched off from other Muskogean groups and were geographically isolated from them for a long time, perhaps supporting their claim of habitation up north in the Wabash River area (Swanton 1946, 23). The Natchez then arrived in the LMV after the Chitimachas, whom they displaced, forcing Chitimacha migration to the south. Tunicas and Siouans apparently did not arrive in the LMV until after the European invasion; in fact, European and Euro-American aggression may have been a prime push factor for their migration into the area. Language evidence suggests that Proto-Tunicas may have migrated from the Rocky Mountains or even farther west. Tunicans lived in the northern periphery of the LMV, near the Arkansas River, at the time of the Spanish invasion, ca. 1541. They migrated southward toward the Red River thereafter. Toponymic data suggest that the ancestors of Biloxis and Ofos originated in the Cumberland Plateau and Appalachian region. Siouans were likely the most recent arrivals in the LMV, the Biloxis around the early seventeenth century and the Ofos a bit later.

In any case language evidence makes it clear that the peoples who settled in the LMV came into contact with each other. We have seen that certain broad-ranging lexical, to phonetic and morphological borrowing was the result of such contact. Such intimate interactions resulted in bilingualism and multilingualism, which in turn led to aspects of their languages sharing certain features discussed in part 2 (reiterated below).

The following lists lay out the features that characterize the LMV as a sprachbund. The list below shows phonetic and phonological features:

1. Vowel nasalization (Atakapa, Biloxi, Choctaw-Chickasaw, MTL, Natchez, Ofo)
2. Alternation of /h/ and /Ø/ in word-initial position (Atakapa, Biloxi, MTL)
3. Bilabial fricative /ɸ/ or labiodental fricative /f/ (Atakapa, Biloxi, Choctaw-Chickasaw, MTL, Ofo)
4. Velar fricative /x/ (Atakapa, Biloxi, Ofo)
5. Retroflex sibilant /ʂ/ (Choctaw-Chickasaw, MTL, Natchez, Tunica)
6. Lateral fricative /ɬ/ (Atakapa, Choctaw-Chickasaw, MTL)

All LMV languages except Chitimacha and Tunica have nasalized vowels. All LMV languages except Biloxi and Chitimacha have /l/. Devoicing of sonorants occurs in Chitimacha, Natchez, and Tunica, but it is now impossible to know if any or all of these languages originally possessed this feature or if it was copied among languages. Ejective stops, labiovelar /kʷ/, velar nasal /ŋ/, liquid /r/ (including /r/ and /l/ opposition), lateral affricate /tl/, preaspirated voiceless stops, and vowel harmony are present in two or fewer languages of the region; in accordance with my definition of a sprachbund (see Kaufman 2014), they are not considered relevant to the LMV language area.

Based on the features as demonstrated in table 3, Choctaw-Chickasaw, Natchez, and Atakapa show the highest total of LMV phonetic features, followed closely by MTL, Ofo, and Tunica. Chitimacha shows the lowest number of LMV phonetic and phonological features, which is interesting considering that the Chitimachas were in the LMV longer than the Natchez (remember that, according to oral narrative, the Natchez moved into Chitimacha territory and pushed the latter farther south). This could indicate either (a) Natchez is indeed remotely related to the Muskogean language family, or (b) Chitimachas simply did not interact as much with their neighbors as did other LMV groups.

This list shows the morphological features of the LMV:

1. Focus/topic/assertive marking (Atakapa, Biloxi, Chitimacha, Choctaw-Chickasaw, Natchez)
2. Definite article (Atakapa, Biloxi, Chitimacha, Choctaw-Chickasaw, Natchez, Tunica)
3. Indefinite animate subject/object preverb or prefix (Atakapa, Choctaw-Chickasaw, Natchez)
4. Indefinite inanimate subject/object preverb or prefix (Atakapa, Choctaw-Chickasaw, Natchez)
5. Reference tracking (Biloxi, Choctaw-Chickasaw, Natchez, Tunica)
6. Verbal number suppletion (Atakapa, Biloxi, Choctaw-Chickasaw, Tunica)
7. Positional verb auxiliaries (Atakapa, Biloxi, Chitimacha, Choctaw-Chickasaw, Natchez, Ofo, Tunica)

As with phonetic features, the highest-ranking LMV languages in terms of shared morphological features are Choctaw-Chickasaw, Natchez, and Atakapa. Next come Biloxi, Tunica, Chitimacha, Ofo, and MTL. MTL, as expected, scores low in the number of LMV morphological features, since there are almost no morphological features in the pidgin. Ofo also ranks low, not so much because it shares fewer morphological features with the rest of the LMV, but because data are simply lacking and indeterminate for several of the features.

The fact that Natchez comes in a close second to Choctaw-Chickasaw in phonetic and phonological as well as in morphological ranking supports Haas's theory that Natchez and the Muskogean languages are distantly genetically related. However, the close ranking could also be due to Natchez speakers having become part of the Choctaw Confederacy after the French destroyed the Natchez homeland. Perhaps the close ranking reflects a combination of both factors.

As we have seen, the least LMV language in phonetic, phonological, and morphological ranking is Chitimacha. Although there are several word borrowings between Chitimacha and Natchez and Atakapa, indicating a certain level of contact among these groups, it appears that Chitimachas for the most part did not interact much with other groups in the region.

Such lack of interaction could have been a conscious cultural choice on the part of Chitimachas, although they did participate in the Mississippian-Plaquemine culture.

The thirteen features from the above lists have been determined to be most characteristic of the LMV as a sprachbund partly because of their overall limited distribution beyond the LMV. Such limited distribution suggests a comparatively well-defined area that once hosted a high volume of ongoing contact.

As in other language areas the LMV shows a sizable number of word borrowings. The highest number of lexical borrowings in the LMV occurs in the semantic realm of zoology, with nineteen terms copied among two or more languages. The next closest category is anatomy, or body parts, with eleven terms copied. Agricultural and food terms rank a close third, with nine terms copied. The borrowing of zoological, agricultural, and food terms is not unusual for peoples coming into a new environment featuring new flora, fauna, and cultural items different from what they were used to. It is easy to copy vocabulary from another group that has been in a particular environment for a longer period of time and already has the relevant terminology for the local flora and fauna. The widespread copying of body part terms, however, is more surprising, since these terms tend to be among the most basic in languages and not as susceptible to borrowing. The copying of anatomical terms may suggest close contact for ritual and ceremonial purposes such as for intergroup dancing.

As between specific LMV languages, Atakapa and Biloxi show sixteen terms copied between them. Biloxi and Choctaw, however, share only six terms. This presents something of an enigma. Biloxis were found living in close proximity to Choctaws ca. 1700. The fact that the number of borrowed lexical terms is greater between Biloxi and Atakapa than between Biloxi and Choctaw suggests that Biloxis were in closer contact with Atakapas, perhaps for a longer period of time than with Choctaws. The Biloxi and Ofo borrowing of the word for 'maize' from a Caddoan language also shows that they were in contact with this region west of the Mississippi River (Caddoans and Atakapans were in close proximity to each other). This suggests that Proto-Biloxis had, at one point, either settled somewhere west of the Mississippi River, thus placing them closer to Atakapans and Caddoans, or that they simply had a fairly strong trade relationship with, or perhaps even a merchant colony in, this region west of the Mississippi. This is probably not surprising since Biloxis, Caddoans, and possibly Atakapans were in or near salt-producing regions; the salt trade may have been a prime motivator for trade relations and interactions. Chitimachas occupied the area of the salt dome now known as Avery Island, currently known for its production of McIlhenny Tabasco Sauce. The salt dome was also located near the Atakapas' eastern border, meaning that Atakapas may have also had access to the saltworks of this island, either in partnership with Chitimachas (which may partly account for the heavy language borrowing between them) or at different periods when the salt dome may have been under control of one or the other group. Both Atakapas and Chitimachas were fisherfolk; salt could have been one means of preserving fish traded to inland groups.

The relatively high number of borrowings between Chitimacha and Natchez (nine) indicates a particularly high level of contact between these two groups. This supports oral history that the Natchez entered Chitimacha territory and then displaced them, forcing the Chitimachas farther south.

I judged the Leipzig-Jakarta basic word list to be superior to the Swadesh basic word list, and used it for this study. With respect to this list, Atakapa, Chitimacha, and Biloxi have the largest number of shared *basic* vocabulary items—nine, eight, and eight respectively. Tunica and Natchez have seven and six respectively. Ofo and Choctaw-Chickasaw rank the lowest, with only one and zero respectively. In addition Atakapa and Chitimacha share basic words with languages on the western periphery of the LMV that I have included in my tentative RGV sprachbund: Coahuiltec, Comecrudo, Cotoname, Karankawa, and Tonkawa. Particularly widespread in the LMV and into the periphery are terms for 'bison/buffalo,' 'bullfrog,' 'cut,' 'goose,' 'metal,' 'robin,' 'split,' 'town,' 'turn,' 'water,' and 'woodpecker.' The widespread copying of these terms across several languages of different genetic stock suggests that these items were particularly culturally relevant.

As stated earlier the "trait core area" (Masica 1976) of the LMV sprachbund appears to be in its easternmost reaches near Mobile Bay, with Western Muskogean languages (Choctaw-Chickasaw and MTL) at the core, scoring 41 on the language feature chart, closely followed by Natchez (36), Atakapa (34), Tunica (32), and Biloxi (31), while Chitimacha scores far lower than the rest of the pack at 19. It is telling that the LMV trait core area lies near Mobile Bay, which has already been described as a principal port on the northern Gulf (Tanner 1989). It is not surprising that a trade language such as MTL would have developed around such a port. The Eastern Muskogean languages, just on the eastern periphery of the LMV, score 34. This indicates a certain level of feature "attrition" just to the east of Mobile Bay, signifying the probable limit of the LMV sprachbund on the east, although several LMV languages to the west of this core area also score about the same as Eastern Muskogean languages. This may suggest that the LMV sprachbund is part of a much larger sprachbund, perhaps including what I term the GA sprachbund, but only further study could ascertain this.

After analyzing the various linguistic features of the LMV, I concur with Masica that "a great many linguistic features *do* pattern areally" (1976, 170; original emphasis). There is indeed enough evidence of areal patterning in the LMV sprachbund to set it on par with others around the world.

It is also clear that what Matras terms "'utterance modifiers'—an extended grouping of discourse-regulating elements, discourse markers, and focus particles" (1998, 281) were likely copied in LMV languages as a means of accommodating the "cognitive pressure" (281) of guiding communication and facilitating comprehension in bilingual and multilingual environments. While such "discourse-regulating elements" have traditionally been little studied in relation to grammar, their presence among languages of the LMV signifies the importance of these elements in contact linguistics.

I concur with Sherzer that "the Southeast . . . is best viewed not as a single linguistic area but rather as several" (1976, 253). I divide these language areas into three: Lower Mississippi Valley (LMV), the prime sprachbund discussed here; Gulf-Atlantic (GA); and Rio Grande Valley (RGV). I have found ample evidence that these language areas overlap, with the GA and RGV stretching to the east and west, respectively, of the LMV.

The RGV sprachbund extends from Karankawa and Tonkawa, overlapping somewhat with Atakapa, on the western periphery of the LMV, west to Comecrudo and Coahuiltec in southern Texas and northeastern Mexico. Unfortunately there is little to no documentation on most of the RGV languages. Several languages are known to have existed in the southern Texas and RGV area on the basis of historical evidence but have no direct attestation (Goddard 1979, 374); the data strongly suggest that these RGV languages "represented many language families" (375). Among the many languages known to have existed in this region, besides Coahuiltec and Comecrudo, are Cotoname, Mamulique, Garza, Solano, and Aranama. A fully developed sign language was attested in Texas in 1740 and "is clearly a significant reflection of the existence of a variety of languages there" (356), not to mention the existence of a probable intensive trading region, again a major impetus for the development of a sprachbund. It is unknown if this RGV sign language was a precursor to the later Plains Sign Language, but evidence of the latter spreading northward from the south would seem to support it.

The GA sprachbund extends from Eastern Muskogean (Alabama, Muskogee [Creek], Koasati [Coushatta], Hitchiti, Apalachee), overlapping somewhat with Western Muskogean (Choctaw-Chickasaw), as far east as the Atlantic Ocean and as far north as the Carolinas. The GA sprachbund includes Cherokee, Yuchi, Timucua, Catawba, and probably several other languages like Westo,[1] Guale, Cusabo, Yamasee, and others that went extinct before being documented along or near the southeastern Atlantic seaboard.

It is difficult, however, to precisely demarcate these hypothesized language areas, since, as the data demonstrate, there is considerable overlap of certain features, some extending far beyond the LMV and others not. These data exhibit isoglosses, or boundary areas, that support Masica's assertion that the distribution of one linguistic feature does not necessarily correlate with the distribution of other features (1976, 171). These data also support the assertion by Campbell, Kaufman, and Smith-Stark that isoglosses typically fail to fall into neat bundles, but often vary in their extensions outward from an areal core (1986, 546). Why some isoglosses correlate and some do not is still beyond explanation (Masica 1976, 171).

While data here reveal three possible language areas (the RGV, LMV, and GA) forming a contiguous contact link from what is now northeastern Mexico all across the northern Gulf to the Atlantic, rigid boundaries do not exist between these language areas. Such contact is supported both linguistically and archaeologically. While, for the most part, there may not have been large migrations of people across this extensive geographic area, it is evident that at least traders, their languages, and cultures were in contact across the region, on land and by water.

Certain features are almost ubiquitous across the three hypothesized contiguous language areas, as the following list indicates:

1. Overall occurrence of /h/
2. Locative suffixes
3. Subject person prefixes
4. SOV constituent order
5. Semi-quinary number system
6. Evidentiality
7. Overall lack of /q/
8. Overall lack of /Θ/
9. Overall lack of /ŋ/
10. Overall lack of glottalized semivowels
11. Overall lack of glottalized nasals
12. Overall lack of tone
13. Overall lack of masculine-feminine gender distinction

Certain of these features likely extend well beyond these three language areas; such features as locative suffixes and subject person prefixes were identified long ago as "widespread" features across North America (Sapir 1922). Whether such extensive features are the result of deep-level linguistic genetic relationship or of borrowing through contact is a question still remaining to be definitively answered, if such an answer is possible.

Examining the periphery of the LMV, including languages that would fit into my newly postulated RGV and GA language areas, we find Yuchi (Euchee) (35) (perhaps not surprising, given that Yuchi has been postulated to be related to Siouan), Eastern Muskogean languages (34), and Quapaw (25) scoring well within reach of some LMV languages and that could be termed "transitional" languages (Campbell, Kaufman, and Smith-Stark 1986, 545). It is arguable whether these languages might be included in the LMV sprachbund rather than on the LMV periphery or in an adjacent GA sprachbund. In order to determine this, the languages comprising the proposed GA sprachbund would need to be analyzed on a scale similar to that in this study in order to more accurately define its center and how far its prospective features extend and overlap with those of the LMV. The RGV sprachbund would similarly need to be analyzed, but such analysis would be hampered by a distinct lack of documentation and data. We can primarily rely solely on "historic evidence" and the fact that a form of sign language was attested in this region (Goddard 1979), besides a few vocabulary items, to infer that the RGV was a region of heavy trade and a probable sprachbund.

It is somewhat surprising to find that Cherokee (24), Catawba (22), and even the more distant Totonac (26) score close to the lowest LMV scores. Catawba, like Yuchi, is considered to be remotely related to the Siouan languages (Biloxi, Ofo) in the LMV. However, the relatively high score of Totonac (on par with LMV languages and even higher than the geographically closer Cherokee and Catawba) presents an intriguing enigma. Totonac people are located in the Mexican Gulf coastal region called Totonacapan, between the modern states of Puebla and Veracruz (Rouy 2005, 187). The Totonacs are believed to have inhabited the great archaeological site of El Tajín, with its iconic Pyramid of the Niches (see fig. 14).

El Tajín developed between 800 and 1200 CE (Ladrón de Guevara 2010, 20).[2] The Totonac people and their language arrived on the Mexican Gulf ca. 850 CE (27),[3] not long after the collapse of the large city-state of Teotihuacan. Why does this central Gulf coastal Mexican language share so many of the features of the northern Gulf languages? The much lower scores of Nahuatl (14) and Huastec (11) would seem to rule out extensive overland trade and migration, though some undoubtedly occurred, between the central Mexican and northern Gulf, since these languages intervened between the two regions. One possible explanation is a maritime trade route between the Mississippi Valley (and Mobile Bay) and east-central Mexico via the Gulf, similar to that proposed by Masica between India and Ethiopia via the Arabian Sea (1976).

Not surprisingly there is evidence of close contact between pairs of LMV languages that were likely in more intimate contact with each other by virtue of their close geographical proximity.[4] Atakapa and Chitimacha may be remotely genetically related, but the similarities between them are more likely due to borrowing. (We have seen that Chitimacha scores much

Fig. 14. Photograph of Pyramid of the Niches, El Tajín, Mexico, the location of Totonacs and possibly Huastec Mayas ca. 800–1200 CE. Photo by Alice Beck Kehoe.

lower than Atakapa in terms of its LMV-ness, making similarities between them more likely due to contact than genetic relatedness.) Biloxi and Ofo obviously share many features by virtue of their shared Siouan ancestry, although in many cases data are lacking for Ofo.

It is beyond the scope of this study to examine the proposed immediate sprachbund neighbors of the LMV, the RGV and GA. Although this analysis has extended somewhat up the Mississippi Valley, into the Plains, the Great Basin, the Atlantic Seaboard, and the Southwest, studies of how these language areas and others may interact with this region overall and just how extensive certain features are in North America remain to be done.

## A CAVEAT

While I have done a thorough analysis of available materials on the eight languages here included, it is impossible for me, not having fluency in and intimate knowledge of most of the languages involved, to avoid possible oversight of certain features or data. For instance, grammars were employed in this analysis with the hope that, if a particular feature were present in a language, it would have been noted by previous scholars. The absence of native-speaker intuition on my part and the previous oversight of potential data on the part of prior scholars may have resulted in certain features being overlooked. Corrections and adjustments may need to be made, hopefully only to a small fraction of this overall analysis.

This survey is not, and cannot be, linguistically complete: many of the indigenous languages of this region went extinct before they could be documented. Unfortunately, we will never know to what degree the undocumented extinct languages may have influenced the documented and analyzed ones.

I have also not delved into dialectal differences where they are known to exist. To echo Masica, this study has aimed to hit the high points and get the basic picture chalked in (1976, 11), without regard to the minute details of dialectal or idiosyncratic speech patterns.

## FURTHER STUDY

This study has left a few issues that warrant further investigation by archaeologists, linguists, and ethnohistorians. Among these issues are the degree of possible contact between the Mississippian LMV and Mesoamerica, the extent of trade across North America, and the degree of contact among Native North American peoples and languages. I hope that archaeologists will examine the possible continuation of certain cultural themes, such as whether the Dallas Phase of the Cumberland Plateau of eastern Tennessee and the Gulf of Mexico represents possible Ohio Valley Siouan cultural continuities (such as housing styles) among migrating Biloxis and Ofos in the LMV.

I agree with White that the procurement and exchange of salt as a component of socioeconomic interaction is an area that needs more investigation and recognition (2005, 310), along with a unified theory of trade in North America. We know that in other ancient civilizations, such as in the Near East and Mesopotamia, trade played a pivotal role, and we have seen that trade played a major role in North American cities such as Poverty Point at least 3,500 years ago. To what degree did indigenous merchants play a role in establishing trading colonies and socioeconomic interaction not only with salt but with other items in North America?

We have seen that language evidence may give us clues as to trans- or circum-Gulf trade and contact. Was the Gulf of Mexico more conducive to trade and contact between the LMV and Mesoamerica than has been previously considered or acknowledged? While most archaeologists will cite the lack of *material* evidence for such interaction, we have seen apparent *linguistic* evidence for such contact that has previously been little acknowledged. As stated in the beginning, if we accept linguistic artifacts to be as legitimate as material artifacts, then the evidence for such contact is apparent.

Could the Totonacapan region of east-central Mexico have been the cultural filter through which the artistic similarities often cited between Mesoamerican and Mississippian spheres (such as the feathered-serpent motif) traveled? Could the very idea of settlements with large leveled plazas as marketplaces and trading centers in the LMV and greater Southeast have started with Totonac trade and contact through Mobile Bay? It is intriguing to note the similarities between the Choctaw-Chickasaw and MTL word *tamaha* for 'town,' its possible borrowing into Siouan languages as variants of *tama*, and its possible origin in Totonacan *tamawan*.

The language issues that warrant further study include the presence of several LMV phonetic and phonological features such as /ʂ/, /ɬ/, ejective stops, /tl/, and vowel harmony in Mesoamerican languages. Do these features represent independent development or do they suggest possible diffusion from, or origin in, Mexico? While phonological features are not easily shared between languages, it is not unknown for such features to be borrowed in cases of heavy contact. The apparent borrowing of certain politicoreligious and artistic features among Mississippian peoples from Mesoamerica, for example, may indicate a higher level of contact between Mesoamerica and the northern Gulf than previously thought or acknowledged, a level of contact that could indeed have affected the relevant languages at deeper levels.

Above all this study raises the issue of how extensive some Native North American language traits became through contact and borrowing. Boas and Sapir both noted that certain traits were widespread across American languages. Boas asserted early on that "a number of traits ... may be enumerated which occur with considerable frequency in many parts of America" (1911, 76). Sapir identified the following widespread American traits:

The incorporation of the pronominal (and nominal) object
    in the verb
the incorporation of the possessive pronouns in the noun
the closer association with the verb-form of the object than the
    subject
the inclusion of a considerable number of instrumental and
    local modifications in the verb-complex
the weak development of differences of tense in the verb and
    of number of the verb and noun
the impossibility of drawing a sharp line between mode and tense
(1922, 282)

Whether such studies would definitively prove widespread North American language diffusion through contact or through deep-level genetics remains to be seen. Further studies may support the idea that, at a certain time depth, it is impossible to distinguish results of borrowing from those of common (genetic) origin (Darnell and Sherzer 1971, 25); furthermore, "it is not possible to group American languages rigidly in a genealogical scheme in which each linguistic family is shown to have developed to modern forms, but we have to recognize that many of the languages have *multiple roots* (Boas [1929] 1940, 255; emphasis mine). While Boas was referring to American languages specifically, it may yet be the case that all of the world's languages have multiple roots, their genetic and contact-induced characteristics being largely inseparable. English is a good example of this: its base Germanic root vocabulary has been heavily augmented and overshadowed by heavy borrowing from Latin and French through contact. Although English started out as a Germanic language, certain features of modern English are now more Latinate than Germanic due to language contact.

In this book we have explored language contact and its results in one geographical location: the Lower Mississippi Valley of North America.

Human history, including in the LMV, involves peoples on the move forming friendships, alliances, trade relationships, and enmities, living peace-
fully together at times while going to war at others. Against this backdrop,
more complex individual relationships—friendships, marriages, and trading compacts—were formed and sometimes severed. We have seen that a
history of contact among peoples affects language, from the loan of a few
words in lighter contact situations to significant grammatical and syntac-
tical change in much heavier contact situations. In certain situations an
entirely new trade, or pidgin, language comes into existence as a second
language while being the first language of nobody.

While linguists try to reconstruct proto-languages in order to establish genetic origins, this book has delved into another, as yet understudied
origin of languages: contact. I hope this book helps spur further studies
in contact linguistics and encourages more interdisciplinary cooperation
among linguists, archaeologists, and ethnohistorians.

## APPENDIX

Sample Texts from the LMV

### ATAKAPA

#### The Western Atakapas

Yokiti išak waši a nep nun nultihinst tul oši nun nultihinst. Tepuk neš hi-hulat. Šešneš hihulat. Kiwilš ol neš, tepuk kuckuc neš hihulat. Moyum kimat cooc konan olol hihulat. Yainso. Lans al, šako, kanan, nohamš ayip, ăndi, pit, yan, yaw laklak, šoknok noktew melmel, enkewišt, anhipon, akip cok, pacal šopš, łakišt, konen ayip, kathopš, nawohox, kuy ol, alin hišom, alin hiškam, hilanwol tey, kulšwalš yains. Yokiti mon šokiti šakkeat šok-koy tanuk mon šokiyay oci tanewc. [Lo šokkoyit hal yokic šakišakip ut. Lo hilay yokiti winewlat. Hiyekiti šakyonhulit. Kákhaw hiyekiti hiyą nun nultihinst.] Tawatwenat Ucutat ut. Šokakulit Ucutat ut. Ciš pum wašwaši pum pumulat. Išak hilay tanuk keat, išak hilay cik ke haceeš. Palnal hilay waši pamnimat. Hilay taxnik pamat, Palnal hilay waši kiš pamnimat; yil lat himatol u tatixintat ha išat pamlikš mon. Kakáw amán an ike ăn tahe ăn taat. Hakit hokišak hokyalulhauxš, hišăncet wet a hinak kišet okyalul inak. Wošiṇa hinakit keš ăn šakyol teš maṇ šakmaṇmaṇit, šakyol katnaw šakhahš. Hatyulšo nohik šakatkopšen hatmelšo; hakit išak kaw hatmelšo pumul naw hakit išatip hatnainst haticon, hakit šiṇšnani tikpum nekin hakit nakšnen.

(Alternate version of bracketed text):

[Lo yokiti hal šokkoyit yukit šakišak ut. Lo hilay yokiti winewlat. Ha ša-kišak hiyekiti šakyoṇšulat. Kakáw kaškin winewlat. Hiyekiti šakyonšulat, nunkin tohulat kákhaw iyecne ut.]

| Yokiti | išak | waši | a | nep | nun | nul-ti-hinst | tul |
|--------|------|------|------|------|------|--------------|-----|
| Indian | person | old | here | below | village | live-3s.PL-IMPF | lake |

| oši | nun | nul-ti-hinst | tepuk | neš | hi-hul-at | šeš-neš |
|-----|-----|--------------|-------|-----|-----------|---------|
| edge | village | live-3s.PL-IMPF | peach | tree | there-plant-PERF | fig-tree |

*hi-hul-at*        *kiwilš*      *ol*      *neš*    *tepuk*   *kuc-kuc*    *neš*
there-plant-PERF   white.man   persimmon   tree   peach   red-REDUP   tree

*hi-hul-at*        *moyu[m]*   *kimat*  *cooc*  *konan*  *ol-ol*      *hi-hul-at*
there-plant-PERF   pumpkin   bean   corn   potato   sweet-REDUP   there-plant-PERF

*ya-ins(o)*  *lans*  *al*    *šako*   *kanan*  *nohamš*  *ay-ip*      *ăndi*
eat-3?   deer   meat   bear   turtle   chicken   swamp-LOC   catfish

*pit*    *yan*    *yaw*   *lak-lak*     *šok-nok*    *nok-tew*   *mel-mel*
perch   bowfin   bass   hard-REDUP   STG-wing   wing-tail   black-REDUP

*enkewišt*  *an-hipon*  *ak-ip*     *cok*     *pacal*  *šopš*  *łakišt*
pheasant   ear-folded   water-LOC   squirrel   ?   ?   ?

*konen*  *ay-ip*     *kathopš*  *nawohox*  *kuy(?)*     *ol*      *alin*
potato   swamp-LOC   lily   chinkapin   prickly pear   persimmon   grape

*hišom*  *alin*  *hiškam*  *hilan-wo*    *tey*  *kulšwalš*
small   grape   large   med.plant-fruit   vine   peanut

*ya-ins*  *yokiti*  *mon*  *šok-iti*     *šak-ke-at*    *šok-koy*
eat-IMPF?   Indian   all   STG-go.before   PL-have-PERF   STG-speech

*tanuk*  *mon*  *šok-iyay*  *oci*    *tanewc*  *Lo*  *šok-koy-(y)it*
one   all   STG-rise.up   above   other   Lo   STG-speech-PERF

*hal*  *yokicšak-išak-ip*  *ut*     *Lo*   *hilay*  *yokiti*
last   Indian   PL-person-LOC   toward   Lo wife   Indian

*wine-ul-at*     *hiye-kiti*  *šak-yon-hul-it*  *kákhaw*  *hiye-kiti*  *hiyaṇ*
find-3subj.PL-CMP   east-people   PL-call-3s.PL-PERF   sun   east-people   there

*nun*  *nul-ti-hi-nst*  *ta-wat-wen-at*  *Ucutat*  *ut*  *šok-ak-ul-it*
village   live-3s.PL-there-IMPF   stand-come-talk-CMP   God   to   STG-green-3s.PL-PERF

*Ucutat*  *ut*  *ciš*  *pum*  *waš-aš-i*  *pum*  *pum-ul-at*    *išak*  *hilay*
God   to   baby   dance   old.very   dance   dance-3s.PL-PERF   man   wife

| *tanuk* | *ke-at* | *išak* | *hilay* | *cik* | *ke-en* | *haceeš* | *Palnal* |
|---|---|---|---|---|---|---|---|
| one | have-PERF | man | wife | two | have-SUB | bad | Palnal |

| *hilay* | *waši* | *pam-nima-(a)t* | *hilay* | *taxn-ik* | *pam-at* | *Palnal* |
|---|---|---|---|---|---|---|
| wife | old | beat-kill-PERF | wife | other-INST | beat-PERF | Palnal |

| *hilay* | *waši* | *kiš* | *pam-nima-(a)t* | *yil* | *lat* | *himatol* | *u* |
|---|---|---|---|---|---|---|---|
| wife | old | woman | beat-kill-PERF | day | three | four | or |

| *ta-tixi-nt-at* | *ha* | *išat* | *pam-lik-š* | *mon* | *kakáw* | *am-n* | *an* | *ike* |
|---|---|---|---|---|---|---|---|---|
| stand-lie-?-PERF | his | head | beat-mash-ASRT | all | water | drink-SUB | ear | rise |

| *ăn* | *tahe* | *ăn* | *ta-at* |
|---|---|---|---|
| and | come.out | and | stand-PERF |

| *hakit* | *hok-išak* | *hok-yal-ul-ha* | *uxc* | *hišăncet* | *wet* |
|---|---|---|---|---|---|
| 3 | REC-person | REC-marry-3s.PL-NEG | be.able | brother | sister |

| *a* | *hinak* | *kišet* | *ok-yal-ul* | *inak* |
|---|---|---|---|---|
| this | like | sister | come-marry-3s.PL | like |

| *wošiṇa* | *(h)inak-it* | *keš* | *ăn* | *šak-yol* | *teš* | *maṇ* | *šak-maṇ-maṇ-it* |
|---|---|---|---|---|---|---|---|
| naked | like-PERF | woman | and | person-bad | hair | long | PL-long-REDUP-PERF |

| *šak-yol* | *katnaw* | *šak-ha-ha-š* | *hat-yul-š-o* | *noh-ik* | *šak-(h)at-kopš-en* |
|---|---|---|---|---|---|
| person-bad | beard | STG-have-NEG-ASRT | RFL-paint-ASRT-? | red.paint-INST | PL-RFL-white-SUB |

| *hat-mel-š-o* | *hakit* | *išak* | *kaw* | *hat-mel-š-o* | *pum-ul* | *naw* |
|---|---|---|---|---|---|---|
| RFL-black-ASRT-? | their | person | dead | RFL-black-ASRT-? | dance-3s.PL | feather |

| *hakit* | *išat-ip* | *hat-na-i-nst* | *hat-icon* | *hakit* | *šiṇ-š-na-ni* |
|---|---|---|---|---|---|
| 3 | head-LOC | RFL-put-there-IMPF | RFL-little | 3 | rattle-DEF-make-NZR? |

| *tik-pum* | *ne-kin* | *hakit* | *nak-š-na-n(i)* |
|---|---|---|---|
| place-dance | land-LOC | 3 | sound-DEF-make-NZR? |

(The following version of the bracketed section was given by Delilah Moss):

| *Lo* | *yokiti* | *hal* | *šok-koy-it* | *yukit* | *šak-išak* | *ut* | *Lo* |
|------|----------|-------|--------------|---------|------------|------|------|
| Lo | Indian | last | STG-speak-PERF | Indian | PL-person | toward | Lo |

| *hilay* | *yokiti* | *wine-ul-at* | *šak-išak* | *Hiye-kiti* |
|---------|----------|--------------|-----------|-------------|
| wife | Indian | find-3s.PL-PERF | PL-person | east-people |

| *šak-yoṇ-š-ul-at* | *kakáw* | *kaš-kin* | *wine-ul-at* | *hiye-kiti* |
|-------------------|---------|-----------|--------------|-------------|
| PL-call-ASRT-3s.PL-PERF | water | high.water-LOC | find-3s.PL-PERF | east-people |

| *šak-yoṇ-š-ul-at* | *nun-kin* | *to-hul-at* | *kákhaw* | *iye-c-ne* | *ut* |
|-------------------|-----------|-------------|---------|------------|------|
| PL-call-ASRT-3s. PL-PERF | village-LOC | sit-3s.PL-PERF | sun | rise-?-EMPH | toward |

The old Atakapa people lived in villages below this place, on the borders of the lakes. They planted peach trees. They planted fig trees. They planted apple trees and plum trees. They planted pumpkins, berries, corn, and sweet potatoes. They ate of them. They ate deer meat, bear (meat), turtles, turkeys, catfish, perch, the choupique, gaspergou, ducks, geese, pheasants, rabbits, water turkeys, squirrels, muscadines, kantak (China briar), marsh potatoes, water chinkapins, chinkapins, cactus pears, persimmons, small grapes, big grape, the soko, and peanuts. The Indians had many chiefs, one being head of all the rest. [Lo was the last head chief. The wife of Lo was a foundling. Her nation was called Easterners (Eastern Atakapa). They lived in villages over yonder toward the rising sun.] The [Atakapa] prayed standing to One-Above. They danced the sacred dance to One-Above. They also danced the young people's dance and the old people's dance. A man had but one wife, and when a man had two it was a bad thing. Palnal's older wife beat him to death. His other wife beat him. When Palnal's older wife beat him to death his body lay on the ground three or four days with the head mashed in. The water he had drunk ran out of his ears. Relatives were not allowed to marry, since it was as if brothers married sisters and sisters married brothers. They went almost naked. Men and women wore their hair long, and the men did not wear beards. They danced painted with red and white paint and, when relatives had died, with black paint and with feathers on their heads, sounding a rattle at the dancing place.

Delilah Moss's version of the bracketed portion:

[Lo was the last chief of the Indians. Lo's wife was a foundling. Her relatives were Easterners (Eastern Atakapa). They found her during a high tide. They called them Easterners (or Sunrise People) because they lived in villages toward the sunrise.]

From Swanton (1932, 9); reviewed and orthography updated by current author.

## BILOXI

*Ayihįdi Ąyaa Tukpê* 'The Wolf That Became a Man'

Ąyaadi wax ni yuke hą uxte yuke hą thao. Eyą kįhį yuke dixyį Ayihįdi tukanitu tukpe eyąhį. Ekeką tukanituyą wo yihi hą "Tukani ko eyą nąx ką nyidǫhi ąkahi ąkihi na," hetu ką, "Ąkįksu wadi kawak yo mąki nani ąkihi utohohiye daha ąkux nedi," edi. Ekehą petuxte wataye wax ade. Tukanituyą yihi hą wax ade ǫ thao kįx ką ahįske wa ąde tha duxke ąde dehedhą ayukuni ti sahiye ti haitha duti ąde ką, "Kô! Tukani kô tha ayukuni ti sahiye duti hąde. Tukani ko haitha hąde ko kadohǫni hanǫ," kiyetu ką "E'ede čikuyixti," hedi. Etike hąda hi kiye hą kiya waxa ade. Ekehą itha kiyowo o kix ką ahįske wadi, čana duxke nedi. Eke hąde ką čipuxi čupą įxkiyaduye ąde ką etike tha duxke ne ką sidiyą kihanetu. "Xooxoo, tukani ko sidi ǫni wo," kiyetu ką, "Xoxo, xoxo," ex dedi. Ekehą Ayihį įčyoxti dedi. Ekeǫnidi ąyaa wax ni yuke oxtetu dixyį ačka wohe ąde xya, etu xa. Exa.

| ąyaa-di | wax | ni | yuke | hą | uxte | yuke | hą | tha-o | eyą | kįhį |
|---|---|---|---|---|---|---|---|---|---|---|
| man-TOP | hunt | walk | move | SS | 3.make. camp | move | SS | deer-3. shoot | then | 3.return |

| yuke | dixyį | Ayihį-di | tukanitu | tukpe | yąhį | ekeką | tukanitu-yą | wo | yihi | hą |
|---|---|---|---|---|---|---|---|---|---|---|
| move | when | Wolf-TOP | 3.uncle | 3.change | there | DS | 3.uncle-DEF | ? | 3.think | SS |

| tukani | ko | eyą | nąx | ką | nyi-dǫhi | ąkahi | ąkihi | na | he-tu | ką |
|---|---|---|---|---|---|---|---|---|---|---|
| uncle | ? | there | sit | DS | 1.2-see | 1.come | 1.think | DECL.M | 3.say-PL | DS |

| *ąk-įksu* | *wadi* | *kawa-k* | *yo* | *mąki* | *nani* | *ąk-ihi* | *u-toho-hiye* |
|---|---|---|---|---|---|---|---|
| 1-want | very.much | STG-ACC | meat | lie | what | 1-think | LOC-trail-CAUS |

| *daha* | *ąk-ux* | *ne-di* | *e-di* |
|---|---|---|---|
| OBJ.PL | 1.come | stand-TOP | 3.say-TOP |

| *ekehą* | *phet-uxte* | *wata-ye* | *wax* | *ade* |
|---|---|---|---|---|
| SS | fire-camp | watch-CAUS | hunt | 3.go |

| *Tukani-tu-yą* | | *yihi* | *hą* | *wax* | *ade* | *ǫ* |
|---|---|---|---|---|---|---|
| mother's.older.brother-3.POSS-DEF | | 3.think | SS | hunt | go | PST |

| *tha-o* | *kįx* | *ką* | *ahįske* | *wa* | *ąde* | *tha* | *du-xke* | *ąde* | *dehedhą* | *ayukuni* | *ti* |
|---|---|---|---|---|---|---|---|---|---|---|---|
| deer-shoot | come | DS | greedy | very | CONT | deer | INST-skin | CONT | that.done | 3.roast | all |

| *sahi-ye* | *ti* | *hai-tha* | *duti* | *ąde* | *ką* | *kô!* | *Tukani* | *kô* | *tha* | *ayukuni* | *ti* | *sahi-ye* | *duti* | *hąde* |
|---|---|---|---|---|---|---|---|---|---|---|---|---|---|---|
| raw-CAUS | all | blood-all | eat | CONT | DS | oh! | uncle | oh! | deer | roast | all | raw-CAUS | eat | CONT |

| *Tukani* | *ko* | *hai-tha* | *hąde* | *ko* | *ka-dohǫ-ni* | *hanǫ* | *ki-ye-tu* | *ką* |
|---|---|---|---|---|---|---|---|---|
| uncle | ? | blood-all | CONT | ? | NEG-see-NEG | perhaps | DAT-3.say-PL | DS |

| *e'ede* | *čkuye-xti* | *he-di* | *etike* | *hąda* | *hi* | *ki-ye* | *hą* | *kiya* | *waxa* | *ade* |
|---|---|---|---|---|---|---|---|---|---|---|
| this.way | sweet-INTENS | 3.say-TOP | so | CONT | FUT | DAT-say | SS | again | hunt | 3.go |

| *ekehą* | *itha* | *kiyowo* | *o* | *kix* | *ką* | *ahįske* | *wadi* | *čana* | *du-xke* | *ne-di* |
|---|---|---|---|---|---|---|---|---|---|---|
| SS | deer | another | 3.shoot | 3.carry.on.back | DS | greedy | very | again | INST-3.flay | stand-TOP |

| *eke* | *hąde* | *ką* | *čipuxi* | *čupą* | *įxki-yaduye* | *ąde* | *ką* |
|---|---|---|---|---|---|---|---|
| this | CONT | DS | blanket | old | RFL-wrap.around | CONT | DS |

| *etike* | *tha* | *du-xke* | *ne* | *ką* | *sįdi-yą* | *ki-hane-tu* | *xooxoo* |
|---|---|---|---|---|---|---|---|
| so | deer | INST-flay | stand | DS | tail-DEF | DAT-3.find-PL | oh-oh |

| *tukani* | *ko* | *sįdi* | *ǫǫni* | *wo* |
|---|---|---|---|---|
| uncle | ? | tail | use | INTER |

| *ki-ye-tu* | | *ką* | *xoxo-xoxo* | *e* | *x* | *de-di* | *ekehą* | *Ayihį* | *įčyo-xti* | | *de-di* |
|---|---|---|---|---|---|---|---|---|---|---|---|
| DAT-3.say-PL | | DS | oh-oh | 3.SG | SS? | go-TOP | SS | Wolf | old-INTENS | | go-TOP |

| *eke-ǫni-di* | *ąyaa* | *wax* | *ni* | *yuke* | *oxte-tu* | *dixyį* | *ačka* | *wohe* | *ąde* | *xya* |
|---|---|---|---|---|---|---|---|---|---|---|
| this-do-TOP | man | hunt | walk | move | 3.camp-PL | when | near | barking | CONT | always |

| *e-tu* | *xa* | *e-xa* |
|---|---|---|
| 3.say-PL | always | 3.say-always |

Some persons who were going hunting, having camped, shot a deer. As they were returning to camp with the game a wolf who had assumed the form of their mother's brother reached there. They thought that he was indeed their mother's brother, so they said, "As you, our mother's brother, live yonder, we thought that we would be coming to see you." The supposed uncle replied, "I have a strong craving for fresh meat, and thinking that perhaps you had shot some animal and that its body was lying here, I have been following your trail until I got here."

Then the men made him watch the camp while they went hunting again. They thought that he was their mother's brother, and while they were walking along in search of game they shot a deer and returned to camp. The Wolf was very greedy, so after flaying the deer he roasted the meat and was eating some of it while it was raw and bloody all over.

Observing this the men said: "Oh! Mother's brother, oh! He is eating the venison that is still raw, though it has been put on to roast. Perhaps he does not see that it is all bloody." But the wolf-man replied, "This way it is very sweet."

They said to him that he should remain, and they went hunting again. They shot more deer, carried them home on their backs, and found that the wolf-man was very greedy. Again he stood flaying the bodies. While he was doing this, he had an old blanket wrapped around himself, and, as he stood flaying, the men discovered his tail. "Oh! Does mother's brother have a tail?" said they to him. On hearing this, he said, "Oh, oh!" and departed. Behold he departed as a very aged male wolf. Therefore when men go hunting and camp there is usually the barking of wolves nearby, they say. That is all.

From Dorsey and Swanton (1912, 65); reviewed and orthography updated by current author.

## CHICKASAW

Excerpt from *Bakbak Ishkobo' Homma' Poma-piisa-chi'*
'Our Guardian, the Redheaded Woodpecker'

Binni'lika̠ Bakbak Ishkobo' Homma' i̠nokhánglocha, pisaka̠, foshi' alhiha' wakaat aba' pílla ayattook oka'ako̠ aba' waa ishtayatook. Pallamihma̠, oka'at aba' waat shotik onattook shotik ombínni'lika̠ i̠hasimbishat akka' pilachittook 'at ompachichi akka' pila aamintika̠.

| *bínni'* | *li-ka̠* | | *Bakbak* | *ishkobo'* | | *homma-'* | *i̠-nokhánglo-cha* |
|---|---|---|---|---|---|---|---|
| sit.SG-CMP.DS | woodpecker | | head | be.red-NZR | | DAT-pity-CONJ.SS | |

| *pisa-ka̠* | | *foshi'* | *alhiha'* | *wakaa-t* | *aba'* | *pílla* | *aya-ttook* | *oka'-ako̠* |
|---|---|---|---|---|---|---|---|---|
| see-CMP.DS | | bird | PL | fly-PRT | up | just | go-PST.REM | water-CONTR.ACC |

| *abaawaa* | *isht-aya-ttook* | | *Pállammi-hma̠* | | *oka'-at* | | *abaawaa-t* | *shotik* |
|---|---|---|---|---|---|---|---|---|
| rise | INST-go-PST.REM | | be.powerful-RL.DS | | water-NOM | | rise-PRT | sky |

| *ona-ttook* | | *shotik* | *om-bínni'li-ka̠* | | *i̠-hasimbish-at* | *akka'* | *pilachi-ttook* |
|---|---|---|---|---|---|---|---|
| reach-PST.REM | | sky | on-sit.SG-CMP.DS | | DAT-tail-NOM | down | send-PST.REM |

| *at-om-pachi-chi* | | *akka'* | *pila* | *aa-minti-ka̠* |
|---|---|---|---|---|
| this.way-on-splash-CAUS | | down | just | LOC-come-CMP.DS |

It was at the time of the great flood that Aba' Binni'li' [God] took pity on the Red-headed Woodpecker, for he watched as the birds flew higher and higher to avoid the rising water. Finally, the waters nearly reached the sky upon which the birds lit as their last hope. Soon, to their great relief, the flood ceased to rise and began to recede.

SUMMARY

The text goes on to discuss the importance of the Red-headed Woodpecker in Chickasaw culture due to this bird's skill and ability during the flood. They are also associated with victory in war and ball play (stickball).

From Galvan (2011, 33). Reviewed by Pam Munro (pers. comm., 2017).

For the full text, see Galvan (2011), *Chikasha Stories: Volume 1*.

## CHITIMACHA

### How the Indian Came (First Telling)

Wetkš hus na·nča·kamankš wetk hi hokmiʔi. Kun ču·k'š še·nink hup hi ničwiʔi. Wetkš we še·nink hi ničwinkiš weyk hi kišutiʔi. Wetkš hesik'en ču·k'š hi ničwiʔi. Tutk te·tiʔi ha še·niš nenču· ʔati nenšwičuki. Wetkš we siksink ni wopmiʔi, him haksi k'am ne, ʔamʔa·ši sanki. ʔišk ku·ketanki ʔap ni·k'šiki. Ha še·niš hi nenču· ʔati kišučuki. Nenšwi k'ihtkš te kunu k'u wesiksink hiš ni wopmiʔi. Tutk we siksi hi natmaʔi, hi nenšwak'a, tewe·š nenču·ʔatii ha še·niš. He·čpicuk, k'ihčuš, we siksinkhiš hi te·tiʔi. K'ihkite hikin, he·čpi ka·kwakiču·š. Tutk kunu·k'u we siksink kap k'aptk we še·ni waʔank hi pešiʔi. Pa·kinekiču·š, ku·kihi nikinčukink'. Hesik'en ku·ki hi nikintkiču·š, kišučuk. Wetkš we siksink hiš hesi k'en ʔapš heyštiʔi. Wetkš ʔap nenčupi. Weyži·k'š kunuk'u panš pinikankš siksi š k'eti k'ayšnaʔa. Siksi k'ečuš, ʔam keysmanki hihčuyi. weyži·k'š huk'u panš pinikank ha·aktiš ʔap nemnaʔa. Ka·kwaki k'an ʔašt ʔuči·k'š panš ne kap načpikminaʔa, tewe·š weytuk'u we ʔasis hank ʔap nenšwiʔi. ʔuč hiš k'an ka·kwiʔi ʔašt ʔuči·k' panš kap načpikmiʔi. Weytʔšin t'a·tk.

| *we-t-k-š* | | *hus* | *na·nča·-ka-ma-nk-š* |
|---|---|---|---|
| DEM.PRO-RFL-LOC-FOC | | 3 | older.sibling-PL-PLURACT-OBJʔ-FOC |

| *we-t-k* | | *hi* | *hok-m-iʔi* |
|---|---|---|---|
| DEM.PRO-RFL-LOC | | to | leave-PLURACT-3s |

| *kun* | *ču·-k'-š* | *še·-ni-nk* | *hup* | *hi* | *ni-čw-iʔi* |
|---|---|---|---|---|---|
| some | go-PRT-FOC | pond-LOC | to/toward | to | water-move.upright-3s |

*we-t-k-š*               *we*        *še·ni-nk*      *hi*
DEM.PRO-RFL-LOC-FOC    DEM.DET    pond-LOC       to

*ni-čwi-nki-š*                    *wey-k*          *hi*
water-move.upright-LOC.TEMP-FOC    DEM.DET-OBJ?    to

*kišut-iʔi*    *we-t-k-š*                *hesi kʼen*    *ču·kʼ-š*       *hi*
swim-3s      DEM.DET-RFL-LOC-FOC    again        go-PRT-FOC      to

*ni-čw-iʔi*                 *tutk*    *te·tiʔi*    *ha*    *še·niš*      *nenču·*
water-move.upright-3s     then     say-3s     this    pond-LOC     too

*ʔati*                *nenšwicuki*                   *we-t-k-š*
large-AOR.INDF.3s    to.water-out-move-1s.FUT       DEM.PRO-RFL-LOC-FOC

*we*          *siksi-nk*      *ni*      *wop-mi-iʔi*        *him*    *haksikʼam*    *ne*
PERS.PRO    eagle-OBJ     thing    hear-PLURACT-3s    2        young.man     and

*ʔam-ʔ-a·š-I*                  *sa-nki*      *ʔiš-k*    *ku·keta-nki*    *ʔap*
what-do-CONT-AOR.INDF.3s    that-LOC    1-OBJ    water        side-LOC       to.here

*ha*      *še·ni-š*       *hi*      *nenču·*    *ʔati*      *kišu-ču-ki*
this    pond-FOC      there    also      be.large-3s    swim-IRR-1s.AGT

*kišu-čuki*       *ne-n-šw-i*             *giht-k-š*          *te*        *kunukʼu*
swim-1s.FUT     to.water-out-move.     want-PRT-when     INTER     QT
                 upright-NOM

*we*          *siksi-nk*      *hiš*      *ni*      *wop-m-iʔi*        *tutk*
DEM.DET    eagle.OBJ?    actor    thing    hear-PLURACT-3s    then

*we*          *siksi*      *hi*      *nat-m-aʔ-i*                      *hi*
DEM.DET    eagle      to       speak-PLURACT-INDIR-AOR.INDF.3s    to

*ne-n-šwa-kʼa*                       *tewe·š*      *nenču·*    *ʔati-i*
to.water-out-move.upright-1s.want    but-FOC      too        large-AOR.INDF-3s

*ha*      *še·ni-š*       *he·č-pi-čuk*            *kʼih-ču-š*         *we*
this    pond-FOC      clear.away-CAUS-1s.FUT    want-FUT-COND    DEM.DET

| *siksi-nk-hiš* | | *hi* | *te·t-iʔi* | *k'ih-kite* | | *hiki-n* |
|---|---|---|---|---|---|---|
| eagle-OBJ?-actor | | to | say-3s | want-1s.PRT | | 1.be-out |

| *he.č-p-i* | | *ka·kwa-ki-ču··š* | | *tutk* |
|---|---|---|---|---|
| clear.away-CAUS-NOM | | know/can-INACT-3s.FUT-FOC | | then |

| *kunuk'u* | *we* | *siksi-nk* | *kap* | *k'apt-k* | *we* | *še·ni* |
|---|---|---|---|---|---|---|
| it.is.said | DEM.DET | eagle-OBJ? | start/sudden | take-PRT | DEM.DET | pond |

| *waʔa-nk* | *hi* | *peš-iʔi* | *pa·kine-ki-ču··š* | | *ku··ki* |
|---|---|---|---|---|---|
| other-LOC | to | fly-3s | be.tired-inactive-3s.FUT-FOC | | water-LOC |

| *hi* | *ni-kin-čuki-nk'* | | *hesik'en* | *ku··ki* | *hi* |
|---|---|---|---|---|---|
| to | to.water-push-1s.FUT-NEG | | again | water-LOC | to |

| *ni-kint-ki-ču··š* | | *kišu-čuk* | *we-t-k-š* | |
|---|---|---|---|---|
| to.water-push-inactive-3s.FUT-FOC | | swim-1s | FUT | DEM.PRO-RFL-LOC-FOC |

| *wesiksi-nk-hiš* | *hesik'en* | *ʔapš* | *hey* | *št-iʔi* |
|---|---|---|---|---|
| DEM.DET | eagle-OBJ?-actor | again | return | pick.up-3s |

| *we-t-k-š* | | *ʔap* | *ne-n-ču-p-i* |
|---|---|---|---|
| DEM.PRO-RFL-LOC-FOC | | to.here | to.water-move.up-CAUS-AOR.INDF.3s |

| *wey-ʔi··k'-š* | | *kunuk'u* | *panš* | *pini-ka-nk-š* | *siksi-š* |
|---|---|---|---|---|---|
| DEM.DET-do-PRT-FOC | | QT | person | red-PL-LOC-FOC | eagle-FOC |

| *k'et-I* | *k'ay-š-naʔa* | | *siksi* | *k'e-ču··š* | *ʔam* |
|---|---|---|---|---|---|
| kill-NOM | be.NEG-when-3.PL | | eagle | kill-FUT-FOC | some |

| *keys-ma-nk-i* | | *hih-čuy-i* |
|---|---|---|
| be.difficult-PLURACT-LOC-AOR.INDF.3s | | be.neutral-FUT-AOR.INDF.3s |

| *wey-ʔi··k'-š* | | *huk'u* | *panš* | *pini-ka-nk* | *ha··aktiš* |
|---|---|---|---|---|---|
| DEM.DET-do-PRT-FOC | | be | person | red-PL-LOC | this-side |

| *ʔap* | *nem-naʔa* | | *ka·kwa-ki* | *k'an* | *ʔašt* | *ʔuči··k'-š* |
|---|---|---|---|---|---|---|
| to.here | out.of.water-3s.are | | know-INACT | NEG | how | do-PRT-FOC |

| | | | | |
|---|---|---|---|---|
| *panš* | *ne* | *kap* | *načpik-mi-naʔa* | *tewe·-š* |
| person | just | STAT/INCHO | begin-PLURACT-3PL | but-FOC |

| | | | |
|---|---|---|---|
| *wey-t-uk'u* | *we* | *ʔasi-s* | *ha-nk* | *ʔap* |
| DEM.DET-RFL-be | DEM.DET | man-FOC | this-LOC | to.here |

| | | | | |
|---|---|---|---|---|
| *ne-n-šw-iʔi* | *ʔuč-hiš* | *k'an* | *ka·kw-iʔi* | *ʔašt* |
| to.water-out-?-3s | who-actor | NEG | know/can-3s | how |

| | | | |
|---|---|---|---|
| *ʔuči.-k'* | *panš* | *kap* | *načpik-m-iʔi* | *wey-t-ʔš-in* |
| do-PRT | person | STAT | begin-PLURACT-3s | DEM.DET-RFL-CONT-adj |

*t'a·-t-k*
there.PROX-RFL-LOC


He left his brothers. He went and went till he came to the edge of a pond. When he got to the edge of the pond, he swam it. Then he went (on) again and came (again) to the edge (of a body of water).

He said, "This pond is too big for me to cross."

Then an eagle met him. The eagle asked, "You, young man, what are you doing there?"

"I have come to the water's side. This pond is too big for me to swim."

"Do you want to cross it?" that eagle asked.

He told the eagle, "I want to cross it, but this pond is too big."

"I'll help you, if you wish," the eagle said.

"I do wish it, if you can help me."

Then they say the eagle took him up and flew toward the opposite side of the pond. "If I get tired, I'll have to drop you into the water" (said the eagle).

"If you drop me back into the water, I'll swim."

Then the eagle picked him up again. Then he got him across.

They say that is why Indians do not kill eagles. If one kills an eagle, he will get into some trouble. That is how Indians came across (to) this side. I do not know how people started up, but that is how the man came over here. Nobody knows how people started up. That is all now.

Story A.1 as told to Morris Swadesh (1939) by Benjamin Paul. Reviewed by Daniel Hieber (pers. comm., 2013).

**CHOCTAW**

Excerpt from *Nanih Waiya* 'Crooked Hill'

Hopaakikaash hattakat yakni paknaka ilappạ ikshottook. Yakni hochokbi nanih notaka aahofobihọ áashattook yakni chilok aayáashattook ilappạ aachukkoayat hofoobihoosh onattook yakni chilok anọka ilappạ okloshi laawakat haknipat shakchi chohmihoosh áashattook.

| hopaakikaash | hattak-at | yakni | | paknaka | ilappạ | iksho-ttook | |
|---|---|---|---|---|---|---|---|
| for.long | time | man-SUBJ | land | above | this | lack-PST.REM | |

| yakni | hochokbi | nanih | notaka | aa-hofobih-ọ | áasha-ttook | |
|---|---|---|---|---|---|---|
| land | cave | mound | under | LOC-deep-OBJ | live-PST.REM | |

| yakni | chilok | aayáasha-ttook | ilappạ | aachukkoa-yat |
|---|---|---|---|---|
| land | hole | dwell-PST.REM | this | passageway-SUBJ |

| hofoobi-h-oosh | ona-ttook | | yakni | chilok | anọka | ilappạ |
|---|---|---|---|---|---|---|
| deep-TNS-PRT.SS | arrive-PST.REM | land | hole | in | this | |

| okloshi | laawa-kat | haknip-at | shakchi | chohmi-h-oosh | áasha-ttook |
|---|---|---|---|---|---|
| other. people | many-SUBJ | body-SUBJ | crawfish | somewhat-TNS-PRT.SS | live-PST.REM |

Long ago, there were no people upon this earth. They lived in a deep place underneath a hill. They dwelled in this cave; here, a deep passageway came out. Inside this cave lived many tribes; their bodies were in the form of crawfish.

SUMMARY

The story goes on to explain that the various tribes, including Cherokees and Creeks, moved out from the cave (mound) in different directions. Then the Choctaws themselves moved out, building their homes near this mound, which the Choctaws call *Nanih Waiya*.

From Haag and Willis (2001, 178). Reviewed by Aaron Broadwell (pers. comm., 2017).

For the full text, see Haag and Willis (2001), *Choctaw Language and Culture: Chahta anumpa.*

## MOBILIAN TRADE LANGUAGE (MTL)

Ino aya bana. Ino čokha ino falama bana. Ino čokha ino aya bana. Anõte nitak tokolo nahili miša ma anõti no mīti … ino čokha ino aya taha. Ino falama … Ino falama. Ino čokha ino mīti … Ino yimikšo … Yako hatak katima lap mīti? Tamaha olčifo ino hakalo bana. [unintelligible] ayomi. Yako hatak čokmakšo. Yako hatak paki lap mīti, ino yokpa fihna. Yako hatak ačokma fihna. Katima oya lap nowa bana, lap aya. Ino čokha ino aya bana. Ino aya bana. Ino nowakšo … Ino nowakšo. Ino čokha ino iyakšo. [unintelligible] lap aya bana [unintelligible]. Lap aya [unintelligible] lap kaniya. Katima õya ino nowa bana. Ino nowa bana. Ino iyi čokmakšo. Katima ino nowakšo fihna. Ino noškobo õya čokmakšo, čokmakšo, čokmakšo. Yako hatak lap kaniya falama lap mīti?

| *ino* | *aya* | *bana* | *ino* | *čokha* | *ino* | *falama* | *bana* |
|-------|-------|--------|-------|---------|-------|----------|--------|
| I | go | want | my | house | I | return | want |

| *ino* | *čokha* | *ino* | *aya* | *bana* | *anõte* | *nitak* | *tokolo* | *nahili* |
|-------|---------|-------|-------|--------|---------|---------|----------|----------|
| my | house | I | go | want | again | day | two | tomorrow |

| *miša* | *ma* | *anõte* | *no* | *mīti* | *ino* | *čokha* | *ino* | *aya* | *taha* |
|--------|------|---------|------|--------|-------|---------|-------|-------|--------|
| after | there | again | I | come | my | house | I | go | PST |

| *ino* | *falama* | *ino* | *falama* | *ino* | *čokha* | *ino* | *mīti* |
|-------|----------|-------|----------|-------|---------|-------|--------|
| I | return | I | return | my | house | I | come |

| *ino* | *yimi-kšo* | *yako* | *hatak* | *katima* | *lap* | *mīti* |
|-------|------------|--------|---------|----------|-------|--------|
| I | believe-NEG | this | man | where | he | come |

| *tamaha* | *olčifo* | *ino* | *hakalo* | *bana* | *[unintelligible]* | *ayomi* |
|----------|----------|-------|----------|--------|--------------------|---------|
| town | name | I | hear | want | [unintelligible] | marriage |

| *yako* | *hatak* | *čokma-kšo* | *yako* | *hatak* | *paki* | *lap* | *mīti* | *ino* | *yokpa* | *fihna* |
|--------|---------|-------------|--------|---------|--------|-------|--------|-------|---------|---------|
| this | man | good-NEG | this | man | afar | he | come | I | glad | very |

| *yako* | *hatak* | *ačokma* | *fihna* | *katima* | *oya* | *lap* | *nowa* | *bana* | *lap* | *aya* |
|--------|---------|----------|---------|----------|-------|-------|--------|--------|-------|-------|
| this | man | good | very | where | all.over | he | travel | want | he | go |

| *ino* | *čokha* | *ino* | *aya* | *bana* | *ino* | *aya* | *bana* |
|-------|---------|-------|-------|--------|-------|-------|--------|
| my | house | I | go | want | I | go | want |

| *ino* | *nowa-kšo* | *ino* | *nowa-kšo* | *ino* | *čokha* | *ino* | *aya-kšo* |
|-------|------------|-------|------------|-------|---------|-------|----------|
| I | travel-NEG | I | travel-NEG | my | house | I | go-NEG |

| [unintelligible] | *lap* | *aya* | *bana* | [unintelligible] | *lap* | *aya* | [unintelligible] |
|------------------|-------|-------|--------|------------------|-------|-------|------------------|
| [unintelligible] | she | go | want | [unintelligible] | she | go | [unintelligible] |

| *lap* | *kaniya* | *katima* | *ōya* | *ino* | *nowa* | *bana* | *ino* | *nowa* | *bana* |
|-------|----------|----------|-------|-------|--------|--------|-------|--------|--------|
| she | lost | anywhere | all | I | walk | want | I | travel | want |

| *ino* | *iyi* | *čokma-kšo* | *katima* | *ino* | *nowa-kšo* | *fihna* |
|-------|-------|-------------|---------|-------|------------|---------|
| my | foot/feet | good-NEG | anywhere | I | travel-NEG | really |

| *ino* | *noškobo* | *ōya* | *čokma-kšo* | *čokma-kšo* | *čokma-kšo* |
|-------|-----------|-------|-------------|-------------|-------------|
| my | head | all.over | good-NEG | good-NEG | good-NEG |

| *yako* | *hatak* | *lap* | *kaniya* | *falama* | *lap* | *mīti* |
|--------|---------|-------|----------|----------|-------|--------|
| this | man | he | leave | back | he | come |

I want to go. I want to return to my home. I want to go to my house. Two days after tomorrow, I come back. After going (to my) home, I return … I return. I come to my house … I don't believe … Where does this man come from? I want to hear the name of (his) town.… married/marriage … This person is bad. I am very glad that this man (from) afar comes (here). This man is very good. He goes wherever he wants to travel. I want to go (to my) home. I want to go. I don't travel. I don't travel. I don't go (to my) home. She wants to go … Anywhere she goes … she gets lost. I want to walk all over. I want to walk. My feet are bad. I do not really travel anywhere. My head all over is bad, bad, bad. Does this man, (once) gone, come back?

From Drechsel (1997, 141–43), as recorded by Crawford (ca. 1978) from his Choctaw consultant Arzelie Langley. Text is retranscribed by current author.

## NATCHEZ

*Hakutama·L* 'Corn Woman' (or, 'The Origin of Corn')

Hakutama·L seNcisu·ne. Hohsaluh ʔawiti· sampitisisu·ne. Hakuya sintokosine ast ʔamasanaL hakuʔe·t lesankik ma·k ʔe·tkasaNcine. ʔasta coʔotkop kawete·tsanaL pato·hal hani·hi·sanohsik santanihkusik sampiksisu·ne. Ma·hakuʔe·tak ayį. Kosekatih sana·ne. Ma·k ʔe·tkasancine. Hakuya popkehaʔa kawete·tsanaL ko·s tehneskuk ta·k kakatehnaL ma·kup kawete·tnalą. Ka·witʔe·tkaʔa·cine ki·sa·tenlu·k ma·ʔeLatanilą. Ka·hisi·tanu hakuya ʔe·tokosine ma·ki·sitenlų. Hisantanu·k sampiksisu·ne. Ale hakuya sitokosik sitancokok ma·kup ʔayʔu·ha·t hisitansuk kinsitompaY wi·kaha·p ʔunuhsak kasituksik ʔale·na ʔasta ʔamasaL suhtik kaʔeLsitaniL kasituksine. Hakuʔe·tak ʔe·tkasucik kapalasilu·ne. KakwaLsite·skuk kaksite·skusikka·ʔeL sitanilą. Tuku·tuku·sihsaL su·yak meʔe·meʔe·siskuk ʔasta ʔayatsu·ne. Nukcaka·ksukuk hakuya ʔasta ka·coʔotsala ma·ksaL ʔast wi·ta·ha hamą. ʔayatsu·ne. Nukcaka·ksukuk popkeha ʔasta ka·coʔotsala maksaL ʔeLsitaniL ka·kwaLsite·skų. Ma·nanê·ta·ciknelu·k temi·hi·nenlu·k nokma·ʔį. Cikilu·k kawete·talą ka·witan kinʔiskwa·t ma·ʔatani. Ka·hisi·tane pato·halą ʔoysu·sine hahku·s ʔiteni·kusa·t ka·sų. Ma·kte ʔeLsitanila ka·sicokǫ. Ma·kup henehpictankik ya·na· ta·pa·taniL ʔe·ta le·pa·tanilą. Ka·hisi·pupu·sį. Ma·kup a·yik ka·ʔe·ta coLiktiʔi·yak hiyapą. Kineceleʔa·yine ma·na kwe·pa·tanu·sik toMsi·Lpa·taniL kinhasku·s pantani·ʔą. ʔaka·hnic suphesku·s pantaniʔą. Ma·kte ta·sitaniL ka·le·sitanilą. ʔAme·kasu·ne ka·kinʔecelasų ma·na kwe·santanu·sik sampiksisu·ne. Kwe·santanu·k lewesantani·ne. Ca·skehą. ʔoksantaniL sanaksine. Kasantompisahkune. Ca·skehą. Wiha·tak ʔoksankik hackaNc kakwe·he·nohcį. Hisi·tanu·k ki·ssitenlu·k ʔeLsitanilne. Ca·skeha·na·N. Kwe·sitanu·k kasupiksik ʔeLsitaniL necsitaniL ca·skehą. Ka·ci·sitankiN.

| | |
|---|---|
| hakutama·L | seNcisu·ne |
| haku-tama·L-ø | se-n-ci-su·-ne |
| corn-woman-ABS | QT-IMPF-sit.SG-NEW.TOP |

*hohsaluh*     *ʔawiti•*     *sampitisisu•ne*
*hohsal-uh*     *ʔawiti•Ø*     *sa-n-piti-Ø-si-su••ne*
girl-DIM     two     QT-IMPF-go.about-ABS-DAT-NEW.TOP-SUB

*hakuya*     *sintokosine*     *ast*
*haku-ya-Ø*     *si-n-toko-Ø-si-ne*     *ast-Ø*
corn-DEF-ABS     QT-IMPF-deplete-DAT-DAT-SUB     fanning.basket-ABS

*ʔamasanaL*     *hakuʔe•t*     *lesankik*     *ma•k*     *ʔe•tkasaNcine*
*ʔama-sa-n-al-k*     *haku-ʔe•t*     *le-sa-n-ki-k*     *ma•k*     *ʔe•tka-sa-n-ci-ne*
carry-QT-IMPF-     corn-house     sit-QT-IMPF-     there     enter-QT-IMPF-AUX-DS
AUX-CONN          AUX-CONN

*ʔasta*     *coʔotkop*     *kawete•tsanaL*     *pato•hal*
*ʔast-a-Ø*     *coʔotkop*     *ka-wete•t-sa-n-al-k*     *pato•hal-Ø*
fanning.basket-DEF-ABS     full     LOC-take.out-QT-IMPF-     sofkee-ABS
                                    AUX-CONN

*hani•hi•sanohsik*     *santanihkusik*     *sampiksisu•ne*
*hani•hi••sa-n-oh-si-k*     *sa-n-tani-hkusi-k*     *sa-m-piksi-su••ne*
make.SG.SUBJ.DU.OBJ-     QT-IMPF-DU-drink-CONN     QT-IMPF-stay.DU-NEW.TOP-SUB
QT-IMPF-?-?-CONN

*ma•*     *hakuʔe•tak*     *ayį*     *kosekatih*     *sana•ne*
*ma•*     *haku-ʔe•t-a-k*     *ay-i-n*     *kosekatih*     *sa-n-a•-ne*
that     corn-house-DEF-LOC     think-3PST-PHR.TRM     empty     QT-IMPF-be.AOR-DS

*ma•k*     *ʔe•tkasancine*     *hakuya*     *popkehaʔa*
*ma•k*     *ʔe•tka-s-an-ci-ne*     *haku-ya*     *popkeh-a-ʔa*
there     enter-QT-IMPF-AUX-SUB     corn-DEF     bean-DEF-COM

*kawete•tsanaL*     *ko•s*     *tehneskuk*     *ta•k*
*ka-wete•t-sa-n-al-k*     *ko•s*     *teh-ne-skʷ-k*     *ta•k*
PST-take.out-QT-IMPF-AUX-CONN     what     get-3-CONN     where

*kakatehnaL*     *ma•kup*     *kawete•tnalą*
*kaka-teh-n-al-k*     *ma•kup*     *ka-wete•t-na-la-n*
PVB-take-3-AUX-CONN     well.then     PST-bring.out-3-AUX-PHR.TRM

ka•wit          ʔe•tkaʔa•cine            ki•sa•tenlu•k          ma•ʔeLatanilą
ka•-wit         ʔe•tka-ʔa•-ci-ne         ki•s-a-teni-lu•-k      ma•-ʔeL-a-tani-la-n
now             enter-3OPT-AUX-SUB       sneak.up-1OPT-DU-      FUT-see-1OPT-DU-AUX-
                                         AUX-CONN              PHR.TRM

ka•hisi•tanu          hakuya          ʔe•tokosine          ma•ki•sitenlą
ka-hi-si-tani-w       haku-ya-Ø       ʔe•toko-si-ne        ma•-ki•s-i-teni-lu-n
PST-say-QT-DU-AUX     corn-DEF-ABS    3OPT-deplete-DAT-SUB FUT-sneak.up-3PST-
                                                           DU-AUX-PHR.TRM

hisantanu•k              sampiksisu•ne              ale        hakuya
hi-sa-n-tani-w-k         sa-n-piksi-su-ne           ʔale       haku-ya-Ø
say-QT-IMPF-DU-AUX-CONN  QT-IMPF-stay-NEW.TOP-SUB   already    corn-DEF-ABS

sitokosik                sitancokok              ma•kup      ʔayʔu•ha•t
si-toko-si-k             si-tani-cokʷ-k          ma•kup      ʔay-ʔi-w-ha•t
QT-deplete-DAT-CONN      QT-DU-know-CONN          well.then   think-PRT-AUX-NEG

hisitansuk                  kinsitompaY            wi•kaha•p      ʔunuhsak
hisi-tani-si-w-k            kin-si-tompay-k        wi•kaha•pʔ     unuhs-a-k
pay.attention-DU-QT-AUX-CONN  STG-QT-play-CONN    yard-edge      DEF-LOC

kasituksik            ʔale•na   ʔasta          ʔamasaL
ka-si-tuksi-k         ʔale•na   ʔast-a-Ø       ʔama-si-al-k
LOC-QT-sit.DU-CONN    now       fan-DEF-ABS    carry-QT-AUX-CONN

suhtik          kaʔeLsitaniL            kasituksine       hakuʔe•tak
su-hti-k        ka-ʔeL-si-tani-l-k      ka-si-tuksi-ne    haku-ʔe•t-a-k
QT-go.SG-CONN   PST-see-DAT-DU-AUX-CONN PST-QT-sit-SUB    corn-house-DEF-LOC

ʔe•tkasucik          kapalasilu•ne          kakwaL-site•skuk
ʔe•tka-su-ci-k       ka-pala-si-lu•-ne      ka-kwaL-si-te•-skw-k
enter-QT-AUX-CONN    LOC-shut-QT-AUX-SUB    LOC-run-QT-DU-AUX-CONN

kaksite•skusik          ka•ʔeLsitanilą          tuku•tuku•sihsaL
kak-si-te•skʷ-Ø-si-k    ka•-ʔeL-si-tani-la-n    tuku•tuku•-si-hsal-k
stick.head.in-QT-AUX-   PST-see-DAT-DU-AUX-     rub.REDUP-QT-AUX-CONN
3DAT-DAT-CONN           PHR.TRM

*su•yak*  *meʔe•meʔe•siskuk*  *ʔasta*  *ʔayatsu•ne*
*su••ya-k*  *meʔemeʔe••si-sk*ʷ*-k*  *ʔast-a-Ø*  *ʔayat-su-••-ne*
breast-DEF-LOC  press-QT-AUX-CONN  fanning.basket-DEF-ABS  stand.astraddle-QT-be-SUB

*nukcaka•ksukuk*  *hakuya*  *ʔasta*  *ka•coʔotsala*
*nuk-caka•k-su-k*ʷ*-k*  *haku-ya*  *ʔast-a-Ø*  *ka••coʔot-sa-la*
PVB-rattle-QT-AUX-CONN  corn-DEF  fan-DEF-ABS  PST-full-QT-AUX

*ma•ksaL*  *ʔast*  *wi•ta•ha*  *hamaN*  *ʔayatsu•ne*
*ma•ksaL*  *ʔast-Ø*  *wi•ta•ha*  *hamaN*  *ʔayat-su-••-ne*
fanning.basket-ABS  another  again    stand.astraddle-QT-be-SUB

*nukcaka•ksukuk*  *popkeha*  *ʔasta*  *ka•coʔotsala*
*nuk-caka•k-su-kw-k*  *popkeh-a*  *ʔast-a-Ø*  *ka••coʔot-sa-la*
PVB-rattle-QT-AUX-CONN  bean-DEF  fan-DEF-ABS  PST-full-QT-AUX

*maksaL*  *ʔeLsitaniL*  *ka•kwaL-site•skụ*  *ma•nanê•ta•*
*ma•ksaL*  *ʔeL-si-tani-l-k*  *ka••kwaL-si-te••-sk*ʷ*-n*  *ma••nane••-ta*
fanning.basket-ABS  see-QT-DU-AUX-CONN  PST-run-QT-DU-AUX-PHR.TRM  ?

*ciknelu•k*  *temi•hi•ne-nlu•k*  *nokma•ʔiN*  *cikilu•k*
*cik-ne-lu••-k*  *temi•hi•-ne-n-lu••-k*  *nok-ma-ʔi-n*  *cik-i-lu••-k*
defecate-3-AUX-CONN  feed.SG.SUBJ.OBJ.DU-3-1OBJ-AUX-CONN  PVB-that-?  defecate-3-AUX-CONN

*kawete•talaN*  *ka•witan*  *kinʔiskwa•t*  *ma•ʔatani*
*ka-wete•t-ʔa-la-n*  *ka•witan*  *kin-ʔi-sk*ʷ*-a•t*  *ma••ʔa-tani-••*
PST-take.out-COM-AUX-PHR.TRM  now  STG-1-eat-NEG  PVB-1OPT-DU-be

*ka•hisi•tane*  *pato•halaN*  *ʔoysu•sine*  *hahku•s*
*ka••hi-si••-tani*  *pato•hal-a-n*  *ʔoy-su••-si-ne*  *hahku•s*
PST-say-QT-DU  sofkee-DEF-ABS  cook-NEW.TOP-QT-SUB  drink

*ʔiteni•kusa•t*  *ka•suN*  *ma•kte*  *ʔeLsitanila*  *ka•sicokọ*
*ʔi-teni••-hkus-a•t*  *ka••su••-n*  *ma•kte*  *ʔeL-si-tani-la*  *ka••-si-cok*ʷ*-n*
3PST-DU-want-NEG  PST-QT-be-PHR.TRM  ?  see-QT-DU-AUX  PST-QT-find.out-PHR.TRM

*ma•kup*      *henehpictankik*      *ya•na•*      *ta•pa•taniL*
*ma•kup*      *henehpic-tan-ki-k*      *ya•na•*      *ta-pa•-tani-l-k*
well.then      ?-DU-AUX-CONN      EMPH      kill-2OPT-DU-AUX-CONN

*ʔe•ta*      *le•pa•tanilą*      *ka•hisi•pupu•sị*      *ma•kup*      *a•yik*
*ʔe•t-a-Ø*      *le•-pa•-tani-la-n*      *ka•-hi-si•-pupu•-si-n*      *ma•kup*      *a•-yi-k*
house-DEF-ABS      burn-2OPT-DU-AUX-PHR.TRM      PST-say-QT-PL.OBJ-DAT-PHR.TRM      well.then      be.AOR-IRR-CONN

*ka•*      *ʔe•ta*      *coLiktiʔi•yak*      *hiyapą*      *kineceleʔa•yine*
*ka•*      *ʔe•t-a*      *colikti-ʔi•-ya-k*      *hi-ya-pa•-n*      *kin-ecele-ʔa•-yi-ne*
this      house-DEF      fire-DECS-DEF-LOC      say-1PT-2OPT-PHR.TRM      STG-grow-3OPT-IRR-SUB

*ma•na*      *kwe•pa•tanu•sik*      *toMsi•Lpa•taniL*      *kinhasku•s*
*ma•na-Ø*      *kwe•-pa•-tani-w-si-k*      *toMsi•L-pa•-tani-l-k*      *kin-ha-skʷ-s*
that-ABS      dig-2OPT-DU-AUX-QT-CONN      raise-2OPT-DU-AUX-CONN      STG-INDF-eat-INF

*pantani•ʔą*      *ʔaka•hnic*      *suphesku•s*      *pantaniʔaN*
*pan-tani•-ʔa-n*      *ʔaka•-hn-ic*      *sup-hesku-ʔis*      *pan-tani•-ʔa-n*
2OPT-DU-be-PHR.TRM      you-ERG      be.busy      2OPT-DU-be-PHR.TRM

*ma•kte*      *ta•sitaniL*      *ka•le•sitanilą*      *ʔame•kasu•ne*      *ka•kinʔecelasuN*
*ma•kte*      *ta-si-tani-il-k*      *ka•-le•-si-tani-la-n*      *ʔame•-ka-si-•-ne*      *ka-kin-ʔecele-a-si-w-n*
?      kill-QT-DU-AUX-CONN      PST-burn-QT-DU-AUX-PHR.TRM      spring-QT-AUX-SUB      PST-STG-grow-?-QT-AUX-PHR.TRM

*ma•na*      *kwe•santanu•sik*      *sampiksisu•ne*
*ma•na-Ø*      *kwe•-sa-n-tani-w-si-k*      *sa-n-piksi-su•-ne*
that.one-ABS      dig-QT-IMPF-DU-AUX-DAT-CONN      QT-IMPF-sit-NEW.TOP-SUB

*kwe•santanu•k*      *lewesantani•ne*      *ca•skehą*      *ʔoksantaniL*
*kwe•-sa-n-tani-w-k*      *lewe-sa-n-tani-•-ne*      *ca•-skeh-a-n*      *ʔok-sa-n-tani-l-k*
dig-QT-IMPF-DU-AUX-CONN      stop-QT-IMPF-DU-AUX-SUB      hoe-DEF-ABS      stick.up-QT-IMPF-DU-AUX-CONN

*sanaksine*      *kasantompisahkune*      *ca•skehą*      *wiha•tak*
*sa-n-ak-si-ne*      *ka-sa-n-tompi-sahku-ne*      *ca•-skeh-a-n*      *wiha•tak*

| QT-IMPF-?-?-SUB | LOC-QT-DU-arrive-SUB | hoe-DEF-ABS | another |
|---|---|---|---|
| *ʔoksankik* | *hackaNc* | *kakwe•he•nohcį* | *hisi•tanu•k* |
| *ʔok-sa-n-ki-k* | *hackan•c* | *ka-kʷ•he•-na-w-t-si-n* | *hi-si•-tani-w-k* |
| stick.up-QT-IMPF-AUX-CONN | who-ERG | LOC-hoe-3-AUX-1DAT-DAT-Q | say-QT-DU-AUX-CONN |

| *ki•ssitenlu•k* | | *ʔeLsitanilne* | *ca•skeha•na•N* |
|---|---|---|---|
| *ki•s-si-ten-lu-k* | | *ʔeL-si-tani-l-ne* | *ca•skeh-a•na••-N* |
| sneak.up.on-QT-DU-AUX-CONN | | see-QT-DU-AUX-SUB | hoe-DEF-nothing.but |

| *kwe•sitanu•k* | *kasupiksik* | *ʔeLsitaniL* | *necsitaniL* |
|---|---|---|---|
| *kwe•-si-tani-w-k* | *ka-su-piksi-k* | *ʔeL-si-tani-l-k* | *nec-si-tani-l-k* |
| dig-QT-DU-AUX-CONN | PST-QT-sit.DU-CONN | see-QT-DU-AUX-CONN | laugh-QT-DU-AUX-CONN |

| *ca•skehą* | *ka•ci•sitankiN* |
|---|---|
| *caskeh-a-n* | *ka•-ci•-si-tan-ki-n* |
| hoe-DEF-ABS | PST-fall-QT-DU-AUX-PHR.TRM |

Now Corn Woman used to live somewhere, so they say, and now she used to go about with two little girls. When the corn ran out on them, Corn Woman would carry the fanning basket in her arms into the corncrib and sit there. Whenever she went in (to the crib) she customarily brought from there a full fanning basket of corn and she used to make sofkee (corn drink) for the two of them, which the two of them used to drink. Yet, they saw that there was nothing in that corncrib. They wondered, if she was taking out corn and beans to eat, where was she getting it? They decided that when she goes back into the crib, they will sneak up on her and see what she does. They said, "When she runs out, we'll sneak up on her and see what she does." They were sitting at the edge of the yard playing when she (Corn Woman) carried the fan into the crib. They were sitting outside when she went into the corncrib and shut the door. They ran toward the crib and stuck their heads in on her. They saw her rubbing herself repeatedly, pressing herself against the fan. She straddled the fan. There was a rustling sound as the corn fan filled up. She did the same with another fan. Again she straddled it and there was a rustling sound as the beans filled the fanning basket. They watched this. Then they ran off. "That one! I declare!" The corn and beans she was feeding them she was defecating out of her into the fans that she brought out. "Now we'll not eat any sofkee (with the corn) she makes." They no longer wanted to drink it after they found out she'd fooled them. "Okay, then you kill me, and you burn the house down. If anything grows on that spot, you must cultivate it. What you raise your-selves will be yours to eat." They killed her and burned her house down. When it was spring, something grew. They stayed there and hoed the spot. They were hoeing, but then they stopped. The hoes were sticking up. They went off to play. When they came back, another hoe would be sticking up. "Who is it that is helping us to hoe?" they said. They snuck up on the spot but they saw only hoes. They stayed there and kept hoeing (the land). They laughed at them (the hoes). Then the hoes fell to the ground.

From Haas's unpublished notes, as told to her by Watt Sam (book 3, 19–29). Glossed and edited with the help of Geoffrey Kimball (pers. comm., 2014).

## TUNICA

### The Origin of the Bean

Tanisaratekahaku 'ohoyahč'eman 'u'nihkeni hinyatihč, tayanera rohpant sehihtepan, yuk'unahč, simink'unani. Tanahta haluht, hahčoni. Hinya-tihč tasatosiniman, tayanera kičun, hopisitihč tahahču hayiht, yakaši-misiteni. Hinyatihč tanisarahč teheyak'oman, tasatosiniman, tapiwan hahk'unani. Hinyatihč 'ašu sahkun, yak'unahč, tasatosiniman hopisitihč tanahta rohpan šimina'arani, hatikan. Tanisarahč, sahkun, 'uhtakan'akihč uhtap'ekeni. Hinyatihč tanahta haihtan, lot'uwanani. Hinyatihč tawišihč 'asani. Hinyatihč tanahta hayiht 'unašahč, tawisihč 'unrikitap'ekeni. Hin-yatihč tokatekahaku 'uwita wič'awani, tanahta hayiht. Hinyatihč tanisa-rahč 'ak'am'ekeni. Hinyatihč tokatekahaku, 'uriš 'uhtam'unani. Hinyatihč sehihtepan, ohoyahč yukatihpowan yakoni. Hinyatihč tihpowistuk'ohoni. Hinyatihč 'uris mar'uwani. Hinya'tihč sehi sahkun, 'uspit'okeni. Hin-yatihč mahon 'unani, 'uris. 'Ašu sahkun, yakateni. Šihpartosu 'ilin, čuyak'akeni. Hinyatihč 'uyanalepihk'atani. 'Uwirahk'atani. Kana lapun, sakuwitin, 'unikateni. 'Aha. Kanahkup'aha, nikoni. Toškaehkint'eku tayiwo hayiht 'uhkaliwit'ahč, lapuhč, 'unikateni. Hinyatihč toškacehkinik 'uhkalin'ukeni, tayi hayiht. Hinyatihč tašihpartosu sahkun, 'uwahkatihč toškačehkint'e kič 'uhtoh'okeni. Hinyatihč 'uyanakateni. Toškačehkiniku, lapuyan, 'uhpohtawit'ahč, samat'ihč, lapuya sak'ik'ahča, 'unikateni. 'Uwet šim 'uwana, tihčet, šimi tiwan'ahani. 'Uyanalepihk'atani. 'Iman tašihparik 'uhtapanč ašu manku piratihč 'usakukani, nikateni. Hinyatihč tiwi'utahani. Hinyatihč hat'ena, 'uyanakateni. 'Iman tašihparik 'uhtapanč, tahč'a manku pirahtihč, 'usakukani, nikateni. Hinyatihč tašihpartosuku, wiyuw'anč 'uhtap'ik'ihč tahč'a manku piratihč, tašihparik 'usak'ik'ahča, 'unikateni. Hinyatihč 'uyanalepihot'otahč, hat'ena, mar'am'ekeni, tayanera kičun.

| *ta-nisaratekaha-ku* | *'ohoyahč-'eman* | *'u'nihk-eni* |
|---|---|---|
| DEF-orphan-M.SUF | his.sister-COM | DU.used.to.be-QT |

| *hinyatihč* | *ta-yanera* | *rohpant* |
|---|---|---|
| now | DEF-ocean | near |

| *sehi-htepan* | *yuk'una-hč* | *šimi-hk'un-ani* |
|---|---|---|
| morning-every | DU.arrive-SUB | play-3.HAB-QT |

| *ta-nahta* | *haluht* | *hahč-oni* | *hinyatihč* |
|---|---|---|---|
| DEF-bank | under | sand-QT | now |

| *ta-sato-sinima-n* | *ta-yanera* | *kičun* | *hopisiti-hč* |
|---|---|---|---|
| DEF-dog-DIM-? | DEF-ocean | from | emerge-SUB |

| *ta-hahču* | *hayiht* | *yaka-šimi-sit-eni* | *hinyatihč* |
|---|---|---|---|
| DEF-sand | LOC | come-play-HAB-QT | now |

| *ta-nisara-hč* | *teheyak-'oma-n* | *ta-sato-sinima-n* |
|---|---|---|
| DEF-girl-F.SUF | her.brother-COM-? | DEF-dog-DIM-? |

| *tapiwan* | *ya-hk'un-ani* | *hinyatihč* | *'ašu* | *sahkun* |
|---|---|---|---|---|
| in.order.to.catch | do-HAB-QT | now | day | one |

| *ya-k'una-hč* | *ta-sato-sinima-n* | *hopisiti-hč* | *ta-nahta* | *rohpan* |
|---|---|---|---|---|
| do-HAB-SUB | DEF-dog-DIM-? | emerge-SUB | DEF-bank | near |

| *šimi-na'ar-ani* | *hatikan* | *ta-nisara-hč* | *sahkun* |
|---|---|---|---|

| play-3?-QT | | again | DEF-girl-F.SUF | one |
|---|---|---|---|---|
| *'uh-taka-n-'aki-hč* | | *uhtap'ek-eni* | *hinyatihč* | *ta-nahta* |
| 3-chase-CAUS-SEM-SUB | | 3-catch-3-QT | now | DEF-bank |

| *hayihtan* | *lot-'uwan-ani* | *hinyatihč* | *ta-wiši-hč* |
|---|---|---|---|
| LOC | run-SEM-QT | now | DEF-water-F.SUF |

| *'as-ani* | *hinyatihč* | *ta-nahta* | *hayiht* | *'unaša-hč* | *ta-wiši-hč* |
|---|---|---|---|---|---|
| was.coming-QT | now | DEF-bank | LOC | DU.come-SUB | DEF-water-F.SUF |

| *'un-riki-tap-'ek-eni* | *hinyatihč* | *t-okatekaha-ku* | *'u-wita* | |
|---|---|---|---|---|
| 3M-overtake-catch-SEM-QT | now | DEF- | orphan-M.SUF | 3M-only |

| *wič-'aw-ani* | *ta-nahta* | *hayiht* | *hinyatihč* | *ta-nisara-hč* |
|---|---|---|---|---|
| climb-SEM-QT | DEF-bank | LOC | now | DEF-girl-F.SUF |

| *'ak-'am-'ek-eni* | *hinyatihč* | *t-okatekaha-ku* | *'u-ri-š* |
|---|---|---|---|
| enter-disappear-SEM-QT | now | DEF-orphan-M.SUF | 3M-house-LOC |

| *'am'-uhk-'eni* | *hinyatihč* | *'u-ki-ku* | *'u-ri-š* |
|---|---|---|---|
| disappear-3-QT | now | 3M-maternal.uncle-M.SUF | 3M-house-LOC |

| *'uh-tam-'un-ani* | *hinyatihč* | *sehi-htepan* | *ohoyahč* | *yuka-tih-po-wan* |
|---|---|---|---|---|
| 3M-live.with-3-QT | now | morning-every | his.sister | arrive-3-see-PURP |

| *ya-k-'oni* | *hinyatihč* | *tih-powi-stuk'oh-oni* |
|---|---|---|
| do-3HAB-QT | now | 3.find-could.not-QT |

| *hinyatihč* | *'u-ri-š* | *mar-'uw-ani* | *hinya'tihč* | *sehi* | *sahkun* |
|---|---|---|---|---|---|
| now | 3M-house-LOC | return-3M-QT | now | morning | one |

| *'u-špit'o-k-eni* | *hinyatihč* | *mahon* | *'un-ani* | *u-ri-š* | *ašu* |
|---|---|---|---|---|---|
| 3M-forget-3F-QT | now | just | sit-QT | 3M-house-LOC | day |

| *sahkun* | *yak-at-eni* | *šihpar-tosu* | *'ilin* | *ču-yak'a-k-eni* |
|---|---|---|---|---|
| one | return-3F-QT | bean-seed | two | take-come-3F-QT |

| *hinyatihč* | *'u-yana-lepi-hk-'at-ani* | | *'u-wira-hk-'at-ani* |
|---|---|---|---|

now       3M-speak-ask-3 F.HAB-3 F.CAUS-QT       3M-ask-3 F.HAB-3 F.CAUS-QT

| *kana* | *lapun* | *saku-witi-n* | | *'u-ni-kat-eni* | *'aha* |
|---|---|---|---|---|---|
| anything | good | eat-2M.HAB-INTER | | 3M-say-3 F.HAB-QT | no |

| *kanahkup'aha* | *ni-k-oni* | *t-oškačehkin-t'e-ku* | *t-ayiwo* |
|---|---|---|---|
| nothing | say-?-QT | DEF-kettle-big-M.SUF | DEF-fire |

| *hayiht* | *'uh-kali-wit'a-hč* | *lapu-hč* | *'u-ni-kat-eni* | *hinyatihč* |
|---|---|---|---|---|
| LOC | 3M-stand-2M.CAUS-SUB | good-SUB? | 3M-say-3 F.HAB-QT | now |

| *t-oškacehkini-k* | *'uh-kali-n'u-k-eni* | *t-ayi* | *hayiht* | *hinyatihč* |
|---|---|---|---|---|
| DEF-kettle-M.SUF | 3M-stand-CAUS-3M-QT | DEF-fire | LOC | now |

| *ta-šihpar-tosu* | *sahkun* | *'u-wahka-ti-hč* | *t-oškačehkin-t'e* | *kič* |
|---|---|---|---|---|
| DEF-bean-seed | one | 3M-break-3F-SUB | DEF-kettle-big | LOC |

| *'uh-toh'o-k-eni* | *hinyatihč* | *'u-yana-kat-eni* | *t-oškačehkini-ku* |
|---|---|---|---|
| 3M-throw-3 F.CAUS-QT | now | 3M-speak-3 F.HAB-QT | DEF-kettle-M.SUF |

| *lapuyan* | *'uh-pohta-wit'a-hč* | *sam-at'i-hč* | *lapuya* | *sak-'ik-'ahča* |
|---|---|---|---|---|
| well | 3M-boil-2M.CAUS-SUB | finish-3 F.COND-SUB | well | eat-2M-FUT |

| *'u-nikateni* | *'uwet* | *šim* | *'u-wana* | *tihčet* | *šimi* | *ti-wan-'ah-ani* |
|---|---|---|---|---|---|---|
| 3M-say-3 F. HAB-QT | he on his part | play | 3M-want | she on her part | play | 3F-want-NEG-QT |

| *'u-yana-lepi-hk-'at-ani* | | *'iman* | *ta-šihparik* | *'uh-tapa-n-č* | *ašu* |
|---|---|---|---|---|---|
| 3M-speak-ask-3 F.HAB-3 F.CAUS-QT | | I | DEF-bean | 3M-plant-1-SUB | day |

| *manku* | *pira-ti-hč* | *'u-saku-k-ani* | *ni-kat-eni* | *hinyatihč* |
|---|---|---|---|---|
| four | turn-3F-SUB | 3M-eat-1.HAB-QT | say-3 F.HAB-QT | now |

| *tiwi-'ut-ah-ani* | *hinyatihč* | *hat'ena* | *'u-yana-kat-eni* | *'iman* |
|---|---|---|---|---|
| hear-3M-NEG-QT | now | once.more | 3M-speak-3 F.HAB-QT | I |

| *ta-šihparik* | *'uh-tapa-nč* | *tahča* | *manku* | *pira-hti-hč* | *'u-saku-k-ani* |
|---|---|---|---|---|---|
| DEF-bean | 3M-plant-SUB | month | four | burn-3F-SUB | 3M-eat-HAB-QT |

| *ni-kat-eni* | | *hinyatihč* | *ta-šihpar-tosu-ku* | *wi-yuw'a-n-č* | *'uh-tap'i-k'i-hč* |
|---|---|---|---|---|---|
| say-3 F.HAB-QT | | now | DEF-bean-seed-M. | 2M-give-1. | 3M-plant-3M. |
| | | | SUF | COND-SUB | COND-QT |
| *tahča* | *manku* | *pira-ti-hč* | *ta-šihparik* | *'u-sak-'i-k'ahča* | *'u-ni-kat-eni* |
| month | four | turn-3F-SUB | DEF-bean | 3M-eat-2M-FUT | 3M-say-3 F.HAB-QT |

| *hinyatihč* | *'u-yana-lepi-hot-'ota-hč* | *hat'ena* | *mar-'am-'ek-eni* |
|---|---|---|---|
| now | 3M-speak-ask-finish-3 F. | once.more | return-disappear-3F-QT |
| | CAUS-SUB | | |

| *ta-yanera* | *kičun* |
|---|---|
| DEF-ocean | LOC |

(Once there) were an orphan boy and his sister. Every morning they would go to the edge of the ocean to play. Under the bank there was sand. Some puppies emerged from the ocean and came to play in the sand. The girl and her brother tried to catch the puppies. One day when they came (there), the puppies came out to play near the bank again. The girl chased one (of them) and caught it. The two (of them) were running toward the bank. The waves were coming (toward them). When they came to the bank, the waves reached them and caught them. Then the orphan boy climbed up onto the bank alone. The girl had gone down (into the water) and had disappeared. The orphan boy went home. He lived with his maternal uncle at (the latter's) home. Every morning he went (there) and tried to find his sister. He could not find her. He went back home. One morning he forgot (to go). He was just sitting at home. One day she came back. She brought two beans. She spoke to him. She asked him a question.

"Have you anything good to eat?" she said.

"No. There is nothing," he said.

"If you place the kettle on the fire, it will be a good thing," she told him.

So he placed the kettle on the fire. Then she broke one of the beans and put it in the kettle.

She spoke to him. "If the kettle boils thoroughly and (the bean) gets done, you will eat well (of it)," she told him.

He, for his part, wanted to play (but) she did not wish to play. She spoke to him. "Four days after I plant the bean I eat it," she said.

He did not hear her.

Then she spoke to him once more. "Four months after I plant the bean I eat it," she said. "If I give you (this) bean and if you plant it, you will (be able to) eat it in four months," she told him.

When she had finished speaking, she went back and disappeared into the ocean once more. Since the orphan boy wanted to play, he did not hear his sister the first time she spoke to him. The Tunica Indians believe that had he been more attentive it would be possible to raise a crop of beans in four days instead of four months.

From Haas (1950).

NOTES

### 1. Geography and Environment

1. The passenger pigeon (*Ectopistes migratorius*) is now extinct but for a time was so numerous as to darken the sky. This development may, however, have been an inadvertent symptom of the ecological upheaval that occurred after the European invasions, since few bones of the pigeon are found in archaeological digs dated prior to 1492 (Mann 2005, 356–57).

### 2. Archaeology and History

1. Although Mexico is geographically part of North America, in this book I use the archaeological term *Mesoamerica(n)* to refer only to Mexico, as opposed to North America north of the modern Mexican border.
2. Peripherally contemporaneous with Mississippian Culture were what archaeologists have termed the Oneota culture, in the northern Plains, and the Fort Ancient culture, in what is now Ohio.
3. Chaco, located in a canyon in modern northwestern New Mexico, was a major Puebloan cliff-dwelling settlement and trading center of the Southwest. There is evidence of heavy trade between Chaco and Mesoamerica.
4. Mesopotamian city-states have been noted as examples of multiethnic communities (Yoffee 1995, 258). It is thus not surprising if indigenous North American cities like Cahokia were similarly multiethnic and multilingual, serving as trade centers for peoples from all directions.
5. Mound-and-plaza architecture later came to symbolize for archaeologists not only the ancient Mississippian but also the ancient Mesoamerican and Peruvian cultures.
6. Though peripheral to this book, evidence of maize also occurs in south-central Florida ca. 500 BCE and in the Dismal Swamp region of coastal Virginia ca. 200 BCE (Fearn and Liu 1995, 110).

### 3. Peoples, Migrations, and Languages

1. Sherzer (after Haas 1958) reports that "the Gulf languages have been shown to form a genetic unit" (1976, 253), including Atakapan, Chitimachan, Muskogean, Natchesan, and Tunican. However, the genetic affinity of this "Gulf language family" has never been proven, and these languages are not considered genetically related in current scholarship, each being still considered unaffiliated, or isolates. Indeed, I believe any similarities among these languages are due to contact and being part of the LMV sprachbund rather than to genetic affiliation.

2. Most of the linguistic examples given in this book use an Americanist transcription, except for the texts in the appendix, in which language-specific orthographies (spelling systems) are used, including updated orthographies for Atakapa and Biloxi.

3. Notable exceptions among Indo-European (IE) languages are Bulgarian and Albanian, both of which have systems of evidentiality apparently borrowed from non-IE Turkish during the reign of the Ottoman Empire (1299–1922). For this reason evidentiality is considered one of the traits of the Balkan sprachbund of eastern Europe.

4. Karankawas have been recognized as belonging to five main groups all speaking the same language: Cópanes, Coapites, Cujanes, Carancaguases, and Cocos (Arnn 2012, 117; Ricklis 1996).

5. The name Calcasieu is derived from Atakapa *katkaš yok*, meaning 'crying eagle.'

6. The Spanish explorer Juan Pardo and his entourage made two forays from the coast of modern South Carolina into modern North Carolina and eastern Tennessee in the years 1566 and 1568. He established Fort San Juan, the first inland Spanish fort, in the Mississippian Culture town called Joara, or Xuala, in present-day North Carolina. These Spanish attempts to extend *La Florida* into an inland empire ultimately failed, but not without forever disrupting the indigenous lifeways of the region. This region contained some of the most influential Mississippian Culture settlements known in the Southeast, at least two of which were ruled over by powerful women.

7. While Hidatsas and Mandans now occupy the same reservation in North Dakota, a Mandan origin story claims that they migrated northward from the mouth of the Mississippi River (see Fenn 2014, 4), bringing maize with them to the northern Plains, where it required adjustment to a shorter growing period. Archaeological evidence places the Siouan Mandans in the northern Plains ca. 1200 CE, implying a northward migration prior to this time. It is possible that the Mandans were members of the LMV sprachbund prior to this migration. The Mandan language is now considered to be its own subbranch of the Siouan language family, no longer part of the Missouri Valley branch of Siouan (Hidatsa, Crow), a former classification based primarily on geography.

8. James Dorsey was not related to the above-named language consultant John Dorsey.

9. For example, the headword *atuti* appears in the revised Biloxi-English dictionary, with one of its translations being 'ripe, done, finished,' while *thohi* occurs with its definitions 'blue, green, purple, of the blue-green color spectrum' and 'unripe.' (A comparison with other Siouan languages demonstrates that the phoneme /t/ here should be aspirated, which, per my revised orthography, is now written <th>.) In the accompanying revised English-Biloxi index, one

can simply look up the word 'ripe' and immediately find Biloxi *atuti*. Similarly one can look up 'blue,' 'green,' and 'unripe,' and immediately find Biloxi *thohi* for each of them. The revised dictionary also includes lexical comparison to other Ohio Valley Siouan languages (Ofo and Tutelo) where available, cross-referencing of vocabulary, and several appendices on body parts, flora and fauna, and medicinal plants.

10. Swanton's orthographic <ŭ> often represents [a], while <u> represents [u], thus making clear the distinction between, for instance, *supi* 'thin' and *sapi* 'black,' the latter agreeing with other Siouan languages (see Kaufman 2007). In Einaudi's orthography, however, both of these words erroneously appear as *supi*, thus possibly misleading researchers in comparative and historical Siouan studies.

11. The exact definition of *Šeyti* given by Swadesh is: "Grand River, all the way from Red River to the Gulf and subsuming a number of stretches separately named in English (Whiskey Bay + Grand River + Belle River + Achafalaya)" (1939, 67).

12. 16SM5 is a numerical designation assigned by the Smithsonian Institution for archaeological sites. I use such numbers in connection to archaeological sites throughout this book.

13. Other indigenous groups to appear sporadically in colonial slave records include Taensas, Mobilians, Natchitoches, Chickasaws, Natchez, Abikas, Cowetas, Altamahas, Paducahs, and Panis or Paniasas (Paniouacha) (Waselkov and Gums 2000, 35).

14. It is probably worth noting here that this time period—the ninth century—approximately coincides with the collapse of the great Mesoamerican city-state of Teotihuacan, which in itself may have led to mass migrations and movements of people out of what we now know as Mexico, perhaps including those who later became Muskogean groups. It is also close to this time period that the great North American city of Cahokia is constructed in the region of what is now St. Louis. This may well be coincidental, of course, but the close chronology may suggest more than mere coincidence.

15. I use the term *Natchesan* in reference to the language family, since *Natchezan* is the archaeological term used to refer to their culture and pottery.

16. I am indebted to Dr. David Costa, a linguist who works primarily on Algonquian languages and has published a Miami-Illinois grammar, for sending me copies of the more than two thousand pages of material (including nearly four thousand lexical items) of which Haas's notebooks are comprised.

17. Other languages of the LMV, such as Natchez (*la·lak*) and Choctaw (*shilaklak*), share similar terms, possibly due to onomatopoeia. But resemblances seem "remarkably precise even if one allows for onomatopoeia" (Haas 1969b, 82), such as among words for 'goose' from the Southeast to California. The 'goose' terms in

Natchez and Choctaw may have been borrowed from Tunica. Other bird names have an equally uneven and widespread distribution, warranting further investigation.

18. Mobila may have been a Muskogean language; it is not to be confused with Mobilian Jargon, or MTL, which was a pidgin language based on Choctaw-Chickasaw and Alabama that served as a lingua franca of the LMV and Southeast.

19. Biloxis and neighboring Pascagoulas both practiced mouth tattooing, which earned them the name "Blue Mouths" (Kniffen, Gregory, and Stokes 1987, 182).

### 5. Phonetic and Phonological Features

1. Labiodental /f/ and bilabial /ɸ/ have both been attested among various Muskogean language speakers, but, at least in modern times, the labiodental /f/ pronunciation seems to predominate (Jack Martin and Aaron Broadwell, pers. comm., 2017).

### 6. Morphological Features

1. The suffix *-ne* "appears frequently in the formation of nouns, with which it has the aspect of an instrumental suffix and may be translated by the prepositions 'to' or 'for'" (Swanton 1929, 129). This seems to be a different suffix, however, from the *-ne* emphatic.

2. Apparently so named in Natchez for its tendency to sting.

3. Watkins (1976) identified *kamškintu* only as 'paddle.' I analyzed it into its component parts.

4. As Haas demonstrated, Koasati (Coushatta), an Eastern Muskogean language, has three pronominal paradigms used according to the particular verb class, one of which has prefixed pronouns except for first-person singular, which is suffixed, just as in the Choctaw-Chickasaw case (1969b, 54–55). Such a paradigm shift from suffixed to prefixed pronominals is thus an internal Muskogean language development rather than being due to the effects of contact with, say, Siouan languages like Biloxi and Ofo, in which all pronominals are prefixed.

5. The Nahuatl numerals from one to ten: *ce, ome, yei, nahui, macuilli, chicuace, chicome, chicuei, chiucnahui, matlactli*. This combination of number systems supports a probable northerly Nahuatl origin in a region where quinary number systems flourished before a southerly migration to Mexico, where vigesimal number systems abound, as in Mayan.

### 7. Word Borrowings and Calques

1. It is unlikely that a similar-looking Algonquian term (e.g., Ojibwe *oodena* [Nichols and Nyholm 1995, 272]) is copied from either Siouan or Western Muskogean due to the Algonquian initial *o(o)*-. Another possibility for the origin of the term

exists, however, which warrants further examination: the Totonacan term *ta-mawan* (*tamāhuan*) means 's/he buys,' while *liitamaw* (*li̱tamáu̱*) and *puutamawan* (*pu̱ta̱mahuán*) mean 'plaza' or 'place to buy' (Aschmann 1973, 110) (the Toto-nac prefix *lii-* is an instrumental prefix while *puu-* is a locative prefix [MacKay 1999, 386, 388]). Assuming that there may have been circum-Gulf navigation and trade, it is possible that this term entered Choctaw-Chickasaw and MTL as *tamaha* from Totonacan *tamawan* as a means of referring to a center for buy-ing, selling, and trading (i.e., a plaza or town center), which may then have been copied into Siouan. Such a scenario might indicate that the term was borrowed into Siouan from Western Muskogean (or MTL) at a time that predated the west-ward migration of Siouan groups from perhaps the Ohio Valley or Appalachian region.

2. Cherokee has a potential cognate for 'maize,' *selu*, shared with Nahuatl *xilotl* 'ear of (tender) corn' (Hall 2012, 61). Cherokees and Catawbas were both located near the head of the Chattahoochee River (near the borders of modern-day North Carolina and South Carolina), which is a tributary of the Apalachicola River originating on the Gulf Coast of present-day western Florida. This indi-cates possible trade routes up these rivers from the Gulf of Mexico.

## Conclusion

1. Bowne (2005) makes a fairly convincing argument, albeit based on very limited data, that the Westos were slave traders of the colonial south who were likely a branch of the Haudenosaunee (Iroquois) Erie group and were thus Iroquoian language speakers (like the Cherokees and Tuscaroras).

2. The original Spanish: "El Tajín se desarolló entre el 800 y el 1200 de nuestra era."

3. The original Spanish: "Los lingüistas han reconocido que la llegada de la lengua totonaca a la costa ocurrió hacia el 850 de nuestra era."

4. We have seen that geographical proximity, however, is not a necessary prerequi-site for language contact, as attested by borrowings among Biloxi and Caddoan and Atakapa. The salt trade may have been one impetus for longer distance contact and interaction. The same holds true for possible contact between the LMV and Mesoamerica, in which long-distance trade and contact may have been conducted by water rather than overland. The establishment of geographically distant merchant colonies by various groups—not only within North America but between the northern Gulf and Mesoamerica—for easier access to various materials is a possibility and something that demands further research.

# REFERENCES

Aikhenvald, Alexandra, and Robert Dixon. 2006. *Serial Verb Constructions: A Cross-Linguistic Typology*. Oxford: Oxford University Press.

Alt, Susan. 2012. "Making Mississippian at Cahokia." In *The Oxford Handbook of North American Archaeology*, edited by Timothy Pauketat, 497–508. Oxford: Oxford University Press.

Arnn, John W., III. 2012. *Land of the Tejas: Native American Identity and Interaction in Texas, A.D. 1300 to 1700*. Austin: University of Texas Press.

Aschmann, Herman. 1973. *Diccionario Totonaco de Papantla, Veracruz*. https://www.sil .org/resources/archives/10932.

Beasley, Virgil, III. 2007. "Feasting on the Bluffs: Anna Site Excavations in the Natchez Bluffs of Mississippi." In *Plaquemine Archaeology*, edited by Mark Rees and Patrick Livingood, 127–44. Tuscaloosa: University of Alabama Press.

Bellwood, Peter, and Colin Renfrew. 2002. *Examining the Farming/Language Dispersal Hypothesis*. Cambridge, UK: McDonald Institute Monographs.

Bense, Judith. 2009. *Archaeology of the Southeastern United States: Paleoindian to World War I*. Walnut Creek CA: Left Coast Press.

Birmingham, Robert, and Lynne Goldstein. 2005. *Aztalan: Mysteries of an Ancient Indian Town*. Madison: Wisconsin Historical Society Press.

Blake, Michael. 2010. "Dating the Initial Spread of Zea mays." In *Histories of Maize in Mesoamerica: Multidisciplinary Approaches*, edited by John E. Staller, Robert H. Tykot, and Bruce F. Benz, 45–62. Walnut Creek CA: Left Coast Press.

Boas, Franz. 1911. *Handbook of American Indian Languages, Part 1*. Washington DC: Government Printing Office.

———. (1929) 1940. *Race, Language, and Culture*. Chicago: University of Chicago Press.

Booker, Karen, Charles Hudson, and Robert Rankin. 1992. "Place Name Identification and Multilingualism in the Sixteenth-Century Southeast." *Ethnohistory* 39 (4): 399–451.

Boszhardt, Robert, Danielle Benden, and Timothy Pauketat. 2015. "Early Mississippian Outposts in the North." In *Medieval Mississippians: The Cahokian World*, edited by Timothy R. Pauketat and Susan M. Alt, 63–69. Santa Fe: School for Advanced Research Press.

Bowne, Eric. 2005. *The Westo Indians: Slave Traders of the Early Colonial South*. Tuscaloosa: University of Alabama Press.

Brackenridge, Henry Marie. 1814. *Views of Louisiana*. Pittsburgh: Cramer, Spear, and Eichbaum.

Brain, Jeffrey. 1988. *Tunica Archaeology*. Cambridge MA: Harvard University Press.

Brain, Jeffrey, and Frank Porter. 1990. *The Tunica-Biloxi*. New York: Chelsea House Publishers.

Brain, Jeffrey, and Philip Phillips. 2004. *Shell Gorgets: Styles of the Late Prehistoric and Protohistoric Southeast*. New Haven: Peabody Museum Press.

Bright, William. 1984. *American Indian Linguistics and Literature*. Berlin: Mouton.

Broadwell, George Aaron. 2006. *A Choctaw Reference Grammar*. Lincoln: University of Nebraska Press.

Brown, Ian, ed. 2003. *Bottle Creek: A Pensacola Culture Site in South Alabama*, edited by Ian Brown. Tuscaloosa: University of Alabama Press.

Brown, James, Richard Kerber, and Howard Winters. 1990. "Trade and the Evolution of Exchange Relations at the Beginning of the Mississippian Period." In *The Mississippian Emergence*, edited by Bruce Smith, 251–80. Washington DC: Smithsonian Institution Press.

Buechel, Eugene, and Paul Manhart. 2002. *Lakota Dictionary*. Lincoln: University of Nebraska Press.

Buikstra, Jane, Lyle Konigsburg, and Jill Bullington. 1986. "Fertility and the Development of Agriculture in the Prehistoric Midwest." *American Antiquity* 51 (3): 528–46.

Byington, Cyrus, and John Swanton. 1915. *A Dictionary of the Choctaw Language*. Washington DC: Government Printing Office.

Cabrera, Dávila. 2005. "Moundbuilders along the Coast of the Gulf of Mexico and the Eastern United States." In *Gulf Coast Archaeology: The Southeastern United States and Mexico, edited by Nancy Marie White*, 87–107. Gainesville: University Press of Florida.

Campbell, Lyle, Terrence Kaufman, and Thomas Smith-Stark. 1986. "Meso-America as a Linguistic Area." *Language* 62 (3): 530–70.

———. 1997. *American Indian Languages: The Historical Linguistics of Native America*. Oxford: Oxford University Press.

———. 2002. "What Drives Linguistic Diversification and Language Spread." In *Examining the Farming/Language Dispersal Hypothesis*, edited by Peter S. Bellwood and Colin Renfrew, 49–63. Cambridge, UK: McDonald Institute for Archaeological Research.

Chafe, Wallace. 1976. *The Caddoan, Iroquoian, and Siouan Languages*. The Hague: Mouton & Co.

Clark, John, and Michelle Knoll. 2005. "The American Formative Revisited." In *Gulf Coast Archaeology: The Southeastern United States and Mexico*, edited by Nancy Marie White, 281–303. Gainesville: University Press of Florida.

Comrie, Bernard. 1989. *Language Universals and Linguistic Typology: Syntax and Morphology*. Chicago: University of Chicago Press.

Conant, Levi. 1896. *The Number Concept: Its Origin and Development*. New York: Macmillan.

Crawford, James. 1978. *The Mobilian Trade Language*. Knoxville: University of Tennessee.

Cristofaro, Sonia. 2000. "Linguistic Areas, Typology and Historical Linguistics: An Overview with Particular Respect to Mediterranean Languages." In *Languages in the Mediterranean Area: Typology and Convergence*, edited by Sonia Cristofaro and Ignazio Putzu, 65–81. Milan: FrancoAngeli.

Darnell, Regna, and Joel Sherzer. 1971. "Areal Linguistic Studies in North America: A Historical Perspective." *International Journal of American Linguistics* 37 (1): 20–28.

Dorsey, James, and John Swanton. 1912. *A Dictionary of the Biloxi and Ofo Languages*. Bureau of American Ethnology, Bulletin 47. Washington DC: Government Printing Office.

Drechsel, Emanuel. 1996. "An Integrated Vocabulary of Mobilian Jargon, a Native American Pidgin of the Mississippi Valley." *Anthropological Linguistics* 38 (2): 248–354.

———. 1997. *Mobilian Jargon: Linguistic and Sociohistorical Aspects of a Native American Pidgin*. Oxford: Clarendon Press.

———. 2001. "Mobilian Jargon in Southeastern Indian Anthropology." In *Anthropologists and Indians in the New South*, edited by Rachel A. Bonney and J. Anthony Paredes, 175–83. Tuscaloosa: University of Alabama Press.

Du Pratz, Le Page. 1751. *Histoire de la Louisiane*. Paris.

Einaudi, Paula. 1976. *A Grammar of Biloxi*. New York: Garland Publishing.

Emeneau, M. B. 1956. "India as a Linguistic Area." *Language* 32: 3–16.

Ethridge, Robbie. 2010. *From Chicaza to Chickasaw: The European Invasion and the Transformation of the Mississippian World, 1540–1715*. Chapel Hill: University of North Carolina Press.

Fagan, Brian. 1995. *Ancient North America: The Archaeology of a Continent*. London: Thames and Hudson.

Fearn, Miriam, and Kam-biu Liu. 1995. "Maize Pollen of 3500 B.P. from Southern Alabama." *American Antiquity* 60 (1): 109–17.

Fenn, Elizabeth. 2014. *Encounters at the Heart of the World: A History of the Mandan People*. New York: Farrar, Straus, and Giroux.

Fox Tree, Erich. 2009. "Meemul Tziij: An Indigenous Sign Language Complex of Mesoamerica." *Sign Language Studies* 9 (3): 324–66.

Friedman, Victor. 2009. "Balkans as a Linguistic Area." In *Concise Encyclopedia of Languages of the World*, edited by Keith Brown and Sarah Ogilvie, 119–34. Amsterdam: Elsevier.

Fritz, Gayle, and Tristram Kidder. 1993. "Recent Investigations into Prehistoric Agriculture in the Lower Mississippi Valley." In *Southeastern Archaeology* 12: 1–14.

Galloway, Patricia. 1994. "Confederacy as a Solution to Chiefdom Dissolution: Historical Evidence in the Choctaw Case." In *The Forgotten Centuries: Indians and Europeans in the American South, 1541–1704*, edited by Charles Hudson and Carmen Chaves Tesser, 393–420. Athens: University of Georgia Press.

———. 1995. *Choctaw Genesis: 1500–1700*. Lincoln: University of Nebraska Press.

Galloway, Patricia, and Clara Sue Kidwell. 2004. "Choctaw in the East." In *Handbook of North American Indians*. Vol. 14, *Southeast*, edited by Raymond D. Fogelson, 499–519. Washington DC: Smithsonian Institution.

Galvan, Glenda. 2011. *Chikasha Stories: Volume 1*. Sulphur: Chickasaw Press.

Gatschet, Albert, and John Swanton. 1932. *A Dictionary of the Atakapa Language: Accompanied by Text Material*. Washington DC: Government Printing Office.

Gatschet, Albert. 1886. Unpublished notes.

Girard, Jeffrey, Timothy Perttula, and Mary Beth Trubitt. 2014. *Caddo Connections: Cultural Interactions within and beyond the Caddo World*. Lanham MD: Rowman and Littlefield.

Goddard, Ives. 1979. *Delaware Verbal Morphology: A Descriptive and Comparative Study*. New York: Garland Publishing.

Goddard, Ives. 1996. "The Classification of the Native Languages of North America." In *Handbook of North American Indians*. Vol. 17, *Languages*, 290–324. Washington DC: Smithsonian Institution.

———. 2005. "The Indigenous Languages of the Southeast." *Anthropological Linguistics* 47 (1): 1–60.

Greenberg, Joseph. (1939) 1961. *Universals of Language*. Cambridge MA: MIT Press.

Griffin, James. 1942. "On the Historic Location of the Tutelo and the Mohetan in the Ohio Valley." *American Anthropologist* 44 (2): 275–80.

Grosjean, François. 1982. *Life with Two Languages: An Introduction to Bilingualism*. Cambridge MA: Harvard University Press.

Gumperz, John J., and Robert Wilson. 1971. "Convergence and Creolization: A Case from the Indo-Aryan/Dravidian Border." In *Pidgeonization and Creolization of Languages*, edited Dell Hymes, 151–67. Cambridge, UK: Cambridge University Press.

Gundel, Jeanette. 1988. *The Role of Topic and Comment in Linguistic Theory*. New York: Garland.

Haag, Marcia, and Henry Willis. 2001. *Choctaw Language and Culture: Chahta anumpa*. Norman: University of Oklahoma Press.

Haas, Mary. 1940. *Tunica*. New York: J. J. Augustin Publishers.

———. 1941. "The Classification of the Muskogean Languages." In *Language, Culture and Personality*, edited by Leslie Spier, A. Irving Hallowell, and Stanley S. Newman, 41–56. Menasha WI: Sapir Memorial Publication Fund.

———. 1946. "A Grammatical Sketch of Tunica." In *Linguistic Structures of Native*

*America*, edited by Harry Hoijer, Leonard Bloomfield, and Mary Haas, 337–66. New York: Johnson Reprint Corporation.

———. 1950. "Tunica Texts." *University of California Publications in Linguistics* 6 (1): 1–174.

———. 1953. *Tunica Dictionary*. Berkeley: University of California Press.

———. 1956. "Natchez and the Muskogean Languages." *Language* 32: 61–72.

———. 1958. "A New Linguistic Relationship in North America: Algonkian and the Gulf Languages." *Southwestern Journal of Anthropology* 14 (3): 231–64.

———. 1969a. "Swanton and the Biloxi and Ofo Dictionaries." *International Journal of American Linguistics* 35: 286–90.

———. 1969b. *The Prehistory of Languages*. The Hague: Mouton.

———. 1970. "Consonant Symbolism in Northwestern California: A Problem in Diffusion." In *Languages and Cultures of Western North America: Essays in Honor of Sven S. Liljeblad*, edited by Earl H. Swanson, 86–96. Pocatello: Idaho State University Press.

———. 1975. "What is Mobilian?" In *Studies in Southeastern Indian Languages*, edited by James Crawford, 257–63. Athens: University of Georgia Press.

———. 1979.

Haas, Mary, and Morris Swadesh. 1968. The Last Words of Biloxi. In *International Journal of American Linguistics*, 34, 77–84.

Hall, Robert. 2012. "Commonalities Linking North America and Mesoamerica." In *The Oxford Handbook of North American Archaeology*, edited by Timothy Pauketat, 52–63. New York: Oxford University Press.

Hardy, Heather. 2005. "Introduction to the Muskogean Language Family." In *Native Languages of the Southeastern United States*, edited by Heather Hardy and Janine Scancarelli, 69–74. Lincoln: University of Nebraska Press.

Hoffman, Michael. 1992. "Protohistoric Tunican Indians in Arkansas." *The Arkansas Historical Quarterly* 51 (1): 30–53.

Hudson, Charles. 1976. *The Southeastern Indians*. Knoxville: University of Tennessee Press.

———. 1990. *The Juan Pardo Expeditions: Exploration of the Carolinas and Tennessee, 1566–1568*. Washington DC: Smithsonian Institution Press.

Huffman, Franklin. 1970. *Modern Spoken Cambodian*. Ithaca NY: Cornell University.

Jaenicke-Després, Viviane, and Bruce Smith. 2010. "Ancient DNA and the Integration of Archaeological and Genetic Approaches to the Study of Maize Domestication." In *Histories of Maize in Mesoamerica: Multidisciplinary Approaches*, edited by John E. Staller, Robert H. Tykot, and Bruce F. Benz, 32–44. Walnut Creek CA: Left Coast Press.

Jefferies, Robert. 1996. "The Emergence of Long Distance Trade Networks in the Southeastern United States." In *Archaeology of the Mid-Holocene Southeast*, edited by Kenneth E. Sassaman and David G. Anderson, 222–34. Gainesville: University Press of Florida.

Johnson, Jay. 1994. "Prehistoric Exchange in the Southeast." In *Prehistoric Exchange Systems in North America*, edited by Timothy Baugh and Jonathon Ericson, 99–125. New York: Plenum Press.

Kaufman, David. 2011. "Biloxi Realis and Irrealis Particles." *Kansas Working Papers in Linguistics* 32: 1–7.

———. 2014a. "The Lower Mississippi Valley as a Language Area." PhD diss., University of Kansas, Department of Anthropology.

———. 2014b. "Another Look at Atakapa." *Kansas Working Papers in Linguistics* 35: 72–78.

———. 2016. "Two Siouan Languages Walk into a Sprachbund." In *Advances in the Study of Siouan Languages and Linguistics*, edited by Catherine Rudin and Bryan Gordon, 39–62. Berlin: Language Science Press.

———. 2017. *Mobilian Trade Language Phrasebook and Lexicon*. Chicago: Exploration Press.

Kehoe, Alice. 1998. *The Land of Prehistory: A Critical History of American Archaeology*. New York: Routledge.

———. 2007. "Osage Texts and Cahokia Data." In *Ancient Objects and Sacred Realms: Interpretations of Mississippian Iconography*, edited by F. Kent Reilly III and James F. Garber, 246–61. Austin: University of Texas Press.

Kidder, Tristram. 1998. "Mississippi Period Mound Groups and Communities in the Lower Mississippi Valley." In *Mississippian Towns and Sacred Spaces: Searching for an Architectural Grammar*, edited by R. Barry Lewis and Charles Stout, 123–50. Tuscaloosa: University of Alabama Press.

———. 2004. "Plazas as Architecture: An Example from the Raffman Site, Northeast Louisiana." *American Antiquity* 69 (3): 514–32.

Kidder, Tristram, and Gayle Fritz. 1993. "Subsistence and Social Change in the Lower Mississippi Valley: The Reno Brake and Osceola Sites, Louisiana." *Journal of Field Archaeology* 20 (3): 281–97.

Kimball, Geoffrey. 1994. *Koasati Dictionary*. Lincoln: University of Nebraska Press.

———. 2005. "Natchez." In *Native Languages of the Southeastern United States*, edited by Heather Hardy and Janine Scancarelli, 385–453. Lincoln: University of Nebraska Press.

Kniffen, Fred, Hiram Gregory, and George Stokes. 1987. *The Historic Indian Tribes of Louisiana: From 1542 to the Present*. Baton Rouge: Louisiana State University Press.

Kroeber, Alfred. 1939. *Cultural and Natural Areas of Native North America*. Berkeley: University of California Press.

Kulick, Don. 1992. *Language Shift and Cultural Reproduction*. Cambridge, UK: Cambridge University Press.

Kurlansky, Mark. 2002. *Salt: A World History*. New York: Walker and Company.

Ladrón de Guevara, Sara. 2010. *El Tajín: la urbe que representa al orbe*. Mexico City: El Colegio de México.

La Vere, David. 2007. *Looting Spiro Mounds: An American King Tut's Tomb*. Norman: University of Oklahoma Press.

Little, Gregory. 2009. *The Illustrated Encyclopedia of Native American Mounds and Earthworks*. Memphis: Eagle Wing Books.

Lockhart, James. 2001. *Nahuatl as Written*. Stanford: Stanford University Press.

MacKay, Carolyn. 1999. *A Grammar of Misantla Totonac*. Salt Lake City: University of Utah Press.

MacLean, John Patterson. 1879. *The Mound Builders*. Cincinnati: Robert Clarke & Co.

Maddieson, Ian. 2013. "Glottalized Consonants." In *The World Atlas of Language Structures Online*, edited by Matthew Dryer and Martin Haspelmath. Leipzig: Max Planck Institute for Evolutionary Anthropology. http://wals.info/chapter/7.

Mann, Barbara Alice. 2003. *Native Americans, Archaeologists, and the Mounds*. New York: Peter Lang.

Mann, Charles. 2005. *1491: New Revelations of the Americas before Columbus*. New York: Random House.

Martin, Jack. 1994. "Modeling Language Contact in the Prehistory of the Southeastern United States." In *Perspectives on the Southeast: Linguistics, Archaeology, and Ethnohistory*, edited by Patricia Kwachka, 14–24. Athens: University of Georgia Press.

Martin, Jack, and Margaret Mauldin. 2000. *A Dictionary of Creek/Muskogee: With Notes on the Florida and Oklahoma Seminole Dialects of Creek*. Lincoln: University of Nebraska Press.

Masica, Colin. 1976. *Defining a Linguistic Area: South Asia*. Chicago: University of Chicago Press.

Matras, Yaron. 1998. "Utterance Modifiers and Universals of Grammatical Borrowing." *Linguistics* 36 (2): 281–331.

———. 2009. *Language Contact*. Cambridge, UK: Cambridge University Press.

Mithun, Marianne. 1999. *The Languages of Native North America*. Cambridge, UK: Cambridge University Press.

Munro, Pamela. 1987. *Muskogean Linguistics*. Los Angeles: University of California Press.

Munro, Pamela, and Catherine Willmond. 1994. *Chickasaw: An Analytical Dictionary*. Norman: University of Oklahoma Press.

Muysken, Pieter. 2008. *From Linguistic Areas to Areal Linguistics*. Amsterdam: John Benjamins.

Nichols, Johanna. 1992. *Linguistic Diversity in Space and Time*. Chicago: University of Chicago Press.

Nichols, John, and Earl Nyholm. 1995. *A Concise Dictionary of Minnesota Ojibwe*. Minneapolis: University of Minnesota Press.

Nicklas, T. Dale. Unpublished ms. No date.

Nicklas, T. Dale. 1994. "Linguistic Provinces of the Southeast at the Time of Columbus." In *Perspectives on the Southeast: Linguistics, Archaeology, and Ethnohistory*, edited by Patricia Kwachka, 1–13. Athens: University of Georgia Press.

Pauketat, Timothy. 2007. *Chiefdoms and Other Archaeological Delusions*. Lanham MD: Altamira Press.

———. 2009. *Cahokia: Ancient America's Great City on the Mississippi*. New York: Penguin.

Payne, Thomas. 1997. *Describing Morphosyntax: A Guide for Field Linguists*. Cambridge, UK: Cambridge University Press.

Peacock, Evan, Wendell Haag, and Melvin Warren Jr. 2005. "Prehistoric Decline in Freshwater Mussels Coincident with the Advent of Maize Agriculture." *Conservation Biology* 19 (2): 547–51.

Perttula, Timothy, and Philip Phillips. 1970. "Archaeological Survey in the Lower Yazoo Basin, Mississippi, 1949–1955." *Papers of the Peabody Museum of Archaeology and Ethnology* 60.

Quintero, Carolyn. 2006. *Osage Grammar*. Lincoln: University of Nebraska Press.

———. 2009. *Osage Dictionary*. Norman: University of Oklahoma Press.

Rankin, Robert. 1988. "'FH' (The Origin of the Ofo Aspirated Fricative)." Paper presented at the 8th annual Siouan and Caddoan Languages Conference, Billings, Montana.

———. 2002. *An Ofo Grammar Sketch and John R. Swanton's Ofo-English Dictionary*. Unpublished manuscript.

———. 2011. "Who Were the Tomahitans?" Paper presented at the 31st annual Siouan and Caddoan Languages Conference, White Cloud, Kansas.

Rees, Mark, and Patrick Livingood. 2007. "Introduction and Historical Overview." In *Plaquemine Archaeology*, edited by Mark Rees and Patrick Livingood, 1–19. Tuscaloosa: University of Alabama Press.

Reilly III, F. Kent, and James F. Garber. 2007. *Ancient Objects and Sacred Realms: Interpretations of Mississippian Iconography*. Austin: University of Texas Press.

Ricklis, Robert. 1996. *The Karankawa Indians of Texas: An Ecological Study of Cultural Tradition and Change*. Austin: University of Texas Press.

———. 2004. "The Archeology of the Native American Occupation of Southeast Texas." In *The Prehistory of Texas*, edited by Timothy Perttula, 181–202. College Station: Texas A&M University Press.

Riggs, Stephen. (1893) 2004. *Dakota Grammar with Texts and Ethnography*. St. Paul: Minnesota Historical Society Press.

Rodning, Christopher. 2003. "Water Travel and Mississippian Settlement at Bottle Creek." In *Bottle Creek: A Pensacola Culture Site in South Alabama*, edited by Ian Brown, 194–204. Tuscaloosa: University of Alabama Press.

Roe, Lori. 2007. "Coles Creek Antecedents of Plaquemine Mound Construction: Evidence from the Raffman Site." In *Plaquemine Archaeology*, edited by Mark Rees and Patrick Livingood, 20–37. Tuscaloosa: University of Alabama Press.

Rowland, Dunbar, and A. G. Sanders. 1927. *Mississippi Provincial Archives, 1729–1740: French Dominion*. Jackson MS.

Rouy, Pablo Valderrama. 2005. "The Totonac." In *Native Peoples of the Gulf Coast of Mexico*, edited by Alan R. Sandstrom and Enrique Hugo García Valencia, 187–210. Tucson: University of Arizona Press.

Rubino, Carl. 2013. "Reduplication." In *The World Atlas of Language Structures Online*, edited by Matthew Dryer and Martin Haspelmath. Leipzig: Max Planck Institute for Evolutionary Anthropology. http://wals.info/chapter/27.

Sapir, Edward. 1922. "The Takelma Language of Southwestern Oregon." In *Handbook of American Indian Languages, Part 2*, edited by Franz Boas, 1–296. Washington DC: Government Printing Office.

Sapir, Edward, and Morris Swadesh. 1946. "American Indian Grammatical Categories." *Word* 2 (2): 103–12.

Sarhimaa, Anneli. 1991. "Karelian Sprachbund? Theoretical Basis of the Study of Russian/Baltic-Finnic Contacts." *Finnisch-Ugrische Forschungen* 50: 209–19.

Saunders, Rebecca, and Christopher Hays. 2004. *Pottery: Technology, Function, Style, and Interaction in the Lower Southeast*. Tuscaloosa: University of Alabama Press.

Schaller, Helmut. 1975. *Die Balkansprachen. Eine Einführung in die Balkanphilologie*. Heidelberg: Carl Winter Universitätsverlag.

Sherzer, Joel. 1976. *An Areal-typological Study of American Indian Languages North of Mexico*. Amsterdam: North-Holland Publishing.

Silver, Shirley, and Wick Miller. 1997. *American Indian Languages: Cultural and Social contexts*. Tucson: University of Arizona Press.

Smith, Bruce. 2009. "Resource Resilience, Human Niche Construction, and the Long-Term Sustainability of Pre-Columbian Subsistence Economies in the Mississippi River Valley Corridor." *Ethnobiology* 29 (2): 167–83.

———. 2011. "The Cultural Context of Plant Domestication in Eastern North America." *Current Anthropology* 52 (Suppl. 4): S471–84.

Southworth, Franklin. 2005. *Linguistic Archaeology of south Asia*. London: Routledge-Curzon.

Southworth, Justin, and David Kaufman. Forthcoming. *Atakapa Ishak Grammar and Dictionary*. Chicago: Exploration Press.

Steponaitis, Vincas. 1986. "Prehistoric Archaeology in the Southeastern United States, 1970–1985." *Annual Review of Anthropology* 15 (1): 363–404.

Sturtevant, William. 2005. "History of Research on Native Languages of the Southeast." In *Native Languages of the Southeastern United States*, edited by Heather Hardy and Janine Scancarelli, 246–98. Lincoln: University of Nebraska Press.

Swadesh, Morris. 1939. *Chitimacha Grammar, Texts, and Vocabulary.* Unpublished manuscript. In Franz Boas Collection of Materials for American Linguistics, MSS. 497.3.B63C.G6.5. American Philosophical Society, Philadelphia PA.

———. 1950. "Salish Internal Relationships." *International Journal of American Linguistics* 16: 157–67.

———. 1971. "What is Glottochronology?" In *The Origin and Diversification of Language,* edited by Joel Sherzer, 271–84. Chicago: Aldine Atherton.

Swanton, John. 1908. "The Language of the Taensa." *American Anthropologist* 10 (1): 24–32.

———. 1952. *The Indian Tribes of North America.* Washington DC: Government Printing Office.

———. 1919. *A Structural and Lexical Comparison of the Tunica, Chitimacha, and Atakapa Languages.* Washington DC: Government Printing Office.

———. 1921. "The Tunica Language." *International Journal of American Linguistics* 2 (1/2): 1–39.

———. 1924. "The Muskhogean Connection of the Natchez Language." *International Journal of American Linguistics* 3 (1): 46–75.

———. 1929. "A Sketch of the Atakapa Language." *International Journal of American Linguistics* 5 (2/4): 121–49.

———. 1943. "Siouan Tribes and the Ohio Valley." *American Anthropologist* 45 (1): 49–66.

———. 1946. *The Indians of the Southeastern United States.* Washington DC: Smithsonian Institution Press.

Tadmor, Uri, Martin Haspelmath, and Bradley Taylor. 2010. "Borrowability and the Notion of Basic Vocabulary." *Diachronica* 27 (2): 226–46.

Tanner, Helen. 1989. "The Land and Water Communication Systems of the Southeastern Indians." In *Powhatan's Mantle: Indians in the Colonial Southeast,* edited by Peter H. Wood, Gregory A. Waselkov, and Thomas Hatley, 6–20. Lincoln: University of Nebraska Press.

Thomason, Sarah. 2001. *Language Contact: An Introduction.* Washington DC: Georgetown University Press.

Thomason, Sarah, and Terrence Kaufman. 1988. *Language Contact, Creolization, and Genetic Linguistics.* Berkeley: University of California Press.

Tomić, Olga. 2006. *Balkan Sprachbund Morpho-syntactic Features.* New York: Springer.

Van Tuyl, Charles. 1980. *The Natchez: Annotated Translations from Antoine Simon le Page du Pratz's Histoire de la Louisiane and a Short English-Natchez Dictionary.* Oklahoma City: Oklahoma Historical Society.

Walthall, John. 1980. *Prehistoric Indians of the Southeast: Archaeology of Alabama and the Middle South.* Tuscaloosa: University of Alabama Press.

Waselkov, Gregory, and Bonnie Gums. 2000. *Plantation Archaeology at Rivière aux Chiens, ca. 1725–1848.* Mobile: University of South Alabama.

Watkins, Laurel. 1976. "Position in Grammar: Sit, Stand, Lie." *Kansas Working Papers in Linguistics* 1: 16–41.

Weinreich, Uriel. 1953. *Languages in Contact: Findings and Problems.* New York: Columbia University Press.

Wells, Douglas, and Richard Weinstein. 2007. "Extraregional Contact and Cultural Interaction at the Coles Creek-Plaquemine Transition: Recent Data from the Lake Providence Mounds, East Carroll Parish, Louisiana." In *Plaquemine Archaeology,* edited by Patrick C. Livingood and Mark A. Rees, 38–65. Tuscaloosa: University of Alabama Press.

Whaley, Lindsay. 1997. *Introduction to Typology: The Unity and Diversity of Language.* Thousand Oaks CA: SAGE Publications.

White, Nancy. 2005. *Gulf Coast Archaeology.* Gainesville: University Press of Florida.

Wilkerson, S. Jeffrey. 2005. "Rivers in the Sea: The Gulf of Mexico as a Cultural Corridor in Antiquity." In *Gulf Coast Archaeology: The Southeastern United States and Mexico,* edited by Nancy Marie White, 56–67. Gainesville: University Press of Florida.

Winford, Donald. 2003. *An Introduction to Contact Linguistics.* Malden MA: Blackwell Publishing.

Yerkes, Richard. 2005. "Bone Chemistry, Body Parts, and Growth Marks: Evaluating Ohio Hopewell and Cahokia Mississippian Seasonality, Subsistence, Ritual, and Feasting." *American Antiquity* 70 (2): 241–65.

Yoffee, Norman. 1995. "The Obvious and the Chimerical: City-States in Archaeological Perspective." In *The Archaeology of City-States: Cross-Cultural Approaches,* edited by Deborah L. Nichols and Thomas H. Charlton, 255–63. Washington DC: Smithsonian Institution Press.

Zaragoza-Ocaña, Diana. 2005. "Characteristic Elements Shared by Northeastern Mexico and the Southeastern United States." In *Gulf Coast Archaeology: The Southeastern United States and Mexico,* edited by Nancy Marie White, 245–62. Gainesville: University of Florida Press.

**Further Reading**

Aikhenvald, Alexandra. 2004. *Evidentiality.* Oxford: Oxford University Press.

———. 2012. *Languages of the Amazon.* Oxford: Oxford University Press.

Anderson, Gregory. 2013. "The Velar Nasal." In *The World Atlas of Language Structures Online,* edited by Matthew Dryer and Martin Haspelmath. Leipzig: Max Planck Institute for Evolutionary Anthropology. http://wals.info/chapter/9.

Booker, Karen, Charles Hudson, and Robert Rankin. 2005. "Muskogean Historical Phonology." In *Native Languages of the Southeastern United States,* edited by Heather Hardy and Janine Scancarelli, 246–98. Lincoln: University of Nebraska Press.

———. 2006. "Areal Linguistics: A Closer Scrutiny." In *Linguistic Areas: Convergence in Historical and Typological Perspective*, edited by Yaron Matras, 1–31. New York: Palgrave Macmillan.

Carter, Richard, A. Wesley Jones, Robert Rankin, John Koontz, and David Rood. 2006. *Comparative Siouan Dictionary*. Unpublished manuscript.

Dryer, Matthew. 2013. "Negative Morphemes." In *The World Atlas of Language Structures Online*, edited by Matthew Dryer and Martin Haspelmath. Leipzig: Max Planck Institute for Evolutionary Anthropology. http://wals.info/chapter/112.

Fogelson, Raymond, and William C. Sturtevant. 2004. *Handbook of North American Indians*. Vol. 14, *Southeast*. Washington DC: Government Printing Office.

Gallois, Cyndy, Tania Ogay, and Howard Giles. 2005. "Communication Accommodation Theory: A Look Back and a Look Ahead." In *Theorizing about Intercultural Communication*, edited by William B. Gudykunst, 121–48. Thousand Oaks CA: Sage.

Galloway, Patricia, and Jason Baird Jackson. 2004. "Natchez and Neighboring Groups." In *Handbook of North American Indians*. Vol. 14, *Southeast*, edited by Raymond D. Fogelson, 598–615. Washington DC: Smithsonian Institution.

Grant, Anthony. 1994. "Karankawa Linguistic Materials." *Kansas Working Papers in Linguistics* 19 (2): 1–56.

Hoijer, Harry. 1949. *An Analytical Dictionary of the Tonkawa Language*. Berkeley: University of California Press.

Kaufman, David. 2007. "A Reanalysis of the Dorsey-Swanton U-Circumflex and U-Brève in Biloxi." *Kansas Working Papers in Linguistics* 28: 1–10.

———. 2008. "Focality and Topicality Marking in Biloxi." *Kansas Working Papers in Linguistics* 30: 150–58.

———. 2015. *Biloxi-English Dictionary*. 2nd ed. Self-published, Lulu.

Mallory, James, and Douglas Adams. 2006. *The Oxford Introduction to Proto-Indo-European and the Proto-Indo-European World*. Oxford: Oxford University Press.

Oliverio, Giulia. 1996. *A Grammar and Dictionary of Tutelo*. PhD diss., University of Kansas, Department of Linguistics.

Phillips, Philip, and James Brown. 1978. *Pre-Columbian shell engravings from the Craig Mound at Spiro, Oklahoma (Part 1)*. Cambridge MA: Harvard University Press.

Phillips, Philip, James Brown, and Eliza McFadden. 1984. *Pre-Columbian Shell Engravings: From the Craig Mound at Spiro, Oklahoma*. Cambridge MA: Peabody Museum Press.

Rankin, Robert. 2006. "Siouan Tribal Contacts and Dispersions Evidenced in the Terminology for Maize and Other Cultigens." In *Histories of Maize: Multidisciplinary Approaches to Prehistory, Linguistics, Biogeography, Domestication, and Evolution of Maize*, edited by John E. Staller, Robert H. Tykot, and Bruce F. Benz, 563–75. Amsterdam: Elsevier.

Rhodes, Richard. 1985. *Eastern Ojibwa-Chippewa-Ottawa dictionary*. The Hague: Mouton.

Schleicher, August. 1850. *Die Sprachen Europas in systematischer Übersicht: Linguistische Untersuchungen*. Bonn.

Schönkron, Marcel. 1991. *Romanian-English English-Romanian Dictionary*. New York: Ungar.

Stolz, Thomas. 2002. "No Sprachbund beyond This Line! On the Age-old Discussion of How to Define a Linguistic Area." In *Mediterranean Languages: Papers from the MEDTYP Workshop, Tirrenia, 2000*, edited by Paolo Ramat and Thomas Stolz, 259–81. Bochum: Universitätsverlag Dr. N. Brockmeyer.

Swadesh, Morris. 1933. "Chitimacha Verbs of Derogatory or Abusive Connotation with Parallels from European Languages." *Language* 9 (2): 192–201.

———. 1934. "The Phonemes of Chitimacha." *International Journal of American Linguistics* 10 (4): 345–62.

———. 1946. "Phonologic Formulas for Atakapa-Chitimacha." *International Journal of American Linguistics* 12 (3): 113–32.

———. 1946. "Chitimacha." In *Linguistic Structures of Native America*, edited by Cornelius Osgood, 312–26. New York: Viking Fund Publications in Anthropology.

Taylor, Allan. 1976. "Words for 'Buffalo.'" *International Journal of American Linguistics* 42: 165–66.

Tomkins, William. (1926) 1969. *Universal American Indian Sign Language*. San Diego: Neyenesch Printers. Reprint, New York: Dover Publications.

Vogel, Virgil. 1983. *Iowa Place Names of Indian Origin*. Iowa City: University of Iowa Press.

# INDEX

Page numbers in italic indicate illustrations. Page numbers appended with an italic *t* indicate a table.

CPSIA information can be obtained
at www.ICGtesting.com
Printed in the USA
LVHW040342300720
661886LV00001B/1